International Research Collaborations

Encouraged by their institutions and governments and aided by advances in technology and communication, researchers increasingly pursue international collaborations with high hopes for scientific breakthroughs, intellectual stimulation, access to research equipment and populations, and the satisfaction of global engagement. Part of the International Studies in Higher Education series, *International Research Collaborations* considers what can and does go wrong in cross-national research collaborations, and how scientists can avoid these problems in order to create and sustain productive, mutually-enriching partnerships.

Unfamiliar approaches to training, legal and regulatory complications, and differences in funding and administration pose challenges for collaborations that are then compounded by the need to satisfy the requirements of different research systems. To help today's international researchers create the best possible partnerships, chapters by funding officers, diplomats, attorneys, publishers, regulators, graduate students and postdocs, industry researchers, administrators, and scholars of responsible research address the following key trouble spots:

- How research is organized and funded
- The legal and normative environments of research
- Differences in regulation and oversight
- Variation in graduate education and postdoctoral training

International Research Collaborations will provide valuable insights to researchers who are collaborating or who intend to collaborate, as well as to administrators, funders, regulators, editors, and policy-makers involved in cross-national research.

Melissa S. Anderson, PhD., is Professor of Higher Education and an affiliate faculty member in bioethics at the University of Minnesota, where she also chairs the University's Senate Research Committee.

Nicholas H. Steneck, PhD., is Director of the Research Ethics and Integrity Program of the Michigan Institute for Clinical and Health Research and Professor Emeritus of History at the University of Michigan.

International Studies in Higher Education
Series Editors:
David Palfreyman, OxCHEPS
Ted Tapper, OxCHEPS
Scott L. Thomas, Claremont Graduate University

The central purpose of this series of a projected dozen volumes is to see how different national and regional systems of higher education are responding to widely shared pressures for change. The most significant of these are: rapid expansion; reducing public funding; the increasing influence of market and global forces; and the widespread political desire to integrate higher education more closely into the wider needs of society and, more especially, the demands of the economic structure. The series will commence with an international overview of structural change in systems of higher education. It will then proceed to examine on a global front the change process in terms of topics that are both traditional (for example, institutional management and system governance) and emerging (for example, the growing influence of international organizations and the blending of academic and professional roles). At its conclusion the series will have presented, through an international perspective, both a composite overview of contemporary systems of higher education, along with the competing interpretations of the process of change.

Published titles:

Structuring Mass Higher Education
The Role of Elite Institutions
Edited by David Palfreyman and Ted Tapper

International Perspectives on the Governance of Higher Education
Alternate Frameworks for Coordination
Edited by Jeroen Huisman

International Organizations and Higher Education Policy
Thinking Globally, Acting Locally?
Edited by Roberta Malee Bassett and Alma Maldonado

Academic and Professional Identities in Higher Education
The Challenges of a Diversifying Workforce
Edited by Celia Whitchurch and George Gordon

International Research Collaborations

Much to be Gained, Many Ways to Get in Trouble

Edited by
Melissa S. Anderson and
Nicholas H. Steneck

Routledge
Taylor & Francis Group

NEW YORK AND LONDON

First published 2011
by Routledge
711 Third Avenue, New York, NY 10017

Simultaneously published in the UK
by Routledge
2 Park Square, Milton Park, Abingdon, Oxfordshire OX14 4RN

Routledge is an imprint of the Taylor & Francis Group, an informa business

First issued in paperback 2011

© 2011 Taylor & Francis

Typeset in Minion by Wearset Ltd, Boldon, Tyne and Wear

Library of Congress Cataloging in Publication Data
International research collaborations: much to be gained, many ways to get in trouble/Melissa S. Anderson and Nicholas H. Steneck, editors.
p. cm. – (International studies in higher education)
Includes bibliographical references and index.
1. University cooperation. 2. Group work in education. 3. Group work in research. 4. College teachers–Professional relationships. I. Anderson, Melissa S. II. Steneck, Nicholas H.

LB2331.5.I528 2010
001.409–dc22

2010000653

ISBN13: 978-0-415-87541-7 (hbk)
ISBN13: 978-0-415-53032-3 (pbk)
ISBN13: 978-0-203-84890-0 (ebk)

Contents

Series Editors' Introduction

This series is constructed around the premise that higher education systems are experiencing common pressures for fundamental change, reinforced by differing national and regional circumstances that also impact upon established institutional structures and procedures. There are four major dynamics for change that are of international significance:

1. Mass higher education is a universal phenomenon.
2. National systems find themselves located in an increasingly global marketplace that has particular significance for their more prestigious institutions.
3. Higher education institutions have acquired (or been obliged to acquire) a wider range of obligations, often under pressure from governments prepared to use state power to secure their policy goals.
4. The balance between the public and private financing of higher education has shifted—markedly in some cases—in favor of the latter.

Although higher education systems in all regions and nation states face their own particular pressures for change, these are especially severe in some cases: the collapse of the established economic and political structures of the former Soviet Union along with Central and Eastern Europe; the political revolution in South Africa; the pressures for economic development in India and China; and demographic pressure in Latin America.

Each volume in this series will examine how systems of higher education are responding to this new and demanding political and socio-economic environment. Although it is easy to overstate the uniqueness of the present situation, it is not an exaggeration to say that higher education is undergoing a fundamental shift in its character, one that is truly international in scope. We are witnessing a major transition in the relationship of higher education to state and society. What makes the present circumstances particularly interesting is seeing how different systems—a product of social, cultural, economic, and political contexts that have interacted and evolved over time—respond in their own peculiar ways to the changing environment. There is no assumption that the pressures for change have set in motion the trend toward a converging model of higher education, but we do believe that in the present circumstances no understanding of "the idea of the university" remains sacrosanct.

Although this is a series with an international focus, it is not expected that each individual volume should cover every national system of higher education. This would be an impossible task. While aiming for a broad range of case studies, with each volume addressing a particular theme, the focus will be upon the most important and interesting examples of responses to the pressures for change. Most of the individual volumes will bring together a range of comparative quantitative and qualitative information, but the primary aim of each volume will be to present differing interpretations of critical developments in key aspects of the experience of higher education. The dominant overarching objective is to explore the conflict of ideas and the political struggles that inevitably surround any significant policy development in higher education.

It can be expected that volume editors and their authors will adopt their own interpretations to explain the emerging patterns of development. There will be conflicting theoretical positions drawn from the multi-disciplinary, and increasingly inter-disciplinary, field of higher education research. Thus we can expect in most volumes to find an inter-marriage of approaches drawn from sociology, economics, history, political science, cultural studies, and the administrative sciences. However, while there will be different approaches to understanding the process of change in higher education, each volume editor(s) will impose a framework upon the volume in as much as chapter authors will be required to address common issues and concerns.

Melissa S. Anderson of the University of Minnesota and Nicholas H. Steneck of the University of Michigan are editors of this fifth volume in the series. This volume has a tight focus on the internationalization of the scientific enterprise, specifically on the ways in which the internationalization of scientific relationships has shaped cross-national collaborations. While international collaborations have proliferated over the past decade, few have paused to make a systematic assessment of their fundamental costs and challenges. These costs are often embedded within the coordination of separate national bureaucracies and funding systems, language differences, and simple geographic distance. But easily identifiable challenges such as these often obscure the underlying reality that science is often conducted differently in different national settings.

The contributors to this volume consider four distinct dimensions along which the character of international research collaborations may be influenced. First, several authors highlight the variety of ways in which countries organize and fund their scientific efforts. Second, this volume touches upon legal requirements and normative expectations that can vary importantly by national setting. Third, considerable attention is devoted to considerations of regulatory differences shaping these cross-national relationships. Finally, the training of post-doctoral fellows and graduate students, the frontline workforce, constitutes a fourth dimension on which the chapters in this volume are organized.

Through their treatment of issues along these four dimensions, Anderson and Steneck provide a powerful examination of potential threats to scientific productivity and integrity in international research collaborations. They also help the reader understand what is being done to address such threats so that these collaborations might be most effectively organized.

As with previous volumes in the series, the above issues are located in different theoretical contexts. Its editors and authors have attempted to establish a dialogue between theory and praxis in order to further our understanding of the internationalization of higher education and, more especially, the role of international organizations in that process. At its best, this is what the study of higher education attempts to achieve.

David Palfreyman
Director of OxCHEPS, New College, University of Oxford

Ted Tapper
OxCHEPS, New College, University of Oxford and CHEMPAS, University of Southampton

Scott L. Thomas
Professor of Educational Studies, Claremont Graduate University, California

Acknowledgments

In October 2008, a conference on Challenges and Tensions in International Research Collaborations was held at the University of Minnesota, Minneapolis, Minnesota, U.S.A. The conference was organized by Melissa S. Anderson of the University of Minnesota and Sandra Titus of the U.S. Office of Research Integrity (ORI). It was funded by a conference grant from the ORI, with additional support from the University of Minnesota's Office of International Programs, Office of the Vice President for Research, and other academic and administrative units. Of the 41 authors represented in this volume, 12 (Adib Abdel-Messih, Belani, Capron, De Vries, Godfrey, Handley, Heitman, Leckie, Lyman, Nebeker, Pais, and Stainthorpe) made presentations at the conference; the chapters here are only loosely based on their conference presentations. For the impetus that the conference gave to this volume, the editors express their sincere gratitude to all who provided financial and personal support.

The editors also express their thanks to Scott L. Thomas, co-editor of the Routledge series on International Studies in Higher Education for his unwavering support and wise guidance; to the authors of particular chapters who stepped up to the challenge of filling in for others on short notice; and to the team of doctoral students (Felly Chiteng Kot, Christine C. Lepkowski, and Krista M. Soria) who provided extraordinary support in the preparation of the manuscript.

Part I

International Research Collaborations

1

What Can Be Gained and What Can Go Wrong in the Context of Different National Research Environments

Melissa S. Anderson

Scientific research is an increasingly international enterprise. Large-scale projects such as the CERN Large Hadron Collider require the participation of teams of physicists from all over the world. Much of biomedical research deals with diseases whose causes, spread and treatment know no national bounds. Major engineering and social-science projects are also likely to be international in scope. Scientists who work in specific disciplinary sub-specialties are often dispersed around the globe. Prompted and enabled by advances in technology and communication, cross-national collaborations have come to characterize much of science.

For the purposes of this volume, international research collaborations are research projects that involve investigators whose primary employment affiliations are in different countries. They range from multi-national projects involving substantial infrastructure development, to mid-range collaborations among several sites or laboratories (including clinical trials), to simple projects involving two scientists from different countries. They may be long-term or limited in duration. These collaborations are subject to challenges common to all collaborative research (Who is in charge? Who will actually do the work? How shall credit be assigned for the products of the collaboration?). There are also complications arising from the cross-national nature of the work. Some of these relate to the team's productivity (How will the investigators deal with the demands of different administrative and regulatory structures? How will international travel and communication affect the maintenance of the collaboration? How will normative differences be negotiated?). Others have to do with ensuring the integrity of the research (How can integrity be ensured when national standards and oversight mechanisms differ widely? How can collaborators verify that research processes and products meet appropriate standards for integrity? When rules and policies differ, whose rules apply?).

This book's purpose is to call attention to challenges that many scientists and their institutions ignore or discount in their rush to establish international partnerships. In a competitive environment nearly devoid of international oversight, research collaborations are sometimes put together in haste, with little thought to what it will take to maintain productivity and integrity throughout the project.

There is often a great deal at stake in international collaborations, due to the substantial investment of funding and effort required to initiate and maintain them. The complications of navigating separate bureaucracies, different funding systems, geographic distance and languages tend to give these collaborations high profiles. There is much to be gained from international collaborations, but when problems arise, they tend to attract a disproportionate amount of attention, especially if something goes seriously wrong.

Problems are often attributed to miscommunication, language barriers, cultural misunderstanding or management issues. Only as a case unfolds does it become apparent that many challenges and problems are due to fundamental, cross-national differences in the way science is organized and done.

In a sense, of course, research is the same everywhere; this fact is what enables global research collaboration in the first place. In another sense, all research is subject to the management styles, expertise, experience, preferences and idiosyncrasies of the individuals involved. Between these extremes, however, are systematic patterns of difference across different research contexts. The systematic differences that are most prominent and detectable in international ("between-nation") collaborations are those related to *differences in national research systems*. These differences and their influences on cross-national scientific collaboration are the subject of this book.

Challenges encountered in cooperative ventures of any kind are compounded by the need to meet the demands of different research systems. For example, one country's stricter human- or animal-subject regulations may impose unfamiliar protocols on all collaborators. Administrative approval processes may appear byzantine to outsiders. Scientists from other countries may make unfounded and risky assumptions about students' training in scientific methods or the responsible conduct of research. Problems like these can derail a project's progress or, worse, lead to allegations of misconduct, mismanagement or illegalities.

The authors of this volume consider four primary dimensions of national research systems relevant to cross-national research collaboration: (1) the organization and funding of research; (2) legal and normative environments; (3) regulatory and publication oversight; and (4) graduate education and postdoctoral training. International variations in these four areas can lead to substantially different assumptions and expectations about how research projects are to be planned, performed and reported. Unless scientists are aware of differences in these assumptions, they may not anticipate or address issues that may arise from these differences in areas such as compliance with national laws and policies, authority within the administrative hierarchy, responsibilities of postdocs, and so on. Such issues can compromise a team's productivity and the integrity of their work.

This volume aims to raise awareness within academic and other research communities of the variety and scope of complications that can and do arise in international research collaborations, as well as strategies that show promise for addressing potential problems. The overarching questions that this volume addresses are:

- What threats to productivity and integrity arise in international research collaborations because of differences in national research systems?
- What can be done to mitigate such threats?

Our contacts with scientists and research administrators confirm that many researchers are eager to initiate cross-national collaborations. Most have not considered fully what they need to know and do to benefit from these projects and to stay out of trouble.

Overview of the Book

The authors of this volume address these issues from varied perspectives. Some are scientists; others have administrative responsibilities at the institutional, national or international level; still others are scholars of international systems or related topics. All consider ways in which international research collaborations are complicated by cross-national differences.

The chapters in the first section, including this one, frame the issues under consideration. The first two are by the book's editors, Melissa Anderson and Nick Steneck, scholars whose research focuses on research integrity, particularly in the international context. Nick's chapter invites consideration of how research integrity, a critical element of any research collaboration, should be handled in the international arena. Gray Handley's broad view of international collaborations and how scientists should approach them derives from his experiences in diplomacy and scientific research, and at the U.S. National Institutes of Health.

The next four parts address the dimensions of the national research systems identified above. The first considers differences in how national systems organize and fund research. David Chapman studies educational systems at the international level, and he and his colleagues focus here on the organizational properties of research in China, India, Germany, Brazil and the United States. Tony Mayer, a geologist with research-administration experience in Europe and Singapore, traces the development of national approaches to funding scientific research. Ping Sun's work at the Chinese Ministry of Education and the Institute of Scientific and Technical Information of China informs his review of national-level research developments in China.

The next dimension of national research systems is the legal and normative environments of research, representing formal and informal ways, respectively, of prescribing appropriate behavior in science. Mark Bohnhorst and colleagues write from their experience as university attorneys or directors of international programs. They discuss legal requirements and issues that international collaborators must consider if they are to stay out of trouble in their own and other countries. Alexander Capron, a legal scholar and former director of an office within the World Health Organization, suggests that the rules and regulations to which cross-national collaborations are subject are inappropriately dominated by U.S. regulatory frameworks. Ray De Vries and his co-authors then argue that norms of scientific research, which are informal but powerful means of defining and promoting proper behavior, need to be negotiated in cross-national contexts. Their chapter draws on their extensive sociological research in international arenas.

The third dimension of national research systems relates to regulatory oversight of research. Christine (Tina) Boesz and Peggy Fischer draw on their experience in the Office of the Inspector General at the U.S. National Science Foundation, as well as their participation in the Global Science Forum's development of guidelines for research integrity worldwide. They discuss the challenges of investigating allegations of research misconduct internationally. The former director of the UK Research Integrity Office, Andy Stainthorpe, then takes a pan-European view of research-integrity efforts. Specific integrity problems associated with research publication are reviewed by Herbert Stegemann and colleagues, who have worked extensively with Latin American journals and international publication associations. Oversight is clearly difficult, since international collaborations are presumably as susceptible to questionable behavior as any other cooperative ventures, and there are no good cross-national mechanisms by which to address problems.

The fourth and final dimension of national research systems is graduate education and postdoctoral training. These differ globally in their relation to national policy and government control, but they are shaped everywhere by the other aspects of national research systems. The first chapter in this section illustrates the distinctive features of doctoral education in seven different countries and suggests how these characteristics may give rise to challenges in cross-national research. The authors of these accounts are doctoral students or postdoctoral fellows, writing about the graduate systems in their own countries. John Godfrey, Assistant Dean for International Education at the University of Michigan, considers postdoctoral training in a cross-national context. Liz Heitman's chapter, written with a colleague, draws on her experience as director of a program in research-ethics education in Costa Rica. It illustrates what is involved in delivering training on ethical issues across national boundaries.

The last part of the book presents advice and recommendations on moving toward successful international collaborations. Camille Nebeker and Stewart Lyman both give advice on how to manage such cooperative work, Camille from the standpoint of institutional research administration, and Stewart from the point of view of industrial research. In the final chapter, the editors draw conclusions about the benefits and challenges of cross-national research. They point out that the benefits of collaboration are more likely to be realized if cooperation is driven by the demands of the research itself, not by a vague assumption that international work always yields superior outcomes. They also review the challenges that are presented in this volume.

The issues addressed above are given immediacy in a set of chapters that appear in the appendix. These chapters by distinguished scientists with wide experience in international research collaborations provide an inside view of cross-national research and the factors that complicate it. Ibrahim Adib Abdel-Messih tells about research in his native Egypt. Prem Pais and his co-authors write about their collaborative experiences in India. Jim Leckie's stories are based on his research projects in Singapore and China. These first-person accounts bear a reminder that the issues here are not merely theoretical, but quite real and with real consequences for the people involved, their colleagues, their subjects and others.

The "much to be gained" referenced in this volume's subtitle is currently driving increased interest and investment in international collaborations. What receives less attention are the "many ways to get in trouble," as presented in this volume. Researchers who are aware of potential challenges and prepared to deal with them are more likely to have positive, productive collaborations. This book is written to that end.

2

Research Integrity in the Context of Global Cooperation

Nicholas H. Steneck

Most researchers presumably set out to conduct research with integrity. There are, of course, exceptions. Estimates are that as many as one in every 100 researchers in the United States deliberately engages in what colleagues believe is serious misbehavior (Martinson, Anderson, & de Vries, 2005). However, the other 99 presumably do the best they can, balancing needs and pressures with their understanding of what is, in some countries, called "good research practice" (GRP), and in others the "responsible conduct of research" (RCR).

Researchers also agree that the standards for "good" or "responsible" practice should be set very high. In its 2001 report on conflict of interest, the American Association of Universities urged the "leaders of the academic community to ensure that research conducted on our campuses meets the highest standards of ethics and integrity and promotes the public health" (American Association of Universities, 2001). The European Commissioner for Science and Research, Janez Potočnik, urged colleagues to think in terms of the "highest standards of integrity" in his 2007 presentation at the First World Conference on Research Integrity (Potočnik, 2007). In principle, high standards for integrity in research are generally expected. However, translating this expectation into practice is not as easy as one might expect. This chapter evaluates the global structures currently in place for setting and maintaining standards for integrity in research, with particular attention to governments, research institutions, and research professionals. The chapter opens with thoughts on what is meant by "integrity" and closes with suggestions for further steps to foster integrity in research around the world.

Integrity, Misconduct, and Questionable Research Practices

Although widely used in discussions of research behavior, the term "integrity" is seldom defined or used in a precise way. It derives from the Latin term "*integritas*," and is intended to convey a sense of soundness, wholeness or completeness. When used in reference to morality, it describes someone who is sound "of moral principle; the character of uncorrupted virtue, especially in relation to truth and fair dealing; uprightness, honesty, sincerity" (*Oxford*

English Dictionary, 1989). Applied to professionals such as researchers, integrity implies someone who is honest, upright, and fair, and meets the responsibilities of her or his profession. Promoting or fostering integrity in research means taking steps to embrace these characteristics and to encourage others to do likewise.

As a goal or principle, *integrity* has an important place in discussions of research behavior. It captures, if somewhat imprecisely, a fundamental responsibility shared by researchers. As a practical standard for developing policies and studying behavior, it has significant shortcomings. Although major departures from best practice, commonly called "research misconduct," may be few in number, minor departures, called "questionable research practices," are not. Research is competitive. For good and bad reasons, significant numbers of researchers—10–20 percent and above—engage in practices that do not meet the standards of "truth and fair dealing; uprightness, honesty, [and] sincerity" (Steneck, 2006). Most researchers would probably be offended if their *integrity* were questioned. They are not intentionally "bad people." But their actions, whether deliberate or inadvertent, do not live up to the high standards set as a goal for research behavior.

The confusion this situation creates is nicely captured in an encounter described to this author by a postdoctoral student. Following a session at a professional meeting, the postdoctoral student reported listening to a group of senior colleagues discussing the individual presentations. They seemed to be agreed that one of the presentations was seriously flawed, so much so that they suspected some of the data had been fabricated or falsified. This was not the first time the flawed data had been presented. The senior colleagues therefore were inclined to ignore the findings, but they apparently were not prepared to report their suspicions. The postdoctoral student wondered why and what she should do, if high standards for integrity are expected. Should she report the suspicions she and apparently her senior colleagues had? If so, where and to whom? And why were the senior colleagues so unconcerned? Didn't they have some responsibility for the integrity of the research process? If researchers are expected to set high standards for integrity for themselves and for research as a whole, why was it acceptable to ignore what the group seemed to agree was an ongoing problem, and to cut corners and bend rules, as researchers too often seem to do?

Governments, research institutions, and research professionals around the world have begun to address and answer these questions, but many challenges remain. There is no doubt that integrity in research, as an overall goal, is important. The need for GRP and RCR is not in doubt. The opposite extreme, research misconduct, is also widely rejected. Governments are today working individually and together to develop ways to address this commonly recognized problem (Organisation for Economic Co-operation and Development & Global Science Forum, 2007, 2008). However, in between the clearly accepted and unaccepted behaviors, there lies a range of questionable research practices that damage the research record, waste public funds, erode public confidence in research, and even, at times, endanger the health of individuals and public welfare more generally. In evaluating what global institutions are doing to address misconduct and promote integrity in research, taking these seemingly minor lapses seriously may be the greatest challenge.

Governments

Worldwide, governments have typically taken a reactive, not proactive, approach to integrity in research. Government research programs usually start with decisions about funding structures, directions, and levels. What research should be supported? How will it be reviewed and the funds distributed? In the United States it was strongly urged during the development of government-supported research in the late 1940s that other matters be left to researchers, who it was generally assumed were honest and could regulate their own behavior (United States Office of Scientific Research and Development & Bush, 1945). Based on this assumption, governments stepped in to regulate behavior or promote integrity only when questions arose about particular misbehaviors.

Governments, obviously, can respond to crises in different ways, depending on how they are organized and their rules for making decisions. The options for dealing with misbehavior in publicly supported research include: (1) clarifying expected standards for behavior; (2) explaining what actions are required when misbehavior occurs; (3) accepting or delegating responsibility for responding; and (4) promoting efforts to foster integrity, usually through education and training. For each option, governments also have the additional option of recommending or requiring particular actions or steps. And finally, since governments are themselves complex, there are different ways in which they can act. They can adopt uniform, government-wide regulations or guidelines or allow individual agencies or programs to adopt their own regulations or guidelines. Given all of these options, it should come as no surprise to anyone entering into a multi-national collaboration to find that they must work with different systems that have different rules that could well conflict with one another. It should also come as no surprise that the systems for confronting integrity issues are not as effective as one might hope. This is true even for the problems that have received the most attention: research misconduct and human-subjects research.

Inconsistent or Absent Misconduct Policies

Anyone entering into an international collaboration needs to be aware of the fact that many countries that fund and encourage research do not have research misconduct policies. Those that do have different policies, including different definitions of misconduct, different places for reporting, and different ways for handling allegations. When they exist, misconduct policies can be difficult to locate and equally difficult to understand. In sum, even though there is widespread agreement about the importance of basic honesty in research, many countries have not defined what they mean by honesty or specified what to do when dishonesty is suspected (ESF, 2008; Organisation for Economic Co-operation and Development & Global Science Forum, 2007). This situation suggests that certain practices may be acceptable in one country but classified as misconduct in another. It can also make it difficult to resolve reports of misconduct in international collaborations.

Ineffective Misconduct Policies

The systems that have been developed to respond to misconduct in research are not effective. In the United States, less than 30 cases of misconduct are confirmed annually, most by the Office of Research Integrity (Office of Research Integrity, 2009) and the National Science Foundation Office of the Inspector General (National Science Foundation Office of Inspector General, 2009). Although there are no firm estimates of the number of federally funded researchers subject to the 2000 U.S. misconduct policy, it is certainly more than 300,000. This means that that the government is at best detecting about one case of misconduct annually for every 10,000 researchers. As noted above, studies of misconduct have put the frequency of misconduct 10–100 times higher (Gardner, Lidz, & Hartwig, 2005; Martinson et al., 2005; Steneck, 2006; Titus, Wells, & Rhoades, 2008). In other words, the system currently in place for discovering, reporting, and investigating misconduct in the United States is missing 90–99 percent of the misconduct that takes place. While these numbers have not been confirmed for other countries, there is no evidence to suggest that the prevalence of misconduct is less in other countries or that other countries are doing a better job of discovering, reporting, and investigating misconduct in research.

Weak Accountability for Integrity in Human-Subjects Research

More effort has gone into developing global standards for good practice in human-subjects research than research misconduct. This effort has led to widely accepted codes of conduct ("Directives for human experimentation: Nuremberg code," 1949; World Medical Association, 1964, 2002), agreements on such things as good clinical practice (European Forum for Good Research Practice, 2009), and a wide range of national and international regulations ("Federal policy for the protection of human subjects," 2001; Food and Drug Administration, 2009). However, as with misconduct, significant challenges remain in relation to the integrity of human-subjects research.

The most significant challenge is accountability. In the United States and many parts of Europe, the rules and regulations for human-subjects research are coupled with provisions for auditing, accreditation, and quality control. In the United States, the Office for Human Research Protection (OHRP) conducts compliance audits (OHRP, 2009) and the Association for the Accreditation of Human Research Protection Programs (AAHRPP) accredits institutional programs (AAHRPP, 2009). The United Kingdom's system of centralized ethics committees (the equivalent of institutional review boards in the United States) allows review of the reliability of the work these committees do on a national basis. These and other national and international efforts have greatly improved the ethics and integrity of human-subjects research on a global basis, but there are still significant gaps in the effectiveness of these systems.

For U.S. researchers entering into global collaborations, two gaps are particularly important. The first is the limited oversight the OHRP is able to provide for a Federal Wide Assurance (FWA) (OHRP, 2009), the guarantee institutions provide that they are following U.S. regulations, principally what is known as the Common Rule ("Federal policy for the protection of human subjects," 2001). FWAs provided by U.S. institutions are monitored, but the OHRP does not have the resources to monitor overseas FWAs. Therefore, just because a foreign institution says it has an FWA does not guarantee that it is following the Common Rule or even that the institution listed as having the FWA has provided or is aware of the listing. An individual researcher can fill out an application for an FWA without anyone checking to see that the information provided is accurate.

The second and certainly not-unexpected gap in accountability is the significant difference in the quality of the systems for protecting human subjects in research throughout the world. Some major research countries that have signed on to international agreements, such as China and Japan, do not have mechanisms for assuring compliance. The same is true and can be more problematic in less-developed research countries or for projects conducted in countries where there is no funding for research. This can lead to problems when getting local approval for collaborative projects or for assuring that the local approval is reliable.

Training

U.S. researchers using U.S. funds to undertake research have an obligation to ensure that U.S. rules are followed, wherever the research is carried out. For researchers using human subjects in their collaboration, this includes the 2000 National Institutes of Health (NIH) requirement that everyone participating in the research—such as local coordinators, anyone collecting data, and so on—must be appropriately trained (NIH, 2000). The integrity of collaborative international projects can depend on the quality of this training. Improper consenting, lost forms, improper data entry and other problems that can arise from poor training can destroy the integrity of the research. Some tools and programs exist to deal with training problems. Without proper training, the various principles and rules for the responsible use of human subjects in research can have only limited impact.

The weaknesses in government systems for promoting integrity and responding to misconduct are significant. Anyone entering into international collaborations needs to understand that she or he could be working in an area where there are no government rules for GRP or where the rules are not enforced. Misconduct may not be investigated if it is reported. Ethics committees may not be properly approved. Intellectual property might not be protected. The systems government have developed for protecting the public's investment in research from all forms of misbehavior do not work nearly as well as they could or should. This, in turn, places a significant burden on the second key player in protecting integrity, research institutions.

Research Institutions

Research institutions are in an ideal position to address problems and promote integrity in research. Researchers work for research institutions. If they engage in misconduct or questionable practices, research institutions can take action. Research institutions can also enforce rules and establish best practices, and they can encourage responsible conduct through education and training. For these and other reasons, they are generally recognized as the institution that should take primary responsibility for protecting the integrity of publicly funded research.

Research institutions throughout the world have been reluctant to accept this responsibility. In the United States, most institutional integrity policies (misconduct, human and animal subject, conflict of interest, and so on) and RCR training programs have been instituted in response to federal regulations. To keep regulation to a minimum, the organizations representing research institutions have resisted new regulations that are in one way or another designed to promote integrity.

There are reasons why institutions have been reluctant to accept too much responsibility for the integrity of the research they sponsor and oversee. Researchers constantly worry that rigid rules for behavior can limit scholarly creativity. Outside rules can also impose uncompensated financial and administrative burdens. In addition, most research institutions (primarily universities) house broad research programs, which makes it difficult for them to have the expertise needed to deal with the various integrity issues that arise in different fields of study. This is a manageable problem for the few cases of research misconduct that large research institutions face each year, but more difficult when it comes to providing guidance on research design, interpretation, publication and authorship issues, conflict of interest, and the like. Putting all these factors together, it is an unfortunate fact that research institutions have been slow to take a leading role in establishing or clarifying best practices and have resisted efforts by governments to impose best practices and other behavior-oriented rules on them.

Research institutions can also have a detrimental impact on integrity in research. Promotion policies can drive research behavior. The more researchers are expected to publish, the more they will publish, sometimes by bending rules and engaging in questionable practices. Funding pressures can drive research agendas and influence research results, as has been documented in many studies of conflict of interest (Friedman & Richter, 2004; Lexchin, Bero, Djulbegovic, & Clark, 2003). American and European researchers complain about funding pressures, Asian researchers about pressures to publish. It is today widely recognized that research integrity has both individual and institutional components (Institute of Medicine, 2002). Institutions that ignore this fact and create environments that set unrealistic expectations run the risk of encouraging their researchers to engage in both questionable practices and research misconduct (Resnik & Shamoo, 2002). Moreover, there is so little coordination across research institutions—both within countries and internationally—that predicting how institutional factors will impact integrity in international collaborations is difficult.

Fortunately, this somewhat gloomy picture of the past contributions of research institutions to research integrity is changing. Throughout the world today there are a growing number of research institutions that are either acting on their own or going beyond what is required to promote integrity in research. Some examples personally experienced include new courses and programs at: Nanyang Technological University in Singapore; Japan's RIKEN Institute and Wasada University; Tsinghua University in China; and Oxford University in the United Kingdom. In 2009 the European Network for Ombudsmen in Higher Education devoted their annual meeting to learning more about integrity in research and their possible role in responding to misconduct and promoting GRP (European Network for Ombudsmen in Higher Education, n.d.).

In the United States, the Council of Graduate Schools, with government funding, has launched a major effort to make training in the RCR an accepted part of graduate training (Council of Graduate Schools, 2009). Two larger international research funders and performers—the Howard Hughes Medical Institute and the Wellcome Foundation Trust—have developed practice guidelines for GRP and for training researchers (Howard Hughes Medical Institute & Burroughs Wellcome Fund, 2006; Wellcome Trust, 2005). These are but a few examples of the many efforts underway to make research institutions more active players in promoting GRP.

Research Professionals

The professional organizations that represent and speak for researchers have sometimes been opposed to formal efforts to promote integrity in research. At the same time, they have also been active players, both within countries and internationally, in addressing specific problems. The four examples below are intended to be illustrative, not exhaustive, with the understanding that many other laudable efforts have been omitted.

The European Science Foundation (ESF), which represents European funding agencies and academies, took the lead in promoting integrity in research in Europe with its 2000 publication: *Good Scientific Practice in Research and Scholarship* (ESF, 2000). It subsequently has spearheaded efforts to coordinate related policy development and training efforts across Europe (ESF, 2008, n.d.) and played a leading role in organizing two world conferences on research integrity (First world conference on research integrity, 2007; Second world conference on research integrity, 2009).

The Committee on Publication Ethics provides "a forum for publishers and Editors of scientific journals to discuss issues relating to the integrity of work submitted to or published in their journals" (Committee on Publication Ethics, n.d.(b)). Since its founding in 1997, it has developed a *Code of Conduct for Publishers* along with guidelines on best practice, retracting articles, boards of directors of learned society journals, research audits, and authorship disputes (Committee on Publication Ethics, n.d (a)). Similar efforts to promote integrity in research have been undertaken by other groups of editors and publishers, such as the Council of Science Editors (Council of Science Editors, 2009), the World Association of Medical Editors (World Association of Medical Editors, 2009), and the International Congresses on Peer Review and Biomedical Publication (International Congresses on Peer Review and Biomedical Publication, 2009). Authorship and publication practices are currently the best-understood aspect of research behavior and have the most complete guidance, largely as a result of the efforts of these and similar groups.

The Society for Scientific Values is a small organization that has taken an active role in promoting "integrity, objectivity and ethical values in the pursuit of science" in India (Society for Scientific Values, 2003). Its approximately 350 members have taken an active role in investigating allegations of misconduct in India. The results of their investigations are posted on the Internet and brought to the attention of related institutions for further action. The organization also publishes an annual newsletter, which keeps Indian scholars abreast of developments in India and globally. A smaller grass-roots effort to call attention to the importance and prevalence of misconduct can be found on a website developed in France, "Scientific Red Cards" (Scientific Red Cards, n.d.).

The European Forum for Good Clinical Practice (EFGCP) was established primarily "to promote good clinical practice and encourage the practice of common, high-quality standards in all stages of biomedical research throughout Europe" (EFGCP, 2009). It recently broadened the scope of its activities to cover research misconduct and currently has an Ethics Working Party drafting recommendations for broadly promoting integrity in research (EFGCP, n.d.). Similar recommendations in the form of a *Code of Conduct* are being developed by an ESF Working Group (ESF, n.d.).

It is difficult to track all of the efforts now underway by research professionals to promote integrity in research. They are often publicized mostly to members and are not undertaken in collaboration with other organizations. As a result, there is a great deal of duplication of effort and sometimes, unfortunately, inadequate quality control. Many researchers were not taught about responsible practices when they were trained and therefore may not have the skills and information needed to provide reliable guidance. This is one reason it is essential to foster international collaboration when developing guidelines and rules, as suggested in the following conclusions and recommendations.

Conclusions and Recommendations

Global research and collaboration would not be possible if every country, institution, and laboratory used different systems for measurement, calibrated instruments differently, or changed the basic laws of nature to suit local customs. The same should be true for the systems and standards used to guide and measure integrity in research. With the exception of conflicts with specific national laws, such as the laws that govern whether misconduct investigations should be made public or kept private, or the requirements of labor contracts, researchers would work globally and collaborate more effectively if the standards for professional behavior were consistent, well-articulated, and subject to some accountability. While strides have been taken to achieve greater clarity and harmony in the professional standards that guide responsible behavior in research, there is still more work to do.

The first challenge researchers face in promoting integrity in research, well before and apart from collaboration, is the need to clarify and reach global consensus on what GRP or RCR requires. Students and young researchers are constantly confused and perplexed by the contradictions they observe in the way research is practiced. They believe that they know what should be done, but when they see the opposite done on a regular basis and presumably accepted, the standards for responsible conduct become confusing. If high standards for integrity are expected of all researchers, the goals for judging behavior must be clearly stated in sufficient detail so there is no confusion when behaviors fall short of the mark.

Second, applying this challenge to international collaboration, an essential step toward fostering integrity is the development of a collaboration template or checklist. Even experienced researchers can miss important responsibilities or fail to clarify key elements of a collaboration before work is started. For students and less experienced researchers, knowing what to expect or, more importantly, what to ask is essential for developing a productive working relationship. What is needed is more than the usual list of regulations posted on institutional compliance pages. A better model to follow would be something along the lines of the Howard Hughes or Wellcome Trust publications mentioned above.

Third, to move beyond standards and guidelines, more needs to be known about actual problems that occur in international collaborations. This book is an important step in this direction, but it is based mostly on experience and anecdotal evidence. The chapters provide many examples of problems that can arise. These problems now need to be put into context, studied, and addressed, based on their impact on what matters most—the reliability and accuracy of the research record.

Fourth and finally, researchers need to think about integrity from a public as well as a professional perspective. This is a lesson researchers involved in the collaborative international study of climate change in the United Kingdom learned only after their private emails and scientific deliberations were stolen from university computers and posted on the web (Kintisch, 2009). In their own minds, these researchers were producing the best science they could to aid public decision-making. When all of their conversations and actions were exposed to scrutiny, the public's perception of their integrity drew a different picture. Whether justified or not, in the end the public's perception matters since most research today is publicly funded.

References

AAHRPP (Association for the Accreditation of Human Research Protection Programs). (2009). *Homepage*. Retrieved December 2009, from www.aahrpp.org/www.aspx.

American Association of Universities. (2001). *Report on individual and institutional financial conflict of interest*. Washington, DC: Association of American Universities.

Committee on Publication Ethics. (n.d. (a)). *Guidelines*. Retrieved December 2009, from http://publicationethics.org/guidelines.

Committee on Publication Ethics. (n.d. (b)). *Homepage*. Retrieved December 2009, from www.publicationethics.org.uk.

Council of Graduate Schools. (2009). *Project for scholarly integrity*. Retrieved December 2009, from www.scholarlyintegrity.org.

Council of Science Editors. (2009). *Homepage*. Retrieved December 2009, from www.councilscienceeditors.org.

Directives for human experimentation: Nuremberg code. (1949). Retrieved December 2009, from http://ohsr.od.nih.gov/nuremberg.php3.

EFGCP (European Forum for Good Clinical Practice). (n.d.). *EFGCP Ethics Working Party*. Retrieved December 2009, from www.efgcp.be/WorkingParties.asp?what=1&L1=5&L2=1.

EFGCP (European Forum for Good Clinical Practice). (2009). *Homepage*. Retrieved December 2009, from www.efgcp.be/Publications.asp?Type=EFGCP%20publications&L1=13&L2=1.

ESF (European Science Foundation). (n.d.). *Member organization forum on research integrity*. Retrieved December 2009, from www.esf.org/activities/mo-fora/research-integrity.html.

ESF (European Science Foundation). (2000). *Good scientific practice in research and scholarship*. Strasbourg: European Science Foundation.

ESF (European Science Foundation). (2008). *Stewards of Integrity*. Strasbourg: European Science Foundation.

European Network for Ombudsmen in Higher Education. (n.d.). *Homepage*. Retrieved December 2009, from www.english.uva.nl/enohe/enohe_network.cfm.

Federal policy for the protection of human subjects, 45 CFR 46, Subpart A (2001).

First world conference on research integrity. (2007). Retrieved December 2009, from www.esf. org/index.php?id=4479.

Food and Drug Administration. (2009). *FDA regulations relating to good clinical practice and clinical trials*. Retrieved December 2009, from www.fda.gov/ScienceResearch/SpecialTopics/RunningClinicalTrials/ucm155713.htm.

Friedman, L. S., & Richter, E. D. (2004). Relationship between conflicts of interest and research results. *Journal of General Internal Medicine, 19*(1), 51–56.

Gardner, W., Lidz, C. W., & Hartwig, K. C. (2005). Authors' reports about research integrity problems in clinical trials. *Contemporary Clinical Trials, 26*(2), 244–251.

Howard Hughes Medical Institute, & Burroughs Wellcome Fund (2006). *Making the right moves: A practical guide to scientific management for postdocs and new faculty* (2nd ed.). Research Triangle Park, NC: Burroughs Wellcome Fund and Howard Hughes Medical Institute.

Institute of Medicine. (2002). *Integrity in scientific research: Creating an environment that promotes responsible conduct.* Washington, DC: The National Academies Press.

International Congresses on Peer Review and Biomedical Publication. (2009). *Homepage.* Retrieved December 2009, from www.ama-assn.org/public/peer/peerhome.htm.

Kintisch, E. (2009). Stolen e-mails turn up heat on climate change rhetoric. *Science, 326*(1329), 5958.

Lexchin, J., Bero, L. A., Djulbegovic, B., & Clark, O. (2003). Pharmaceutical industry sponsorship and research outcome and quality: Systematic review. *BMJ, 326*(7400), 1167–1170.

Martinson, B. C., Anderson, M. S., & de Vries, R. (2005). Scientists behaving badly. *Nature, 435*(7043), 737–738.

National Science Foundation Office of Inspector General. (2009). *Homepage.* Retrieved December 2009, from www.oig.nsf.gov.

NIH (National Institutes of Health). (2000). *Required education in the protection of human research participants* (No. OD-00-039). National Institutes of Health.

Office of Research Integrity. (2009). *Homepage.* Retrieved December 2009, from http://ori.dhhs.gov.

(OHRP) Office for Human Research Protection. (2009). *Homepage.* Retrieved December 2009, from http://www.hhs.gov/ohrp.

Organisation for Economic Co-operation and Development, & Global Science Forum. (2007). *Report from the workshop on best practices for ensuring scientific integrity and preventing misconduct.* Paris: Organisation for Economic Co-operation and Development and Global Science Forum.

Organisation for Economic Co-operation and Development, & Global Science Forum. (2008). *Co-ordinating committee for facilitating international research misconduct investigations.* Paris: Organisation for Economic Co-operation and Development and Global Science Forum.

Oxford English Dictionary (2nd ed.). (1989). Oxford: Clarendon Press.

Potočnik, J. (2007). European research: Towards the highest standards of integrity. Retrieved from www.esf.org/activities/esf-conferences/details/2007/confdetail242/invited-papers-biographies.html.

Resnik, D. B., & Shamoo, A. E. (2002). Conflict of interest and the university. *Accountability in Research, 9*(1), 45–64.

Scientific red cards. (n.d.). *Homepage.* Retrieved December 2009, from www.scientificredcards.org.

Second world conference on research integrity. (2009). Retrieved December 2009, from www.wcri2010.org.

Society for Scientific Values. (2003). *Homepage.* Retrieved December 2009, from www.scientificvalues.org/aims.html.

Steneck, N. H. (2006). Fostering integrity in research: Definitions, current knowledge, and future directions. *Science and Engineering Ethics, 12*(1), 53–74.

Titus, S. L., Wells, J. A., & Rhoades, L. J. (2008). Repairing research integrity. *Nature, 453*(7198), 980–982.

United States Office of Scientific Research and Development, & Bush, V. (1945). *Science, the endless frontier: A report to the president.* Washington, DC: U.S. Government.

Wellcome Trust. (2005). *Guidelines on good research practice.* London: Wellcome Trust.

World Association of Medical Editors. (2009). *Homepage.* Retrieved December 2009, from www.wame.org.

World Medical Association. (1964, 2002). *Declaration of Helsinki: Ethical principles for medical research involving human subjects.* Helsinki: World Medical Association.

3

Considerations upon Setting Out to Collaborate Internationally

F. Gray Handley

As academic institutions expand their engagement in international health research, it is important for scientists to understand that there are special complexities and challenges involved. In some cases, these require new perspectives and ways of interaction quite different from those used in domestic academic and research settings. Fortunately, there are also resources and allies within and outside the scientific community that can help in this endeavor.

In the past, knowledge of how best to undertake international research was gained largely through long experience and usually by trial and error. When few scientists were engaged internationally, this approach seemed to work. Even when mistakes were made, their impact was limited. Now, with so many engaged in international academic and research activities, it is increasingly important to share and use optimal approaches to advance scientific progress while avoiding unnecessary controversy, counterproductive practices, and harm to research partners.

In the twenty-first century, scientists and institutions that support international research are being asked to find answers to some of the most complex questions that have faced humankind. Compelling questions related to climate change and energy, a healthy environment, emerging and re-emerging disease threats, communications, security, an adequate supply of food and fresh water, as well as other fundamental human concerns, now require globally informed answers. Researchers working internationally are being asked to pursue these problems, and the public is watching as never before. This presents remarkable opportunities in a world that is open to scientific cooperation and, perhaps more than ever, willing to fund it. In considering how we undertake such cooperation, it is useful to have an understanding of motivations, risks, varying perspectives, and potential outcomes.

Why do investigators choose to work internationally? In nearly every case, researchers are driven by the desire for knowledge. They seek to advance their fields of science, and increasingly this work can be done best through international engagement. Many also are motivated by a sense of global citizenship, humanitarian concern, and a desire to see other countries reap the benefits of development and science-driven progress. For some, there are cost-efficiencies to be realized through international collaboration that are too attractive to ignore. Some institutions or private concerns are particularly interested in international research because they see opportunities for income. In the fields of biomedical and public health research, there are some transnational disease threats, such as pandemic influenza, which can only be addressed by global networks of researchers. Climate scientists have similar requirements. There may even be a few scientists who see such research collaboration as an important contributor to harmonious international relations.

All these reasons for engagement in international research are compelling and valid. For a growing number of scientists, they influence research directions and career choices. As with nearly all scientists, researchers working internationally seek to maximize productivity, hope to have an impact on their fields, and are fully committed to pursuing their investigations ethically.

With all these factors in mind and informed by a variety of perspectives, this chapter focuses on four primary ideas.

First, for humanitarian, economic, and security reasons, international research is in the public spotlight as never before. National leaders, some of the world's richest individuals, and even rock stars think what scientists do is important, and they tell the world. This spotlight presents challenges and opportunities that make many investigators uncomfortable. They see it as a distraction or something to be avoided at all costs. Others contend that the research community should welcome this attention, because it can generate widespread support for the expansion of the global scientific enterprise. In any case, reaping its potential benefits requires skills and partners to which many scientists are not accustomed.

Second, international research is apt to be more successful and greatly enhanced when scientists keep an array of different perspectives in mind as they design, implement, analyze, and report global research and training activities. Many investigators working internationally have benefited from the perspective of experienced diplomats and other members of their nation's overseas community.

Third, scientists working internationally and the institutions that support them need to understand local cultural and political contexts and to anticipate unintended consequences. Critically important histories, traditions, and relationships are often invisible to expatriate investigators. These can often contribute to unintended consequences in research, and some can be severely damaging to local collaborators, research subjects, or even individuals and institutions with no obvious connection to the immediate research activity. It is important that scientists working internationally and the institutions that support them strive to be aware of the elements of local contexts, and to anticipate and address their role in unintended consequences.

Finally, investigators working internationally need to consider carefully and repeatedly their roles and responsibilities subsequent to the completion of research projects. This concern takes on special importance as more inter-national research is focused on prevention and intervention trials where there can be harsh consequences if follow-on requirements for the research popula-tion are not considered and adequately addressed. Such attention is also essential to help ensure that when scientists return to a locale or when the next generation of scientists follows the pioneers, international colleagues and research sites welcome additional collaboration. Bioethics standards increas-ingly require that international researchers consider responsibilities that may extend beyond the publication of research findings or the issuance of a degree.

Several examples illustrate the relevance of these ideas and may provide insights for individuals interested in international engagement. The first case illustrates the impact that increased public attention can have on global bio-medicine and public health.

A few years ago, two couples from the United States visited South Africa on a fact-finding trip. One couple was the parents of Bill Gates, Jr., the found-ing chief executive director of the Microsoft Corporation. Their role was to help decide priorities for the new Bill and Melinda Gates Foundation. They were accompanied by Jimmy and Roslyn Carter, the former president and first lady of the United States. A team of diplomats and public-health special-ists briefed them about the complex politics of South Africa and its eagerness to be considered a rising power. They also presented research findings that showed that South Africa had more individuals infected with the human immunodeficiency virus (HIV, the cause of AIDS) than any other country in the world. The team further explained that recent findings from research in Uganda demonstrated that mother-to-child HIV transmission could be dras-tically reduced using a very simple and virtually free antiretroviral inter-vention. The briefing team also mentioned that South Africa's official policy did not include the provision of this drug in its public antenatal clinics. After the briefing and a few questions, this group of U.S. elders visited with Nelson Mandela and Thabo Mbeki, who was the South African president at the time. They then flew on to Nigeria.

You can imagine the briefers' surprise when they watched the evening news and saw former President Carter lambasting President Mbeki from the Abuja airport for not taking care of his people and not making use of good scientific findings to prevent HIV infection in infants. Carter also implied that President Mbeki's overall approach to AIDS was uninformed by science and the evidence base it had produced, which of course sounded a lot like conde-scending imperialism to President Mbeki—whether justified or not.

It was no surprise that the next interaction between U.S. health diplomats and the South African Minister of Health, a political ally of President Mbeki, included a chilly lecture on public health as a domestic issue and not a foreign policy matter, a "reminder" that not all health research is transferable, in the minister's opinion, and a quick dismissal. From that day forward, the U.S. science and public-health community faced special scrutiny whenever new AIDS research activities were proposed or launched.

AIDS was already the main focus of U.S.-supported research in South Africa and a key foreign-policy issue between South Africa and the United States. With the involvement of South African scientists, often working with U.S. colleagues, the value of antiretroviral therapy was directly demonstrated in South African populations and eventually was widely introduced through a cooperative South Africa–United States partnership supported by the president's Emergency Plan for AIDS Relief. This joint program ultimately met both South African and U.S. objectives. When a group of leading members of the U.S. Congress visited South Africa some years later, President Mbeki thanked the United States for its support of South African AIDS programs and research. Getting to that point required careful coordination and respectful engagement. It is not clear what role President Carter's blunt comments might have played.

What was learned by those involved in this international health interaction? The experience with President Carter demonstrates that the "apolitical" and convincing arguments of science can be used as a political tool, and in this case the South African and world media took advantage of the incident to describe President Mbeki as an "AIDS denialist." Whether scientists are comfortable with it or not, many areas of international science (climate change research being another good example) are now part of the global political dialogue.

Another lesson to draw from this series of events is that the "celebrity spotlight," which is a defining feature of modern life, shines on work that used to appear primarily in scientific journals and conferences. Such attention brings with it powerful but unpredictable forces, with both risks and potential benefits. Well-informed researchers are actually finding remarkable advantage in this, because opinion-leader attention can generate an unusual level of public support, fresh funding, and the rapid translation of findings into practice or product. In the South African case, the incident and the glaring public spotlight it brought may have improved the chances that a recalcitrant minister would not interfere with antiretroviral therapy to treat HIV infections. Finally, the outcome of this chain of events demonstrated that by combining the authority of scientific discovery with foreign-policy skills and diplomatic approaches, both international research and science-based service delivery could thrive, even in a highly charged political atmosphere.

This example also offers insights into the value of considering and understanding foreign-policy and science-diplomacy perspectives when planning for and engaging in international research. From the diplomats' point of view, the science world is sometimes seen as politically naïve or intent on avoiding appropriate scrutiny. Nothing disturbs some diplomats more than government-supported visitors about whom they hear only when there is an outcry in the media or some other controversy. Nearly every diplomat has stories about scientists who finished their work and left behind only bad feelings about data, or about samples taken out of the country inappropriately or even illegally, or about scientific credit not shared with local collaborators. Although modern standards of research and research ethics make these practices uncommon, there have been cases where the foreign ministries or departments of state and embassy officials either curtailed or forbade research, because it was perceived that local sensitivities or needs had not been considered or that research participants would be left without appropriate ongoing care and support once the research was complete.

On the other hand, the diplomatic community is beginning to see international scientific collaboration as one of the key sectors for bilateral and multilateral engagement. Some of the more enlightened ambassadors have scientific goals integrated into their plans for host-country engagement. A strong science base is now recognized as an engine of development and a harbinger of improved population health and social well-being, especially in countries with emerging economies such as Brazil, China, India, and South Korea, which are now investing heavily in research and education. Senior ambassadors are often thrilled to have scientists from their home countries working in their host countries. However, they expect these investigators to understand the rules of diplomatic engagement (including keeping embassies informed) and to pursue their research following the same ethical and professional standards they would use at home.

Because diplomats are giving increasing attention to scientific engagement, it is important for scientists to be aware of diplomats' perspectives on international research. Where scientists see intriguing questions that will advance human understanding in their fields, diplomats want to know why the project requires international involvement and how pursuit of the research and its results might improve (or at least not damage) relations with the host country. Where scientists are sometimes focused on the accurate and methodologically sound collection of data, diplomats worry that researchers may choose to work internationally to escape the ethical constraints of studies done at home. Where some scientists feel their work is complete and all obligations are met once their findings are published, diplomats sometimes find themselves surprised to have to contend with foreign scientists or populations that feel ill-used and abandoned when the research protocol is fully executed. In addition, the end-users of research, those involved in the translation of research findings into practice or products, often see the work of both scientists and diplomats as incomplete. For many of them, international research is only justified if findings are made known, understood, and acted on in international settings where they can lead to improved health or other progress.

In addition to considering various perspectives, international investigators need to give careful attention to cultural factors and sensitivities when planning and implementing research. This is illustrated in a case shared by a colleague with long years of health-program engagement in Africa.

An American nursing professor and investigator was teaching research at a nursing college in sub-Saharan Africa on her first international assignment. She and one of her students decided to compare the care provided by traditional midwives in home deliveries with that provided by professional nurses in government hospitals. The focus was on assessing a variety of clinical and psychosocial interventions, and the research protocol included videotaping interactions for later analysis. They secured all the necessary consents from patients, health facilities, midwives, and the nursing college. The college principal was enthusiastic about the study because she felt the videotapes would be useful for training purposes. The study went well and the findings were to be presented at a seminar to which senior government health officials and college leaders were invited.

The seminar was well attended. The researcher presented the study, its hypothesis and methodology, and its findings; then, for background, they showed video clips. The audience sat in stunned silence as they watched government nurses providing care that could only be described as appalling, by any standard. The traditional midwives, on the other hand, looked like angels of mercy.

The discussion afterwards did not focus on research results that might improve training or care, or even on how to engage midwives in the health-care system. The participants wanted to know who owned the videotapes. Where would they be kept and who would have access to them? Had the women's rights been violated? Had the clients' husbands signed consent forms? What about the rights of the health workers? Did the hospital leadership give permission for the taping? The videotapes were confiscated by the principal. The study was never published, and the American professor was left wondering what she could have done differently and whether, as an expatriate, she should have conducted this study at all given the sensitivities involving cultural practices, professional boundaries, and local capacity to deliver care.

This example raises issues about perspective and partnership. How important is it to see international research and training engagement from many perspectives? Are there others outside the usual range of consultation whose engagement could help define research objectives and improve research outcomes?

From the perspective of the agency that funded this research, the methodology was reasonable, all appropriate ethical standards were met, the research was publishable, and the findings could have had an impact on clinical practice. The researcher's home institution probably also found it reasonable and might have even considered it a contribution toward her bid for tenure. But from the point of view of the diplomats in the researcher's home country, had they known about this study, they might have been able to warn the investigator about a government hypersensitive to criticism of public-sector employees, about tensions between Western-style medicine and traditional-care providers, and even about local customs that could require a husband's involvement in informed consent. From the end-user perspective, this research was a recipe for public embarrassment or possibly even official sanction.

Was the research question itself flawed? Would the investigator have used a different methodology or presented the findings differently if she had had the benefit of other perspectives? When an investigator seeks to undertake any international research, the challenge is to remember what makes international research complex. To do such research well requires considering its design, methodology, hypothesis, data, and even analysis from many perspectives. Usually the most important perspectives are those of the host country's collaborating partners and their institutions. With their help, international investigators may better understand both the local academic and wider sociocultural contexts, as well as the political realities that surround health research. The cultural and political context in which international research occurs may be very different from the prevalent research norms and conditions in researchers' home countries.

In addition to local research collaborators—who of course have their own personal interests at stake and may have reasons to accommodate or resist expatriate investigators' plans—to whom can an investigator turn to fill knowledge gaps or confirm impressions? In some cases it is very informative to consult with the expected end-users of the research, but they are often inaccessible. In some places the diplomatic community also can offer an unbiased take on local conditions, politics, and practices that can help increase the likelihood of success as research is designed and implemented. Often, staff at embassies or at governmental or private organizations with an interest in public health or science may be able to make an important contribution that can enhance the development of research methodology, sampling strategies, and the procurement of required permissions. Although few scientists use this option, it can be helpful for scientists to seek out and rely on the advice of compatriot government officials or others who are scientifically literate, have had extensive international experience, and have developed local contacts and knowledge. Such advice can be especially helpful in understanding the motivations of local collaborators and research contexts, especially where corruption or domestic politics may be invisible to a visiting foreign collaborator.

Another critical factor to consider in international research and training is the anticipation of unintended consequences and the value of paying attention to a broad environmental context, which is often difficult to identify, as the next case illustrates.

The northeastern part of India borders Myanmar. This is a frontier area of dense jungle and mountain lakes crossed by a few legal and many more illegal trade routes that carry manufactured goods from India eastward and, too often, heroin, gemstones, and living contraband westward. It is also one of the regions of India most affected by AIDS due to intravenous (IV) drug use increases 20 years ago. When Indian researchers at outposts in the border state of Manipur noticed these trends, they invited experienced international colleagues to measure the prevalence of HIV among the IV-drug-using population. The researchers worked with local social workers to find networks of young drug users, most of whom were adolescents or unemployed young men in their twenties. The investigators' interventions helped the subjects understand the value of using sterile needles and linked them to the few non-governmental organizations working with that disenfranchised population. The Indian and non-Indian researchers shared the same goals: to document the size of the problem, collect HIV samples to track the origins of the virus strain, and connect research subjects to care.

A year or two after initiation of the project, during an assessment visit, the non-governmental organizations involved in outreach to the still-growing IV-drug-using population were asked about the impact of the earlier research. The organizations reported that many of the drug users who were identified through the research (the ones who were still alive) had been placed in prison by their families. When interviewed, a research participant's mother said that the shame of drug abuse is worse than going to prison, even though many of the incarcerated never return from prison. In addition, many of the locals seemed to see this result of the study and its identification of research subjects as a perfectly reasonable outcome for individuals identified as having a drug-abuse problem. Their HIV status just made them seem even more diminished as reliable family members and contributors to society.

Although research-funding bodies rarely consider ethically reviewed research itself to be potentially risky, in many countries international research occurs within a context where the collection of data or the identification of risk factors can place both scientists and human-study participants at real jeopardy. Sometimes local collaborators do not want foreign colleagues to know the challenges they face, for fear that revelations might threaten funding or discourage continuation of the joint research. International investigators and funding agencies need to be especially attentive to ensure that international research does no harm. As the public watches more closely and higher expectations are placed on international research, even a few cases in which there are adverse, unintended consequences can cause major disruptions in the ability of scientists to continue their global efforts with widespread cooperation.

Of course, it is actually far more common for unanticipated consequences of international research to be positive. In Kolkata (previously Calcutta) there was a very different outcome from earlier research among another disenfranchised population at high risk of acquiring HIV. Twenty years ago, Kolkata sex workers were recruited to participate in Indo-U.S. HIV prevention trials with the cooperation of trusted community members who assisted with recruitment and data collection. Although research data were protected, there were still some issues with the police. Nevertheless, findings were published and shared widely with the community, and many of those who helped with the study emerged as leaders among the commercial sex workers. Over the last 20 years, members of the trade union of Kolkata sex workers have applied the findings of that early research, and the HIV prevalence rate among Kolkata sex workers remains among the lowest in the world for such a high-risk group. In Kolkata everyone has been surprised by the impact of research on the lives of uneducated and underprivileged women at great risk. The empowerment of sex workers was certainly not an intended consequence when U.S. and Indian investigators set out to test a behavioral intervention to evaluate strategies that would encourage condom use.

Such outcomes are a reminder of why international research is so important and what makes it and the scientists who pursue it an invaluable resource for many communities. Another example from Africa illustrates this point.

Recently in Kenya, South Africa, and Uganda, international teams of investigators working with sample populations of uncircumcised young men in communities with high HIV/AIDS prevalence offered half of them the option of being circumcised and the other half intensified, HIV-prevention counseling and condoms, which is the standard of prevention care. Those who chose medically supervised circumcision and those who did not were followed and monitored for the acquisition of HIV and other health-related outcomes. The men who acquired HIV were placed into long-term care, with antiretroviral treatment available, as medically appropriate, along with ongoing counseling.

It was found that the young men who received the circumcision intervention had a 60 percent reduction in the likelihood that they would become HIV-infected over the duration of the study. This was a far better prevention outcome than anticipated. The intention of the research had been to understand why there are uneven patterns of infection among communities in Africa where few differences in other behaviors are observed. As a result of the research, the focus of HIV-prevention service providers shifted, and adult males sought medically supervised circumcision all across southern Africa.

This research generated considerable global interest. It touched on some deeply ingrained cultural beliefs and practices, immediately engaged the interest of policy-makers, and confronted the researchers with complex communications challenges. Questions were raised about the exploitation of African research subjects, why some men were allowed to become HIV-infected, and what happened to them after the study. There was worry among policy-makers that the public would misunderstand the results, and that men would resort to unsafe circumcision and post-circumcision behaviors, thinking that the procedure would fully protect them.

How did the researchers and the funding organizations address these challenges and questions? First, none of the research subjects were abandoned, because the research plan included full access to HIV care and antiretroviral treatment for all participants for as long as they would need it. Second, the teams of African and non-African scientists jointly released the research findings, demonstrating that there was evident and fair co-ownership of the research methodology and the results. Leaders at the U.S. National Institutes of Health, which partially funded these studies, were careful to share credit for the findings across the research teams in four countries. Third, in releasing the results, the investigators identified possible unintended consequences, including the risks associated with non-medical circumcision and the urgent need to convey to the public that circumcision is not 100 percent protective.

Perhaps most importantly, the investigators also engaged African health-policy-makers in advance so they understood the ramifications of the research and could plan a politically beneficial public response. During the research, local surgeons and research teams had been trained. As follow-on data collection continued, the research communities welcomed the scientists' continuing engagement as circumcision services were offered even outside of the research protocol.

Finally, the investigators and the National Institutes of Health worked with public affairs experts in the U.S. embassies to assure accurate local reporting, which helped curtail sensational coverage of potentially explosive issues. These investigators left behind goodwill and an enthusiasm about international research. They set the stage for their results to move rapidly into practice, while making clear the challenges this step would pose. They also strengthened local research and intervention capacity and engaged political leaders in a way that made possible a positive response to potentially difficult findings.

From these examples, several ideas emerge as potentially useful to individual scientists and their institutions, as engagement in international research and training rapidly expands.

The world is watching and expectations are high. The spotlight on science has risks if international research teams are not working in genuine partnership, with the highest ethical standards and full transparency. This worldwide attention also has huge potential benefits if scientists can respond with sophistication to funding organizations that hope to foster the expansion of international research. A way forward is to find allies who will help researchers become more comfortable with this more-public role and its pressing demands.

As the biomedical and public-health research communities plan and implement international research, it is increasingly important that those engaged examine all aspects of that work from as many perspectives as possible. This is a challenge for investigators and for funding organizations, but it can mean the difference between success and failure. The key perspectives are those of the foreign collaborators and research participants, the end-users of research, local decision-makers, and collaborating institutions. Among the valuable and often overlooked perspectives are those of colleagues in foreign affairs and international development, who have great international experience and understanding.

The engagement of such colleagues, even those from non-scientific backgrounds, is also potentially very useful as investigators contend with unanticipated consequences that may arise from international research or from the ripples caused even by the pursuit of international cooperation in some countries. For international research to prosper, investigators must anticipate, be aware of, and directly address such consequences, positive or negative.

As national boundaries become less of a hindrance to scientific collaboration and as international research is increasingly productive and visible, unprecedented opportunities are opening up for investigators who can expand their skill sets to respond to the social and political complexities posed by multi-national collaboration. The scientists who succeed best in this new environment will be those who achieve both scientific and global partnership goals: completing their research objectives while also fostering sustained research capacity for their partners; pursuing strategies that ensure research findings are translated into publicly visible advances; and creating a legacy of goodwill, thereby building strong foundations for a future of rapidly expanding global cooperation.

Part II

Differences in the Organization and Funding of Research

4

National Variations in the Organization of Scientific Research

David W. Chapman, Ingo Stolz, and Olena Glushko

The world may be flattening due to forces of globalization (Friedman, 2007), but a tilt is emerging in the conduct of scientific research around the world. Research has, for many decades, been dominated by the United States and Europe. While these countries remain dominant, the trend is changing. Rapidly emerging economies, particularly in Asia, are increasingly the producers of scientific research. Governments in a number of these rapidly emerging economies are investing heavily in building research capacity.

As the research enterprise has broadened to a wider set of countries, cross-border collaboration has expanded. Such collaborations are motivated by opportunities to tap multiple sources of funding, spread financial risk, and sustain working relationships among researchers. In some cases, research has moved abroad in response to government regulatory policies (Senker, Enzing, & Reiss, 2008). For example, restrictions on stem-cell research during the Bush presidency in the United States led some companies to move their research in this area to other countries. International collaborations are facilitated by the increased simplicity and low cost of communication and the ease with which multi-national corporations can direct their research funds to take advantage of favorable economic and legal contexts.

This chapter characterizes the nature of current cross-national research collaborations from the perspective of national variation. It reviews changes now underway in the manner and extent to which scientific research is being pursued across countries. To that end, it presents an overview of the size of, and emerging trends in, the research and development (R&D) endeavor across countries, the distribution of research funds across sectors and institutions, and the growth of cross-national collaboration in research. The central argument is that four trends are currently shaping cross-national research collaboration. First, aggregate funding for scientific research has grown rapidly over the last decade. Second, funding patterns reflect a shift away from those countries that have previously dominated, toward newly emerging economies. Third, across virtually all countries, most funding for scientific research is provided by private companies with governments playing a secondary, though still important, role. Finally, the shifting patterns in where and how research is being conducted have implications for cross-national research collaboration.

Who Sponsors Scientific Research? Who Conducts It?

Most scientific research is funded by governments or private-sector companies. The research is typically conducted by private-sector enterprises, universities, free-standing research institutes, or directly by governments themselves, though the prominence of each group differs by country. Among member countries of the Organization for Economic Co-operation and Development (OECD), the majority of R&D is both funded and conducted by private-sector business and industry (OECD, 2008a); higher-education institutions play a much smaller role. The relative role of the private sector, government, and higher education in conducting scientific research varies greatly across countries. Government research in Indonesia, for example, constitutes 81 percent of the gross domestic expenditure on R&D, while it represents only 13 and 3 percent in Korea and Hong Kong, respectively (Gill & Kharas, 2006). With notable exceptions, the higher-education sector in most countries is an important but minor player in the research endeavor.

Research in Private-Sector Business and Industry

By far the biggest sponsors of scientific R&D are private-sector business and industry. In OECD countries almost 69 percent of R&D is performed by large businesses (OECD, 2008b), though in many countries small- and medium-sized enterprises also play an important role. Regardless of a business' size, the majority of the research they sponsor is linked to product development. Undertaking the research "in-house" often permits greater secrecy in product development and greater control over ownership of resulting ideas and products than doing the research at a university would allow. Conducting research in-house also allows multi-national corporations to shift the location of the work, to take advantage of favorable national, economic, and regulatory environments.

Over the last two decades, the role of business and industry in supporting research has grown dramatically. Between 1995 and 2006, the percentage of the gross expenditure on R&D funded by industry in OECD countries rose from 60 percent to 64 percent (OECD, 2008b). Similar rates of growth occurred in the European Union (from 52 percent to 54 percent), and the United States (from 60 percent to 65 percent) (OECD, 2008b). The growth of private-sector support for research has been even more dramatic in China, increasing from 58 percent to 70 percent in just seven years (UNESCO, 2009a).

Research in Universities

Higher-education systems are differentiated, with scientific research typically concentrated at top-tier universities and usually connected, in some fashion, to the advanced training of emerging researchers. Depending on the country, research in public universities is supported by government either through the university budget or through competitive grant systems. To the extent that private universities are major centers of scientific research, as in the United States, most research funds come through university researchers competing for government or private research contracts.

Higher-education institutions play an important, but seldom dominant, role in the conduct of research in most countries. Nevertheless, the relative share of R&D performed in higher-education institutions increased in some countries between 1996 and 2007, as in the Slovak Republic (20 percent), Lithuania (19 percent), Latvia (14 percent), the Czech Republic (8 percent), South Africa (8 percent between 1997 and 2006), Canada (7 percent), and Ireland (6 percent) (UNESCO, 2009a). The comparable increase was slower across OECD countries by only about 1 percent between 1995 and 2006 (OECD, 2008b). The OECD posits that the strong growth in R&D funds flowing to higher education may reflect the growing recognition of the important role of higher-education-based R&D in national economic growth. In relative terms, however, funding for higher-education-based research has been losing ground to the private sector. In short, while the amount spent for university research over the last decade in most countries has continued to grow, the amount being spent on research conducted by business and industry has grown faster. The net effect is that university-based research has been losing its market share of the total funds being invested in research.

Though businesses undertake most of their own research, they sometimes outsource part of it to university researchers. In that respect, higher-education institutions are in a position to gain from increased research spending on the part of businesses. This is not, however, the general pattern. The increased funding for business-sponsored R&D has not necessarily resulted in research gains for higher-education institutions. In fact, the percentage of higher-education R&D funded by industry generally has been stagnant over the most recent years of measurement, though it varies by country. For example, in the early 2000s, large firms were more likely to collaborate with higher-education institutions in Scandinavia, Belgium, the Netherlands, and Luxembourg, but less likely in the United Kingdom, Canada, and Australia (OECD, 2007).

Research in Research Institutes

The Soviet model, widely employed in Central Asian countries, is that research is conducted at separate institutes that may be either university-affiliated or free-standing. In these countries, the scientific-research endeavor is separated from the instructional mission of the university. Research institutes are most often funded by the government. This pattern is beginning to change, however. In some countries across Central Asia (in Kazakhstan, for example), the trend is now to integrate research institutes into universities.

Research in Government Research Facilities

Worldwide, government supports university-based research, but also conducts research directly. In the United States the government conducts its own research through laboratories at, for example, the National Institutes of Health (NIH), the National Aeronautical and Space Administration (NASA), and the Los Alamos National Laboratories, though these organizations often work closely with academic institutions and researchers.

In Europe, a new type of research center, the "pan-European research facility," is emerging ("Legal accord," 2009, p. 764). Future European research infrastructures, such as the European Spallation Source, will be granted the status of an international organization, and exempted from value added tax and excise duty ("Legal accord," 2009). At present, the European Commission is designing a standard legal framework governing all pan-European research facilities, which will make it easier for nations to develop large, shared projects ("Legal accord," 2009). These research institutions represent an emerging type of research collaboration with government sponsorship. There is a trend, moreover, toward a decrease in university–industry collaborations in Europe. Gilbert (2008) argues that the credibility of the European Commission's efforts to promote research collaborations between academia and industry is under threat, because universities cannot afford to take part.

In summary, cross-national research collaboration is most likely to occur in projects undertaken by private-sector companies and by universities. Research institutes and government research facilities may also engage in international research collaborations, but their interests are typically better served by keeping their research in-house, since government-conducted research is often linked to national interests. Similarly, free-standing research institutes are generally government-funded and also tend to focus on topics of national relevance.

Shifting Patterns in Where Research is Conducted

The global distribution of investment in R&D is changing, with non-OECD economies now becoming important R&D spenders, while expenditures in many OECD countries are stagnant or falling. The net result is that non-OECD countries account for a sharply growing share of the world's R&D. From 12 percent of the world's R&D expenditures in 1996, non-OECD countries now account for 18 percent (OECD, 2008a). For example, in China, gross expenditure on R&D increased by about 19 percent annually between 2001 and 2006 (OECD, 2008a), and by 2007 reached $105 billion in purchasing power parity (UNESCO, 2009a). Despite the global financial crisis, the Chinese government budget for scientific research grew by 26 percent from 2008 to 2009. Similarly, between 2004 and 2006, gross expenditure on R&D in

South Africa rose by 31 percent (UNESCO, 2009a). Gross expenditure on R&D increased from $9 billion to $24 billion in Russia between 1996 and 2007, while in 2007 India spent $25 billion in purchasing power parity (UNESCO, 2009a).

Where are Researchers Prepared?

The patterns in research funding described above are clear. The countries that already account for the most substantial production of researchers are those in which funding for research is growing at the slowest rates. The countries making the most substantial investments in scientific research tend to be those with smaller supplies of highly trained researchers. For example, the number of graduates in science and engineering across Asia is low relative to Europe and North America, though the proportion of graduates in science and engineering versus other fields is roughly comparable across those regions (NSF, 2004). Across Asia, enrollment growth in mathematics, science, and engineering appears to be flat; absolute numbers of graduates in these fields are increasing, but only at about the rate of overall enrollment increases in higher education (UNESCO, 2005).

Encouraging enrollment growth in science and technology is not a sufficient strategy for promoting scientific research. Once enrolled, students must have a rigorous program of study and research. In many low-income countries, that is not consistently the case. A characteristic of many countries is that relatively little research is currently conducted in public universities. Business and industry observers express concern that much of the research that is conducted is of low quality, due to, among other things, the theoretical nature of much university research, the lack of qualified instructors, old and outdated equipment, and differences in the timeframes and results orientation of academics and industry (Chapman, 2007). These weaknesses are exacerbated by the lack of linkages between universities and industry, the fragmentation of research efforts, weak commercialization and exploitation of R&D, and the lack of connection between regional economic strengths and research excellence (LaRocque, 2007). A report by the not-for-profit National Bureau of Economic Research argues that the quality and amount of university research is shaped by three factors: (1) research funding; (2) the ability of the university to decide on its own programs, hiring, and budgets; and (3) the level of competition the university faces in securing resources, faculty, and students ("University research," 2009, p. 1207). The report stresses that all three conditions must be favorable; if one of the three is missing, research output and quality drop ("University research," 2009).

The *Global Competitiveness Report* indicates that scientific research institutions in both East and Southeast Asia are of low quality, particularly in countries such as the Philippines, Indonesia, and Thailand, compared to those in more industrialized countries (LaRocque, 2007). This may explain why an analysis of university-based R&D, compared to business and government R&D across Asia, suggests that, with a few notable exceptions (e.g., Hong Kong), university-based research lags well behind research done in business and frequently behind government-based research.

National Variation in Emphasis on Scientific Research

Countries differ in the emphasis they assign to scientific research. These differences are not easily categorized and are not necessarily related to geographical region. For example, East Asia includes the country with the largest population in the world (China) along with some of the smallest (Laos, Mongolia). It includes some of the most affluent (Japan, Singapore, South Korea) and some of the poorest (Cambodia, Laos). It includes some of those countries investing the most in expanding research (China) and some investing the least. Similar differences can be observed across Latin America and the Middle East. The economic condition of countries may be a more meaningful variable by which to categorize countries, but even that dimension is ebbing in relevance as research investments in some of the richest countries are leveling off, while some less-affluent countries, such as China, are increasing their research investments. That said, in characterizing the research profile of countries, eight factors are of particular relevance: (1) policy development; (2) governmental initiatives to expand scientific R&D; (3) rate of increase in investment in R&D; (4) quality of research training; (5) access to research funding; (6) opportunities to participate in national and international research collaborations; (7) incentive systems for participation in scientific research; and (8) extent and effectiveness of research-oversight mechanisms. The following snapshots of R&D efforts in five countries (India, the United States, China, Germany, and Brazil) illustrate differences in how research is organized, funded, and conducted along these dimensions at the national level.

Research in India: Behind but on the Move

R&D in India is still surprisingly weak compared to OECD and peer non-OECD countries. With an overall research expenditure of 0.8 percent of the gross domestic product (UNESCO, 2009a), India is in the lowest quartile internationally, and even ranks last in regard to both business investment and higher-education investment in research (OECD, 2008a). Further, in recent reports, India ranked last in the number of triadic patents per million population (OECD, 2009a), last in the number of scientific articles per million population (OECD, 2008a), second to last in international ratings of the prominence of Indian scientific articles (OECD, 2007), last in the number of researchers per 1,000 people employed in the country (OECD, 2007), and last in the number of PhD degrees awarded as a percentage of the relevant age cohort (OECD, 2007). The situation is further exacerbated by the out-migration of highly educated Indians. Two-thirds of the doctoral students from India who graduate from U.S. institutions receive a postdoctoral appointment in the United States (OECD, 2007).

The Indian government has a unique responsibility for alleviating this rather bleak picture, due to its unusually strong involvement in scientific research. Over three-quarters of the gross domestic expenditure on research is funded and performed by the government (as of 2004, UNESCO, 2009a). India therefore ranks among the top countries, worldwide, in the share of research that is funded and performed by government institutions. By comparison, the role of Indian higher-education institutions in research is negligible, with not even 5 percent of the gross domestic expenditure on research going to projects that are funded and performed by universities.

Indeed, the Indian government has initiated steps to improve the current status of Indian research through funding and policy. Gross investment in R&D in India more than tripled between 1996 and 2007, from $7.6 billion to $24.8 billion in purchasing power parity (UNESCO, 2009a). Also, India has created a competitive tax environment for investments in research (OECD, 2008a) and introduced a Science and Technology Plan in the Tenth Five-Year Plan from 2002 to 2007 (Planning Commission, 2002). This plan focuses explicitly on the development of indigenous technologies; the interface between industry, research institutions, and academe; international cooperation; and the development of human resources (Planning Commission, 2002). The Science and Technology Policy 2003 of the Indian Department of Science and Technology stated that the level of investment in research and technology should be raised to at least 2 percent of gross domestic product at the end of the Tenth Plan (Department of Science and Technology, 2003). This goal, however, has most likely not been achieved, with a gross expenditure on research of 0.8 percent of the gross domestic product in 2007, which even represents a slight decrease from that of 2005 (UNESCO, 2009a).

Positive trends are nevertheless emerging. A reduced share of patents involving international co-invention "may indicate that [India] is strengthening [its] domestic technological capabilities" (OECD, 2008a, p. 44). The foreign ownership of Indian inventions has declined considerably, while the Indian ownership of inventions made abroad has increased (OECD, 2007). Also, the annual rate of growth in patenting between 1997 and 2004 was the second largest in the world, trailing only China's (OECD, 2007).

These positive trends suggest that India could position itself as a future world power in research. In order to achieve such a position, however, India will have to make an even greater effort to unleash its innovative potential. This might mean taking action to increase the involvement of businesses and higher-education institutions in research, to educate larger proportions of its population for future research, to reverse the national loss of highly trained scientists, and to broaden the indigenous market for research and technologies. It is rather doubtful, however, that the initiatives taken under the Science and Technology Plan and the Science and Technology Policy 2003 will prove to be sufficient for that purpose.

Research in the United States: Ahead but Losing Ground

An increasingly shrill chorus of commentators announce "the end of America's era as the scientific hegemony" (Hollingsworth, Muller, & Hollingsworth, 2008, p. 412). The United States is far from losing its dominant position in R&D. It remains among the top 10 countries in the world in its rate of gross domestic expenditure on R&D (OECD, 2008a), even though R&D intensity in the United States decreased from its peak of 2.76 percent in 2001 to 2.62 percent in 2006 (OECD, 2008a). In 2007 the United States ranked seventh among OECD countries in gross domestic expenditure on R&D (OECD, 2009b) and accounted for 32 percent of global R&D expenditure (UNESCO, 2009b).

The United States also leads the world in terms of availability of highly qualified human resources in the field of R&D. In 2004, out of the 150,000 doctoral degrees in science and engineering awarded worldwide, more than 26,000 doctoral degrees were earned in the United States, while Russia awarded 16,000, China conferred almost 15,000, and Germany awarded more than 12,000 (NSF, 2008a). Overall, the United States represented 20 percent of world researchers in 2007 (UNESCO, 2009b).

Furthermore, the United States leads in research output. In 2005 the United States alone produced 205,320 journal articles (29 percent of the world output) in science and engineering (NSF, 2008a). The European Union collectively only slightly outperformed the United States by producing 33 percent of the world output (NSF, 2008a). Moreover, between 1995 and 2005, the United States' index of highly cited articles (a measure of research impact) increased from 1.73 to 1.83, while the European Union's index went from 0.75 to 0.84, and the Asia-10's[1] index grew only from 0.39 to 0.41 (NSF, 2008a).

U.S. productivity is, in many respects, a function of the U.S. investment in science and engineering. Expenditures for R&D conducted in the United States have followed a pattern of nearly continuous growth since 1953, when such data were first collected (NSF, 2008a). While the U.S. expenditure on R&D has climbed steadily, the growth has been driven mostly by increases in R&D expenditures in the business sector, which in 2006 performed 71 percent of U.S. R&D and funded 66 percent of U.S. R&D (NSF, 2008a). The academic sector is the second to business, but ahead of the federal government in R&D performance. In 2006 colleges and universities received $48 billion for R&D from all sources of funding (NSF, 2008b). Higher-education R&D output represented 14 percent of the total U.S. R&D (NSF, 2008a). Still, this output is only one-fifth as large as the R&D output of the business sector (NSF, 2008a). However, this indicator may under-represent the importance of university-based research, since industry concentrates on applied research, whereas colleges and universities lead the nation in basic research, conducting 56 percent of basic research in the United States (NSF, 2008a).

Although the business sector is the primary driving force of R&D in the United States, the experience of other countries (China and India, for example) demonstrates that government policies play a crucial role in expanding R&D. In the United States, the American Recovery and Reinvestment Act (ARRA) of 2009 added $18.4 billion to the federal R&D budget in fiscal year 2009, representing a 12.5 percent increase in government support for R&D (AAAS, 2009). Much of the money went to the National Science Foundation, the National Institute of Standards and Technology, the NIH, the Department of Energy, and NASA (AAAS, 2009). From there, much of it went to higher-education researchers. The proposed budget for fiscal year 2010 continues R&D as a national policy priority in the United States. It would further increase federal R&D funding by $148 billion, a 0.3 percent increase over fiscal year 2009 (AAAS, 2009).

Despite these recent governmental efforts to stimulate R&D in the United States, the fiscal year 2010 budget will continue the long-term, downward trend in federal research funding, and the federal research portfolio will be 6.8 percent below the 2004 level in inflation-adjusted dollars (AAAS, 2009). Joint efforts by the federal government, industry, and state governments are therefore necessary to improve the efficiency and effectiveness of R&D investments in the United States, and to prevent the United States from losing its status as a world scientific superpower.

Research in China: A Force to be Reckoned With

The speed with which China has emerged as a scientific power represents one of the most dramatic shifts in worldwide R&D (Hollingsworth et al., 2008). In 2000, China had the fourth-largest expenditure on R&D in the world at $45 billion. By 2005 Chinese expenditures on R&D had increased to $115 billion, placing it third in the world in R&D expenditures (NSF, 2008a). R&D intensity more than doubled in China between 1996 and 2007 (UNESCO, 2009b). Research funding in China heavily favors applied R&D, aimed at short-term economic development. In 2003–2004, its basic-research share was only 6 percent of total R&D (NSF, 2008a).

China's R&D funding pattern is similar to that of other countries. In 2005 industry funded 67 percent of R&D while government funded 26 percent (NSF, 2008a). However, universities played a less prominent role in conducting research in China, compared to their role in other leading research countries. Most Chinese R&D (68 percent) was conducted by the business sector, with another 22 percent conducted directly by the government. Higher education accounted for only 10 percent of the country's R&D (NSF, 2008a).

One indicator of China's success as an emerging science power is the growth of highly qualified human resources. As a result of major educational reforms of the late 1990s, the number of recipients of four-year degrees increased from 405,000 in 1998 to 1.2 million in 2004, and 37 percent of degrees were in engineering (NSF, 2008a). At the same time, China joined the largest producers of science and engineering doctoral degrees, awarding almost 15,000 in 2004 (NSF, 2008a). The number of science and engineering doctoral degrees conferred in China increased more than six-fold between 1993 and 2004 (NSF, 2008a), giving China the world's second-largest pool of human resources in science and technology (OECD, 2008a). In 2007 China represented 20 percent of world researchers compared to 14 percent in 2002 (UNESCO, 2009b).

The increase in PhDs is reflected in research output. China's production of science and engineering articles has increased significantly since 1995 and is second only to Japan's among the Asia-10 countries. In 1995, China produced less than 2 percent of the world's science and technology articles; by 2005 it produced 6 percent of the world's output (NSF, 2008a). By 2005 China entered the "top 15" for triadic patents (OECD, 2008a).

China attributes much of its success in economic and scientific development to its governmental policies. The two main goals of research policy in China are promoting independent innovation and enhancing competitiveness (ERAWATCH, 2009). Two main policy documents: the *Medium and Long-term National Plan for Science and Technology Development 2006–2020* and China's *National S&T Development Plan for the 11th Five-year Period 2006–2010* (ERAWATCH, 2009) specify the anticipated progress of R&D over the next 15 years and five years, respectively. Among the goals of these plans are that: (1) R&D as a percentage of gross domestic product will reach 2 percent in 2010 and 2.5 percent in 2020; (2) the level of reliance on foreign technology will decrease to 40 percent by 2010 and 30 percent by 2020; (3) the share of science and technology's contribution to economic growth will reach 45 percent by 2010 and 60 percent by 2020; (4) China will become a "top 10" country in terms of the number of citations to scientific publications by 2010 and a "top five" country in 2020; and (5) China will become a "top 15" country in terms of the number of invention patents issued by 2010 and a "top five" country by 2020 (ERAWATCH, 2009).

Both plans also identify four areas of primary importance in China's R&D for the next 15 years. First, China intends to advance key technologies in the manufacturing industry, information technology, and agricultural industry, which are perceived as priority industries for research policy. Second, China plans to address environmental issues. Specifically, China intends to develop clean energy and energy-efficient technologies to reduce energy consumption and optimize energy structure. Third, China aims to develop human resources. To achieve this objective, China plans to support and develop top-level universities, research institutes, and research programs, and, as a result, increase the share of science and technology personnel as a percentage of the country's population. Finally, China aims to enforce national security, giving priority to pharmaceutical and medical-equipment technologies for coping with major diseases (ERAWATCH, 2009).

The *Medium and Long-term National Plan for S&T Development 2006–2020* and China's *National S&T Development Plan (2006–2010)* set ambitious goals for developing China's capacity for research and innovation (ERAWATCH, 2009). The OECD has observed, however, that continued expansion of China's research enterprise should be accompanied by changes in the infrastructure for financing R&D, greater protection of intellectual property rights, and increased support for entrepreneurship (OECD, 2008a).

Research in Germany: A Renewed Surge

Germany traditionally has been a top producer of R&D. It boasts a well-established system of research and innovation, has a large and growing share of total OECD technology exports, and is fourth in patenting worldwide, in population-adjusted terms (OECD, 2008a). Gross investment in research has increased by 61 percent in one decade, to $69.7 billion in 2007, in purchasing power parity (UNESCO, 2009a), which again places Germany fourth worldwide. In the same period, businesses have strengthened their involvement in research to almost 70 percent of the gross expenditure on research performed by the private sector (UNESCO, 2009a).

There are signs, however, that this well-established system of innovation might not have been nourished adequately. German productivity performance has decreased compared to that of other OECD countries (OECD, 2008a). The tertiary graduation rate in Germany is among the lowest in the OECD area (OECD, 2008a), and the number of research personnel has grown very slowly compared to that in other OECD countries (OECD, 2008a). Higher-education institutions have slowly but steadily decreased their involvement in research in the last decade. In 2007, 16 percent of the gross expenditure on research was performed in a university setting, down from over 18 percent in 1996 (UNESCO, 2009a).

These trends have prompted new policies regarding the organization of science, which are intended to ensure that Germany remains one of the most competitive research players. Four initiatives play especially important roles. First, the *High-Tech Strategy*, launched by the federal government in 2006 committed €15 billion to fund research in 17 fields, including health, energy. and security (Federal Ministry of Education and Research, 2006). The government's goals are to increase investment in research to 3 percent of the gross domestic product by 2010, improve cooperation between science and industry, and accelerate the practical application of research findings. Second, the *Initiative for Excellence*, launched in 2005 by federal and state governments, is aimed at enhancing research at higher-education institutions (Federal Ministry of Education and Research, 2005). Through a competitive application process, €1.9 billion are to be awarded by 2011 to the most innovative research universities and research programs. Another €2.7 billion, pledged in April 2009, will extend the program to 2017 (Federal Ministry of Education and Research, 2009b). Third, the federal 2008 *Strategy for the Internationalization of Science and Research* gives researchers opportunities for increased international collaborations (Federal Ministry of Education and Research, 2008). This strategy is intended to facilitate employment of international researchers in Germany. Fourth, the *Higher Education Pact 2020*, sponsored by federal and state governments, is intended to increase higher-education enrollment by 275,000 (Federal Ministry of Education and Research, 2009a). Between 2011 and 2015, more than €5 billion will be spent on this initiative.

Overall, Germany's investments are aimed at making it a more competitive market for scientific R&D. Programs and policies have been launched especially within the higher-education system (Mayer & Ziegele, 2009). These initiatives are driven mainly by federal and state governments. This is a new approach for Germany, since German higher education has been widely regarded as a state matter. Nevertheless, broader reforms are still needed to lower regulatory and administrative barriers to entrepreneurship and to foster further competitive and innovative R&D (OECD, 2008a).

Research in Brazil: Energy and Direction

Brazil is the research leader in Latin America, but Brazilian research still falls behind in global comparisons. In 2006, 1 percent of the gross domestic product was invested in research (UNESCO, 2009a), which is high compared to any other Latin American country, but low compared to the OECD average of 2.26 percent (OECD, 2008b). Several other statistics also show the gap between Brazil and many of its peer nations worldwide. In 2004 less than 8 percent of the 25–64 age group had attained a postsecondary degree, and less than 11 percent of university graduates had received degrees in science and engineering (OECD, 2008a). Brazil also faces a shortage of researchers and an exodus of those it has. In 2006 the country had only 1.48 researchers per 1,000 total employment (OECD, 2008a). Those scholars and researchers are increasingly leaving to go to the United States (OECD, 2007). The average annual emigration growth rate to the United States among Brazilian scholars was 4 percent between 1995 and 2006; of those who left, about 30 percent did not intend to return (OECD, 2007).

Brazil accounts for only 0.31 triadic patents per million inhabitants (OECD, 2008a), representing only 0.1 percent of the patents worldwide in 2005 (OECD, 2009a). By comparison, the OECD average is 43.9 triadic patents per million inhabitants (OECD, 2009a). Brazilian innovations are often owned by foreign stakeholders, mostly European and U.S. partners (OECD, 2007). More specifically, 39 percent of domestic innovations are owned by foreign owners, as compared to the OECD average of 16 percent (2001–2003).

Similarly, 28 percent of Brazilian patents that are filed have foreign co-inventors, as compared to an OECD average of 7 percent (OECD, 2007). Finally, there is little cooperation between business and higher education in the area of research and little cooperation among businesses with each other (OECD, 2008a).

In 2007 a four-year plan for science, technology, and innovation was approved in order to improve the status of Brazilian research (Ministry of Science and Technology, 2007). The plan is to invest $23 billion, focused primarily on: (1) the development of research personnel; (2) investments in research, especially in the fields of biotechnology, nanotechnology, information technology, energy, climate change, and the Amazon River ecosystem; (3) enterprise innovation; and (4) sustainable development (OECD, 2008a; Science and Development Network, 2007).

This four-year plan promises to reinforce and accelerate some already-positive trends in Brazilian research. These trends include a 33-percent increase in academic patenting between 2004 and 2005, a 60-percent increase in academic revenue through technology licensing in that same time period, and an increase to 1.4 percent of world scientific publications in 2005 (OECD, 2008a).

Nevertheless, Brazil might have to alter more of the structural features of its research environment if it is to advance further. Research in Brazil remains funded mostly by the government (50 percent in 2006, UNESCO, 2009a). Brazilian businesses now fund almost 50 percent of the research, but they still see economic risks, lack of financing, and the shortage of skilled labor as factors that impede innovation (OECD, 2008a). As a consequence, "fostering productivity-enhancing innovation in the business sector is an important challenge" (OECD, 2006). The yet-to-be-implemented 2008 program, *Politica de Desinvolvimento Produtivo* (Ministério do Desinvolvimento, Indústria e Comércio Exterior, 2008), is intended to help meet this challenge by encouraging greater cooperation between the private sector and various government agencies responsible for innovation policy (OECD, 2009c).

Overall, research in Brazil still has a way to go; however, the 2008 *Politica de Desinvolvimento Produtivo* and the 2007 four-year plan show that first steps are underway. The research world might increasingly look to Brazil in the future.

Implications for International Research Collaborations

The preceding discussion supports five propositions relevant to the expansion of international research collaborations.

First, national differences in research productivity reflect differences in national policies regarding how research is funded and conducted; however, these national differences are not necessarily geographically or economically based.

Second, countries vary in the extent to which government ideology operates as a filter on researchers' choice of research topics. This difference is likely to affect university-based more than private-sector researchers, since university-based researchers are less mobile.

Third, most research worldwide is funded by private-sector business and industry and is generally driven by a profit motive. One consequence is that, to protect proprietary rights, such research is often less transparent in the way it is conducted. This is not necessarily sinister, but it does have implications for the ability of other researchers to review research protocols and attempt to replicate findings. The proprietary nature of private-sector research can make monitoring the conduct and integrity of research more challenging.

Fourth, businesses and industries that operate in multiple international locations are in a position to assemble and support multi-national research teams and to move their research to the most research-friendly environments. Two potential consequences follow. Multi-national companies can "shop around" for the venue that offers the greatest regulatory latitude, if that is an advantage for either the company or the researchers involved. Also, researchers from multiple countries may join together in their orientation to their sponsor's objectives, perhaps without a full appreciation for the legal and ethical differences associated with the venues in which they are actually conducting the research.

Fifth, while governments can and do encourage research through direct funding, the adoption of government policies that promote and encourage private-sector investment in research (for example, taxation policies, policies on intellectual property rights) can be an even stronger accelerator.

Note

1.   Asia-10 includes China, India, Indonesia, Japan, Malaysia, the Philippines, Singapore, South Korea, Taiwan, and Thailand.

References

AAAS (American Association for the Advancement of Science). (2009). *AAAS report XXXIV research & development FY 2010*. Retrieved September 25, 2009, from www.aaas.org/spp/rd/rdreport2010.

Chapman, D. W. (2007). Higher education, part 3. In V. Ordonez, R. Johanson, & D. W. Chapman, *Investing in education in the Asia-Pacific region in the future: A strategic education sector study*. Manila: Asian Development Bank.

Department of Science and Technology. (2003). *Science and technology policy 2003*. Retrieved October 10, 2009, from http://dst.gov.in/stsysindia/stp2003.htm.

ERAWATCH. (2009). *ERAWATCH research inventory report: China*. Retrieved September 25, 2009, from http://cordis.europa.eu/erawatch/index.cfm?fuseaction=ri.content&topicID=4&countryCode=CN.

Federal Ministry of Education and Research. (2005). *Bund-Länder-Vereinbarung über die Exzellenzinitiative des Bundes und der Länder zur Förderung der Wissenschaft und Forschung an den deutschen Hochschulen [Agreement between federation and states regarding the initiative for excellence of federation and states for advancing science and research at German higher education institutions]*. Retrieved November 25, 2009, from www.bmbf.de/pub/vereinbarung_exzellenzinitiative.pdf.

Federal Ministry of Education and Research. (2006). *The high-tech strategy for Germany*. Bonn, Germany: Federal Ministry of Education and Research.

Federal Ministry of Education and Research. (2008). *Strengthening Germany's role in the global knowledge society: Strategy of the federal government for the internationalization of science and research*. Bonn, Germany: Federal Ministry of Education and Research.

Federal Ministry of Education and Research. (2009a). *Higher education pact*. Retrieved July 27, 2009, from www.bmbf.de/en/6142.php.

Federal Ministry of Education and Research. (2009b). *Initiative for excellence*. Retrieved July 27, 2009, from www.bmbf.de/en/1321.php.

Friedman, T. L. (2007). *The world is flat: A brief history of the twenty-first century*. New York: Farrar, Straus & Giroux.

Gilbert, N. (2008). European funding plan "unviable." *Nature, 456*(7222), 551.

Gill, I., & Kharas, H. (2006). *An East Asian renaissance: Ideas for economic growth*. Washington, DC: World Bank.

Hollingsworth, J. R., Muller, K. H., & Hollingsworth, E. J. (2008). The end of the science superpowers. *Nature, 454*(7203), 412–413.

LaRocque, N. (2007). *The role of education in supporting the development of science, technology and innovation in developing member countries: An issues paper*. Manila: Asian Development Bank.

Legal accord eases path to Europe's research facilities [News in Brief]. (2009). *Nature, 459*(7248), 764.

Mayer, P., & Ziegele, F. (2009). Competition, autonomy and new thinking: Transformation of higher education in federal Germany. *Higher Education Management and Policy, 21*(2), 51–70.

Ministério do Desenvolvimento, Indústria e Comércio Exterior. (2008). *Política de desenvolvimento produtivo [Productive development policy]*. Retrieved November 25, 2009, from www.mdic.gov.br/pdp/index.php/sitio/inicial.

Ministry of Science and Technology. (2007). *Science, technology and innovation for Brazil's development: Investing and innovating to grow: 2007–2010 action plan*. Retrieved November 25, 2009, from www.brasilemb.org/index.php?option=com_content&task=view&id=215&Itemid=194.

NSF (National Science Foundation). (2004). *Science and engineering indicators 2004*. Retrieved January 18, 2009, from www.nsf.gov/statistics/seind04/c2/c2s5.htm.

NSF (National Science Foundation). (2008a). *Science and engineering indicators 2008: Volume 1*. Retrieved January 18, 2009, from www.nsf.gov/statistics/indicators.

NSF (National Science Foundation). (2008b). *Science and engineering indicators 2008: Volume 2*. Retrieved January 18, 2009, from www.nsf.gov/statistics/indicators.

OECD (Organisation for Economic Co-operation and Development). (2006). *OECD economic surveys: Brazil*. Paris: OECD.

OECD (Organisation for Economic Co-operation and Development). (2007). *OECD science, technology and industry scorecard 2007: Innovation and performance in the global economy*. Paris: OECD.

OECD (Organisation for Economic Co-operation and Development). (2008a). *OECD science, technology and industry outlook*. Paris: OECD. Retrieved January 18, 2009, from www.sourceoecd.org/scienceIT/9789264049918.

OECD (Organisation for Economic Co-operation and Development). (2008b). *Main science and technology indicators*. Paris: OECD.

OECD (Organisation for Economic Co-operation and Development). (2009a). *OECD factbook 2009: Economic, environmental, and social statistics*. Paris: OECD.

OECD (Organisation for Economic Co-operation and Development). (2009b). Science and technology: Research and development. In *OECD factbook 2009: Economic, environment, and social statistics*. Paris: OECD. Retrieved on October 20, 2009, from http://puck.sourceoecd.org/pdf/factbook2009/302009011e-07-01-01.pdf.

OECD (Organisation for Economic Co-operation and Development). (2009c). *OECD economic surveys: Brazil*. Paris: OECD.

Planning Commission. (2002). *Tenth five year plan: 2002–2007*. Retrieved October 10, 2009, from http://planningcommission.gov.in/plans/planref/fiveyr/10th/volume2/v2_ch10_1.pdf.

Science and Development Network. (2007). *Brazil launches US$23 billion science plan*. Retrieved October 10, 2009, from www.scidev.net/en/news/brazil-launches-us23-billion-science-plan.html.

Senker, J., Enzing, C., & Reiss, T. (2008). Biotechnology policies and performance in Central and Eastern Europe. *International Journal of Biotechnology, 10*(4), 341–361.

UNESCO. (2005). *Global Development Report 2005.* Montreal: Institute for Statistics.

UNESCO. (2009a). *UNESCO Institute for Statistics database.* Retrieved October 29, 2009, from http://stats.uis.unesco.org/unesco/ReportFolders/ReportFolders.aspx?IF_ActivePath =P,54&IF_Language=eng.

UNESCO. (2009b). *A global perspective on research and development. UIS Fact Sheet. October 2009, No. 2.* Retrieved October 20, 2009, from www.uis.unesco.org/template/pdf/S&T/ Factsheet_No2_ST_2009_EN.pdf.

University research [News in Brief]. (2009). *Nature, 458*(7242), 1207.

5

Evolution of National Funding Systems for Research

Tony Mayer

Over human history, our curiosity has driven us to explore new intellectual horizons and solve new technological problems. These endeavours have been undertaken for a variety of motives ranging from pure altruism and "blue skies" enquiry to the solution for applied problems.

For the past 300–400 years we have seen the emphasis change from the "gentleman" scientist or philosopher (and they were mostly gentlemen throughout this period) to the professional researcher, and the rise of the research "enterprise" supported by the public purse, as well as directly commissioned research by industry and commerce. The days of the "dilettante" researcher who could support himself by private means are now long gone, and the public funding of research has arisen in its place, especially from the beginning of the twentieth century to the present. We have come a long way from the first "professional" scientist, Robert Hooke, the paid "servant of the Royal Society", whose task was to prepare experiments for the Fellows on a regular and frequent basis.

What has driven this inexorable development? First, research has become more complex and more and more expensive, demanding sophisticated equipment and substantial infrastructures, including major international research collaborations that are beyond even the means of a single state to support, such as the International Space Station, ITER (the International Thermonuclear Experimental Reactor) and CERN (originally Conseil Européen pour la Recherche Nucléaire, though the name changed to the current Organisation Européenne pour la Recherche Nucléaire).

But what motivated the original move to publicly funded research? Certainly perceived economic benefit has been seen as an increasingly strong driving force and remains a key political justification for public investment in research. Then there are the demands of an increasingly technologically complex modern society, with its new demands for advances in such areas as medicine and information technology.

In order to support research, governments have devised a variety of funding structures and methodologies that have been based on two inter-linked principles. The first is that of the "self-governing republic" of science. In other words, researchers have successfully contended that they are the only people, especially within their specialisations, able to judge proposals and understand their scientific and technological content; that is, they govern science through peer review. The second is that this is a public good available for the benefit of society at large and so justifies the use of tax-payers' money. Research, then, is a national interest. Both come together in the words of Winston Churchill who, repeating those of Haldane, said that "scientists should always be on tap but not on top". This pithy statement also indicates that the final decision rests with politicians, and this brings with it its own dangers. Haldane (1918) enunciated this view in his report, which says:

> Although the operations of the Medical Research Committee [discussed below in the description of the UK funding system] are within the province of the Minister ... the Minister relies on the MRC to select the objects upon which they will spend their income and to frame schemes for the efficient and economical performance of their work.

In the UK, this became known as the Haldane Principle of scientific independence, and yet it introduces the political element by placing ultimate responsibility for funding within the hands of the politician.

Now the justification for public investment is based on the claim that there is a direct linear relation between research investment, innovation, new economic development and, ultimately, employment. The other major driver has been that of national emergency (including war). In fact, many of the biggest boosts for research funding have resulted from the First and Second World Wars and the Cold War.

What follows are brief accounts of the evolution and current funding systems of two "mature" and large countries that have been world leaders in research, namely the United Kingdom and Germany, and that of a small and new—but increasingly influential—"player", Singapore. The chapter may serve to show the differences as well as the similarities in history, philosophy and motivation that have influenced the development of their respective research-funding systems.

United Kingdom

After more than two centuries of largely privately funded endeavour, public (i.e. government) funding started in earnest with the establishment of the Medical Research Committee in 1913, motivated by increasing concerns about health. The committee finally emerged as the Medical Research Council (MRC) in 1918, after the experiences of the First World War. MRC was established under a Royal Charter guaranteeing its "sovereign" status and operating under the Haldane Principle.

At the same time, developments in other areas of research demanded new action from government. While several research services had been funded by the public purse for some time (examples are the Royal Astronomical Observatories, the Meteorological Office and the Geological Survey), the pace of publicly funded activities increased substantially with the creation of the National Physical Laboratory in 1899 and the Development Commission in 1909. In other words, government-funded research was becoming larger and more complex. With pressures from war and from the research community itself, in 1916 the government created a new ministry to oversee all these activities—the Department of Scientific and Industrial Research. One should note the inclusion of industrial research in this title. This ministry brought together many national laboratories and services. Although a department of state under a minister who was the de facto Minister of Science, it was only one of that minister's responsibilities. The governance of the Department of Scientific and Industrial Research therefore tended not to be a political matter, and scientific decision-making was largely left in the hands of directors and the senior colleagues of institutes. This model for the government funding of research institutions was "exported" to other parts of the then British Empire, and one can still see here the origins of such organisations as the Commonwealth Scientific and Industrial Research Organisation (CSIRO) in Australia (established in 1926), the Crown Research Institutes in New Zealand (also established in 1926) and the Council for Scientific and Industrial Research (CSIR) in South Africa (established in 1945).

At the same time, the development of the research council model had also taken place with the conversion of the Medical Research Committee into the MRC, followed by the creation of the Agriculture Research Council in 1923. The so-called Development Commission and similar bodies looked after other research activities.

The most significant year in the formation of the modern British funding system was 1965, when a system of research councils covering most of the research spectrum was created, very much taking the lead from what had gone on in the United States in the immediate post-Second World War period with the establishment of the National Science Foundation (NSF). What emerged was the creation of new councils alongside the MRC and the Agriculture Research Council. These were the Natural Environment Research Council, the Social Science Research Council and, by far the largest, the Science Research Council. The creation of the research councils was accompanied by a major increase in public funding for research. All the councils were bodies created under a Royal Charter outside the civil service but with comparable terms for their employees as public servants. Each council was somewhat different, with the Agriculture, Medical and Natural Environment Research Councils combining the grant-agency function with that of an institutional body as national research-performing organisations. The other two councils were grant agencies, although the Science Research Council had responsibility for major research infrastructure establishments and was the subscribing body to CERN and the European Space Agency (ESA).

Then, in 1972, following a new political direction, there was a sense that some change was inevitable. The government considered that it should have a far greater say in the programmes of the research councils as the proxy customer for research. Consequently, following the report of Lord Victor Rothschild (1971), head of the Central Policy Review Staff—the government's "think tank"—the concept of the customer–contractor relationship in research was enunciated and so had implications for the development of basic research. This resulted in major portions of the budgets of Agriculture, Medical and Natural Environment Research Councils being transferred to a variety of government departments that were designated as the customers of research. This created many funding and bureaucratic difficulties, but one benefit was the creation of Chief Scientist posts in those ministries whose work included substantial technological components. Earlier there had only been a Chief Scientific Advisor in the Ministry of Defence.

This was the first of many changes that affected the British research council system over the next 35 years. There has been a constant urging by governments of both the left and right to reorganise British research funding under the guise of increasing efficiency and making research "more relevant". The danger is that this starts to earmark and influence the directions of funding and ultimately the science being undertaken, whose priorities then become subservient to political direction.

The next major reorganisation took place in 1994 with the splitting up of the Scientific Research Council, which had become the Science and Engineering Research Council following the Rothschild (1971) review. Its life sciences were transferred to what had become the Agriculture and Food Research Council. This new structure became the Biotechnology and Biological Research Council. The physical sciences were split between a body responsible for physical sciences (including chemistry and mathematics) and engineering—the Engineering and Physical Sciences Research Council—and one responsible for so-called "big science"—the Particle Physics and Astronomy Research Council—with the large facilities falling under a Council for the Central Laboratories of the Research Councils. The other councils remained unchanged, noting that the Social Science Research Council had successfully fended off an attempt by the Thatcher government to close it down and had become the Economic and Social Research Council. These changes were accompanied by a further change with the creation of the post of Director General of the Research Councils, sitting in a ministry, to oversee the budgets and operation of the research councils. Then, in 2006, there was a further structural change with the merger of the Particle Physics and Astronomy Research Council and the Council for the Central Laboratories of the Research Councils, creating the new Science and Technology Facilities Council.

While this account has dealt with science and technology, we also need to look at arts and humanities and their research funding. This had remained very much within the ministerial purview until, in 1998, an independent body was formed from within the university funding sector to provide competitive funding for arts and humanities research. This board subsequently evolved into the Arts and Humanities Research Council (AHRC) in 2005 to give the current research-funding structure in the United Kingdom, with seven separate sectoral research councils. They come together formally as Research Councils UK, a body that can provide common approaches across the councils and can act as a single point of contact and interlocutor with government through the Director General for Science and Research (formerly the Director General of the Research Councils).

When the research councils were formed and the Department of Scientific and Industrial Research dissolved in 1965, the government research laboratories were transferred to their appropriate ministries. So, for example, the Building Research Establishment and the Hydraulics Research Station both became part of the then Department of the Environment. Since then, the policy of successive governments has been to privatise such assets.

It is noteworthy that the creation of devolved governments in Scotland, Wales and Northern Ireland has led to the break-up of centralised university funding into its regional components, but the research councils have been retained at a fully national level, which is seen as essential in providing a significant pool for competitive research funding.

In summary, through the establishment of a successful research-funding model through the first half of the twentieth century and later an updated system with independent research councils, there has been a continual desire of governments to reorganise research funding, coupled with the constant stated desire to make such funding economically and societally relevant. This has also been accompanied, after the initial funding "burst" in the late 1960s, with a long-term decline in research funding until the start of the twenty-first century. Such changes have been disturbing to the system, with the community having to adjust to new funding situations and competitions at the macro level. This period has also seen an increasing trend towards viewing research in terms of innovation, economic payoff and employment, all much more short-term and thus more political, with governments seeking to influence the major research-funding priorities via a top-down approach.

Germany

The German research system is also a mature system, dating back to the early part of the twentieth century. However, unlike the United Kingdom's, it has experienced the dark period and trauma of the National Socialist (Nazi) regime and the Second World War. It has now evolved into an independent, stable and much-envied research-funding system. The German funding system embraces both the national research-performers as well as the grant-funding for the universities.

Starting in 1911, the first significant development was the establishment of the Kaiser Wilhelm Society for the Advancement of Science (Kaiser Wilhelm Gesellschaft zur Förderung der Wissenschaften), which supervised a series of constituent research institutes, funded originally from government, industry and private donors. Eventually, in 1934, the Kaiser Wilhelm Society succumbed to the Nazi regime. After the Second World War, with the reconstruction of Germany, a new body with a similar nature was formed at the instigation of Max Planck. This organisation later took his name to become the Max Planck Society (Max Planck Gesellschaft or MPG) and later absorbed the surviving Kaiser Wilhelm Society institutes. MPG has now evolved into a well-respected, research-performing organisation with guaranteed independence.

In fact, this independence extends across the whole German research system and stems from the establishment of the Basic Law (Grundgesetz) in 1958, whose fundamental provisions guarantee the freedom of art, scholarship, research and teaching. It also sets out the shared competence for research funding between the Federal Ministry for Education and Research (Bundesministerium für Bildung und Forschung) and the state (Länder) governments in a fully federal system. This provides checks and balances within research funding and so ensures the constitutional independence of the various research-performing and research-funding bodies. The driving force to ensure this independence came from the political distortions arising from the Nazi regime and the resultant perversion of research and research institutions.

The keystone in the funding ecosystem in Germany is the German Research Society (Deutsche Forschungegemeinschaft or DFG), which is the primary competitive funding agency for the German universities. The universities themselves are the members of the organisation and provide its governance and quality control. The DFG itself has long antecedents and originally evolved from the Emergency Association for German Science (Notgemeinschaft der Deutschen Wissenschaft), established in the aftermath of the First World War to raise funds to support research. The DFG eventually emerged from this structure in 1929. After the Nazi period, the Notgemeinschaft was re-established in 1949, leading to the creation of the modern DFG, which extended its funding operations to the whole of Germany following re-unification in 1990.

The other components of the German research system are both national research-performing organisations, but again with scientific independence and jointly funded between the Federal and the Länder governments. They are the Helmholtz Association of German Research Centres (Helmholtz Gemeinschaft Deutscher Forschungszentren), which brings together the former civil nuclear research laboratories and the German Aerospace Centre (Deutsches Zentrum für Luft und Raumfahrt), and the Leibniz Scientific Association (Wissenschaftsgemeinschaft Gottfried Wilhelm Leibniz), which consists of the 84 non-university research institutes spanning the whole research spectrum. Again, while heavily dependent on national (i.e. Federal) funding, these organisations are co-funded by the Länder.

Finally, there is an independent advisory structure, the German Science Council (Wissenschaftsrat), with the task of providing high-level scientific advice to both the Federal and Länder governments and to the research community in general. The council covers the universities, the research-performing organisations and major research infrastructure investment, with the specific mandate of ensuring German research competitiveness.

The evolution of research funding and structures in Germany closely parallels that of the United Kingdom in the early years of the twentieth century. Similarly, as in the United Kingdom, it represents a long and proud tradition. However, it has also experienced the disrupting effects of the First and Second World Wars and the trauma of the Nazi period from 1934 to 1945. Recognising what happened has ensured that systems are in place, starting with the Basic Law, to ensure the independence of research and the independence of the performing and funding organisations. This is coupled with the shared funding competence between the Federal and Länder governments, which also provides further independence, especially for the MPG and the DFG. Thus, there is seemingly less top-down setting of research agendas and more of a bottom-up approach.

Funding at the European Level

The description of the funding ecosystems in two of Europe's leading research countries also requires mention of development of funding at the European level, especially through the European Union Framework Programmes. This is again a shared competence between the European Commission and the Member States. Originally, research at the European level was established through the European Coal and Steel Community and the European Atomic Energy Community. The latter led to the direct support of major research laboratories carrying out research into peaceful uses of nuclear energy. Otherwise the European Commission was confined to only supporting coordination activities. This changed in 1985 with the adoption of the Single European Act that led to the creation of the Framework Programmes and the ability to fund research directly, although on a cost-sharing basis. Now the Framework Programme has evolved, if one takes this as a single entity, into the world's largest funding programme, with an annual expenditure of approximately €7 billion. While representing perhaps 5 per cent or so of the total public expenditure on research across the European Union, it is actually more significant, as much of national spending is tied up in fixed costs such as maintenance of research institutes and the salaries of the staff. Therefore, in practical effect, the Framework Programme is very significant as it represents an estimated 25–30 per cent of the manoeuvrable funds available across the

European Union. It is especially significant in the smaller countries and those with a low investment in research in terms of the percentage of gross domestic expenditure on research and development in the gross domestic product.

The competence was based on the need to increase Europe's industrial competitiveness and later to support the development of a European Union policy. Thus, from the outset, even though there was a significant component of basic research, the programme followed the strategic and economic benefit justification for expenditure. Unlike many national programmes, there is a major participation of industrial companies in the Framework Programme. Until recently, a fundamental condition for funding was to establish trans-frontier collaborations.

Since 2000 a new concept has been developed, that of the European Research Area (ERA). This is meant to be the arena for the totality of research funding in the European Union, and includes the Framework Programme, the Member States' funding and other players and coordination and collaboration activities. The ERA has now achieved a constitutional status within the European Union through the Lisbon Treaty (2009). Within the ERA and the Framework Programme, a new funding development is that of the European Research Council (ERC), which was launched in 2007 after prolonged pressure from the European research community at large. It has a very distinct mandate from the rest of the Framework Programme, especially in that the principle of trans-frontier collaboration no longer applies, the basis of decision-making is peer review and excellence, and the ERC also supports basic research. It has been described as being akin to European football's Champions League. Thus it mimics and supplements the basic research-funding mechanisms that can be seen in the British research councils and in Germany's DFG.

Finally, to complete the European picture, there are the research coordination mechanisms, such as the European Cooperation in Science and Technology (COST) and the European Science Foundation, which do not fund research directly but provide the wherewithal for research collaboration, inter-laboratory visits, exchanges and similar actions that are especially difficult to fund at the national level. Funds for establishing collaboration and attending international research meetings are normally excised from applications by national funding agencies. Therefore, these collaboration and coordination funders, while deploying relatively small amounts of funds, play a very significant role in the development of research collaboration within Europe.

Singapore

Singapore is very much the "new kid on the block". The contrast with the United Kingdom and Germany could not be more pronounced. Singapore is a small city state, the only state of its kind without a natural hinterland and therefore having to look to a "global hinterland". It is small in geographical and population terms, with a population of 4.5 million, contrasted to 61 million in the United Kingdom and 82 million in Germany. However, there are many states in Europe with a similar or even smaller population, such as the Republic of Ireland at 4.2 million, Norway at 4.8 million and Denmark at 5.5 million. Until recently, however, Singapore had only two universities, in contrast to the other countries listed here, so the research community, including those in the institutes of the Agency for Science, Technology and Research, was rather small. Singapore forms a sharp contrast with the United Kingdom and Germany in terms of its political system and cultural background, but, in crude economic terms, Singapore is a success story with its gross domestic product per capita ranking the country between third and fifth in the world (whereas Germany ranks between fourteenth and twenty-sixth place and the United Kingdom between fifteenth and twenty-fifth).

The progress made by Singapore, especially over the two decades from 1990 to 2009, is truly impressive and remarkable. With the single-minded aim of developing Singapore as a knowledge-based economy, the government has embarked on a series of five-year plans for science and technology which have taken Singapore into the top league of countries in terms of its investment in research. Starting from the base of 0.2 per cent of gross domestic expenditure on research and development in 1967, when the Science Council was established (two years after independence), the level of investment in 2007 was 2.6 per cent and the intention is to try to reach 3 per cent by 2010.

This investment has been coupled with a strategy of building the research base through talent recruitment at three levels. Schemes have been introduced to attract individual talent at both the junior and senior levels and recruit world-leading institutions to set up bases in Singapore or to enter into partnership with local institutions. Examples of the latter are Massachusetts Institute of Technology, Imperial College London, Stanford University, Duke University, Technion, Haifa, INSEAD (*Institut Européen d'Administration des Affaires*—European Institute of Business Administration) and the Swiss Federal Institute of Technology (ETH—Eidgenössische Technische Hochschule Zürich). A condition of such support is that faculty members from these institutions are required to spend substantial amounts of time in Singapore and conduct the research programmes within Singapore.

The funding system is very much geared to addressing research with an anticipated economic benefit, even if this is in the longer term. Furthermore, most of the research funding is geared to science and technology rather than to the social sciences and the humanities.

Singapore's research system, like those of other countries, is divided between a national research performer—the Agency for Science, Technology and Research (A*STAR), funded through the Ministry of Trade and Industry—and the university sector, funded by the Ministry of Education.

A*STAR has its origins in the Science Council founded in 1967, with its first institute being the Institute of Molecular and Cell Biology, set up in 1987.

The Science Council itself evolved into the National Science and Technology Board in 1991 (later re-named A*STAR) and the first physical sciences institute, the Singapore Institute of Manufacturing Technology, was founded in 1993. In 2000 two supervisory bodies, the Biomedical Research Council and the Science and Engineering Research Council were formed, and A*STAR took on its present form. The two councils have the task of overseeing the work of the relevant A*STAR institutes and funding research in the universities, on a competitive basis, to supplement the work of the agency. A*STAR itself has the mandate to conduct and fund research and exploit its economic potential for the benefit of the country. A*STAR has also taken on an educational aspect with the establishment of the A*STAR Graduate Academy, aimed at sponsoring research students at universities, especially overseas, in partnership with local universities.

The university sector in Singapore is dominated by two very large and highly ranked research institutions, the National University of Singapore and the Nanyang Technological University. Of these, the National University of Singapore is the more comprehensive, but both incorporate business schools and social sciences. More recently, the Singapore Management University, with a specific mandate to promote business studies, social sciences and related disciplines, was created and a fourth university, to be known as the Singapore University of Technology and Design, in partnership with the Massachusetts Institute of Technology, is under development. Having more academic institutions creates a larger community and will encourage greater competition and collaboration.

Competitive research funding for the university sector derives from the Ministry of Education, in what is known as Tier 2 funding, and from the National Research Foundation, which falls under the Prime Minister's Office and was created in 2006 as part of the five-year plan to boost research investment. The National Research Foundation promotes economically important, strategic research areas through a variety of significant funding instruments that involve bringing in senior researchers to spend substantial amounts of time in Singapore. Together with the Ministry of Education, the National Research Foundation sponsors a very substantial funding scheme, the Research Centres of Excellence scheme, which provides $S150 million over 10 years, with each centre being led by a world-leading researcher. In this way, Singapore catapults its way into a world-leading position and can use these senior research personalities to nucleate very major research activities starting from a relatively low base.

In summary, the Singapore research-funding system has been designed in a purposeful way to develop the national research base very rapidly, with the clear aim of fostering a future knowledge-based economy. It is based on talent recruitment and backed by a substantial financial investment. Thus, it contrasts significantly with the very mature research-funding systems in the United Kingdom and Germany.

Summary

Government funding of research is seen as a public good and has been so regarded from the early days of the twentieth century. Already, by that time, a number of public research institutions carrying out a variety of strategic tasks had been established, and, in the United Kingdom, these were brought together under a single structure within government. At the same time, the need to establish a system for funding research—particularly in the universities in specific sectors, especially medicine—in which scientific decisions are made by specialists in the field concerned, had also been accepted. Hence, we see the creation of the Medical Research Committee, later the MRC, in the United Kingdom in the years prior to the First World War. Together, after the war, these formed the Department of Scientific and Industrial Research, which provided a funding and structural model for other countries in various British dominions. Similar developments, especially with regard to research institutes, were taking place in Germany, although a formal structure for university funding in the form of the DFG was not established until the late 1920s. In both countries, the First World War had given a boost to the concept of public funding of research in institutes and universities. Unfortunately, German research structures and funding then entered the dark days of the Nazi regime, which lasted until the end of the Second World War. Research-funding systems were re-established in Germany after the Second World War, certainly encouraged by the United States as part of its generous Marshall Plan for the reconstruction of Europe and the start of the Cold War. In this respect, the report by Bush (1945), *Science, the Endless Frontier*, was a seminal work in influencing research communities worldwide. In Germany, tarred with its experiences of the 1930s, the desire to re-create research-funding structures was based very much on ensuring the independence of research, even though the taxpayer was the funder. Part of this independence is based on a constitutional provision, the Basic Law, and partly through the joint funding of the DFG, the MPG and other institutes from both the Federal and Länder governments. With this structure in place, there has been stability in the German research-funding system not seen in the United Kingdom.

In contrast, the United Kingdom has seen continual reorganisation of the funding system following the creation of the research council system in 1965. This has been driven by the political view that research should be seen not just as a public good, but also as the driver for innovation. The Rothschild report of 1971 started this approach with the introduction to government-funded research of the customer–contractor principle. This approach has continued up to the present day. Governments have also been tempted to set strategic research goals as part of the successive reorganisations of the British science system, which has seen an increasing influence from the private sector as a result.

Singapore contrasts with both the United Kingdom and Germany in size, but also in its late start and very rapid rise in the research "league tables". It has now become a significant player on the world scene. In this case, however, the motivation is very much geared to the promotion of the knowledge-based economy and an innovation payoff.

The use of tax payers' money always carries with it the need for accountability, but the success of research funding has to be based on trust in the scientific and scholarly research communities who have to make decisions based on peer review. The search for innovation and economic benefit encourages governments to set research targets and interfere with the scientific and scholarly process, and this is a danger that all the actors need to be aware of. Constant reorganisation also has a disturbing effect on research communities, and in this sense the German research-funding system is an enviable example for others to follow.

International Collaboration: A Difficult Activity to Promote

In terms of international research collaboration, the problem is that national funding systems are just that. They are designed to support researchers within the country concerned, and there may be legal difficulties in the transfer of funds across national boundaries. In addition, expert committees within national structures tend to see international collaborative projects in some way as pre-empting the wholly national applications, and there is a reluctance to accept the peer-review procedures and outcomes of agencies in other countries. As a result, collaborative proposals run the risk of multiple-jeopardy in terms of peer review as each agency conducts its own assessments. In fact, the problems are similar to those of cross-disciplinary proposals within national systems. Singapore is in a different position, in that it is importing collaborations into its national system.

Of course there are major projects such as CERN or the International Space Station which are international, but in these cases major budget decisions have been made to pool resources from national sources.

In the case of European Union programmes, there is one central budget and one peer-review system, so some of the problems of multiple peer reviews and reluctance to fund something outside one's control and responsibility do not arise.

In terms of monitoring and evaluation and, of course, dealing with problems including misconduct, there is again a problem between the national responsibilities of each agency. There have been reported incidents where one agency is unable to pursue an investigation because the counterpart funding agency is unwilling or legally unable to cooperate.

One attempt to bring national funding agencies together has been the scheme introduced by the European Science Foundation, known as EURO-CORES (European Collaborative Research Scheme). After much discussion and negotiation, the national funding agencies have agreed to accept a single, centrally organised peer review, although funding decisions on specific proposals or parts thereof still remain at the national level as there is a reluctance to allocate national funds into a single "pot". However, reporting and evaluation are established as a central responsibility.

Conclusion

In sum, national funding systems have evolved to meet perceived national needs and in response to the political environment and imperatives. This variation in structures means that the components of top-down and bottom-up research tend to reflect the national approaches.

As national funding structures predominate, the support for international collaborative research is more difficult to achieve. There is an increasing desire within the research community to undertake international collaborative research, along with an increasing trend for multi-disciplinarity. The European Union Framework Programme represents a large and successful international research-funding operation, but it is functioning essentially as a single system and resembles a national funding structure. There is a general difficulty in obtaining funding for coordination activities, although Europe has developed a means of dealing with this through a limited number of organisations with special networking support mechanisms. One attempt to develop international research funding—EUROCORES—demonstrates the difficulties inherent in such an endeavour. Monitoring, evaluation and the investigation of problems such as misconduct suffer similarly.

To resolve such difficulties requires a number of inter-linked actions. There has to be greater trust and openness between funding and performing organisations and a willingness to accept the best practice from whichever agency has the most advanced procedures. This ranges from accepting each other's peer-review mechanisms to establishing common monitoring and evaluation procedures and a willingness to cooperate in investigations of breaches of good practice. Agencies should ensure that the institutions performing research have common standards of education and training in good research practice, and there should be fora for such exchanges of best practice to be considered and promoted. There should also be a greater willingness to support coordination activities as a precursor to international research collaboration, especially through the specialist structures that have been established.

References

Bush, V. (1945). *Science, the endless frontier: A report to the President.* Washington, DC: United States Government Printing Office.

Haldane Report, The. (1918). *Report of the machinery of government committee under the chairmanship of Viscount Haldane of Cloan* (Cd. 9230). London: Her Majesty's Stationery Office.

Rothschild Report, The. (1971). *A Framework for government research and development* (Cmnd. 5096). London: Her Majesty's Stationery Office.

6

National Systems for Scientific Research in China

Ping Sun[1]

This chapter analyzes issues in international research collaborations that emerge from variations in aspects of national research management systems and research practices, in the context of collaborations between China and other countries. It also discusses strategies for promoting extensive and in-depth collaborations. The chapter begins with a brief introduction to the Chinese research management system and the main features of international scientific and technological cooperation involving China, and then puts forward some suggestions on how to enhance collaborations. Finally, it discusses what roles governments should play in facilitating international research collaborations.

A Brief Introduction to the Chinese Research Management System

The Funding of Research

Funding of research and development (R&D) in China comes from five major sources: the central government, local governments, businesses, financial institutions, and foreign investment. In 2007, the total R&D expenditure in China was ¥371.02 billion ($54.56 billion[2]), and the proportion of expenditures among different groups was as follows: businesses, 72 percent (¥268.19 billion or $39.44 billion); research institutions sponsored by the government, 19 percent (¥68.79 billion or $10.12 billion); universities, 8 percent (¥31.47 billion or $4.63 billion); and others, 1 percent (¥2.57 billion, or $0.38 billion) (National Bureau of Statistics, Ministry of Science and Technology, & Ministry of Finance of China, 2009).

Researchers from universities normally apply for competitive research funds from the National Natural Science Foundation of China (NSFC) and through scientific and technological programs administered by the Ministry of Science and Technology, other commissions or ministries, and relevant departments at the provincial level. The amounts of grants vary according to different funds, projects, disciplines, and the nature of the research activities. Taking the 2008 NSFC grants as an example, the successful applicants received an average grant of ¥323,500 ($47,500) for minor projects, ¥1,834,700 ($269,800) for major projects, and a uniform ¥10 million ($1,470,600) for one of the 17 key projects (NSFC, 2009a). The 2008 investment of the central government in national scientific and technological programs was ¥17.575 billion ($2.585 billion). The major programs or projects included the National High-tech R&D Program (Program 863), the National Basic Research Program (Program 973), the National Sci-Tech Pillar Program, National Sci-Tech Infrastructure Construction Projects, and policy steering programs and special grants (Department of Development Planning, Ministry of Science and Technology of China, 2009).

Research institutions and researchers also carry out research projects commissioned by businesses and other agencies. In addition, the Chinese government, universities and research institutions provide various special funds for attracting talented researchers from overseas and for carrying out innovative research.

Many national scientific and technological programs of China, such as Program 863 and Program 973, are open to institutions and scientists from the European Union (Ministry of Science and Technology of China, 2009b, p. 655). Government departments and funding agencies also allocate special funds for international research collaborations. For example, the Chinese Ministry of Science and Technology allocated a special grant of around ¥300 million ($44 million) each year from 2006 to 2008 for the International Scientific and Technological Cooperation Program (Ministry of Science and Technology of China, 2009b, p. 636). Under the Sino–E.U. Scientific Technological Partnership Cooperation Program, both sides will jointly sponsor projects in agreed-upon research priority areas and provide funding of no less than €30 million each year (Ministry of Science and Technology of China, 2009b, p. 656). Generally speaking, the funding, which can be used for international research collaborations in China, are from various sources, and the amounts have been increasing.

Scientific Research Institutions

Researchers undertaking basic research in China are mainly from universities and research institutions. The advantage of universities is their potential to aggregate researchers in multiple disciplinary areas. The implementation of two university-oriented initiatives, Project 211[3] and Project 985,[4] has significantly improved the infrastructures, facilities, and disciplinary development in many universities. Now, many key national laboratories, which are administered by the Ministry of Science and Technology, are based in universities, and research-funding conditions for major universities have been improved.

The number of research institutions sponsored by the government decreased after a "system transferring" reform during 2001 and 2004, in which some institutions became scientific and technological enterprises or changed their affiliations. The institutions designated as engaging in basic research or providing public services, namely public-interest institutions, remain sponsored by the government. Now there are about 100 research institutions sponsored by the central government. These and other public-interest institutions at local levels can focus on key research areas and major research projects. For example, the Chinese Academy of Sciences (CAS) is a prominent comprehensive R&D center in physical sciences and innovative high-technology fields, and its research centers and institutions are fully supported by public funds. The CAS has made substantial contributions in basic research, defense science and technology, high-tech R&D, and advanced training of researchers. The research institutions that transformed into technology-oriented enterprises need to take on commissioned projects or provide paid services.

The research-funding agencies have made efforts to mobilize researchers from various institutions around some major research programs, such as Program 973, Major National Sci-Tech Special Projects, and to construct public-service systems, such as systems for sharing scientific and technological resources, including research literature, scientific data, large-scale instruments and equipment.

Primary Features of International Scientific and Technological Cooperation in China

For Chinese institutions, the goals of international scientific and technological cooperation, which appear in various policy papers and research literature, include: (1) enabling the implementation of mega-science projects that require large-scale facilities and investment; (2) solving common or global problems effectively and sharing the benefits; (3) utilizing talented researchers, facilities, and research materials from other countries in research projects; (4) enhancing institutional strength in specific research fields or in general; (5) creating opportunities for young scientists to work with top-level researchers; and (6) promoting the development of diplomatic relations and expanding the cooperation to other fields.

For a developing country like China, international scientific and technological cooperation can be most valuable. They can call researchers' attention to research projects, new directions, innovative approaches that are being proposed and developed elsewhere in the world. These connections can be especially valuable in the areas of highest national priority. For example, the Asia 3 Foresight Program, initiated by three major funding agencies in China, Japan, and Korea, is aimed at advancing world-class research by scientists in certain priority areas (Ministry of Science and Technology of China, 2009b, p. 666).

China has established a number of laws, regulations, and guidelines associated with international scientific and technological cooperation. It is widely accepted that the principles of cooperation should be own-needs driven, based on equality, reciprocity, and mutual benefit, and sharing research achievement. These principles are also reflected in some criteria for reviewing the proposals of international research cooperation projects, such as the research basis and conditions of the collaborating parties; the significance and foundation of the collaboration; and the rationality and feasibility of the collaboration (NSFC, 2009b), to ensure that the collaborations are substantiated.

Major Approaches and Foci of Cooperation

The Chinese government encourages international scientific and technological cooperation and exchanges in all funded programs, if no confidentiality or security issues are involved. Currently, China has signed inter-governmental agreements for scientific and technological cooperation with about 100 countries (Ministry of Science and Technology of China, 2007). Universities, research institutions, and businesses are also encouraged to carry out international cooperation. There are four main models of international cooperation:

1. Cooperation under the framework of inter-governmental agreements for scientific and technological cooperation, such as the agreements between China and the United States, or between China and Japan, which include research collaborations, personnel exchanges, and so on.
2. Self-initiated cooperation between the Chinese and foreign universities, research institutions, businesses, research teams and researchers of different countries, such as the cooperation between the Chinese Academy of Sciences and the Max Planck Society (MPG) of Germany (Ministry of Science and Technology of China, 2009b, p. 641) and numerous other institutional and personal collaborations.
3. International research collaboration platforms, such as joint research institutions, joint funding for international collaborative projects, and the cooperation of two groups of universities from China and foreign countries, which are often facilitated by the governments, such as the "10 + 10 Program" between 10 universities in China and 10 campuses within the University of California system (Perlin, 2008).
4. Government-initiated international research collaboration programs, such as mega-science projects within China's strength areas, including a Chinese medicine project (2006) and a re-usable and new energy project (2007) (Ministry of Science and Technology of China, 2009b, p. 646).

Strategies and Priority Areas for Cooperation

The practices of international scientific and technological cooperation in China have undergone tremendous changes, from individual visits of scientists at an earlier stage, to collaboration on a personal or project basis, to large-scale cooperation and the establishment of joint research institutions. In December 2007 China established an inter-ministerial coordination mechanism for international scientific and technological cooperation. The participating departments and organizations share their visions and develop practical strategies jointly (Ministry of Science and Technology of China, 2008).

According to the *Implementation Outlines for International Scientific and Technological Cooperation in the Eleventh Five-year Plan*, which China is implementing, China is seeking breakthroughs in three areas: (1) expanding areas of cooperation; (2) creating innovative means of cooperation; and (3) increasing the effectiveness of cooperation. Strategies for cooperation will be adjusted accordingly. The strategic goals of cooperation will switch from general-purpose cooperation to national development strategy- and demand-oriented cooperation. The means of cooperation will change from being project-based to incorporating projects, research talent and development of the research base. The emphasis in cooperation will shift from importing technology to a combination of technology transfer and personnel mobilization in both directions. The major players in cooperation will expand from government and research institutions to a broader set of participants, with governments assuming leading roles. Decision-making related to the tasks of cooperation will switch from a bottom-up approach to a national-development, strategy-oriented, top-down decision-making mechanism.

The key areas of international scientific and technological cooperation, as suggested in the aforementioned *Implementation Outlines*, include:

1. the development of clean energy and advanced nuclear energy, energy conservation and resource-saving, clean production and recycling economy, water resources protection, and comprehensive utilization of mineral resources;
2. the prevention and treatment of major chronic and epidemic diseases, the technologies for modernizing Chinese medicine and developing biomedicine, techniques for processing agricultural products, green agriculture, agricultural mechanization, and informatization;
3. the development and application of information technology, new material technologies, key technologies for green manufacturing, and advanced manufacturing;
4. life sciences, nanotechnology, space and air technologies, marine technologies, essential subjects, and major frontier issues.

(Ministry of Science and Technology of China, 2009b, p. 637)

Many of these research priority areas are the same as those set by developed countries and international organizations, thus broadening prospects for Sino-foreign international scientific and technological cooperation.

Challenges to Sino-Foreign Research Collaborations and Relevant Strategies

There are always problems that can hamper international research collaborations, no matter what countries are involved. Such issues center around different research-management regulations, mismatch of expectations, disputes about the distribution of research benefits and intellectual property, and communication problems related to language and culture. Problems can be solved or alleviated if relevant parties are aware of them beforehand and take appropriate steps before the problems become intractable.

Identifying Potential Partners

Choosing collaborative partners in another country is a prominent challenge due to asymmetrical information and other complicating factors. For example, it is relatively easy to identify researchers who are prolific authors in certain areas, but the most-published authors may not have the particular expertise needed for a given project. At the other extreme is the potential partner (whether a research institution or a researcher) that has been highly and deservedly successful in obtaining grants or participating in extensive international relations. Such a partner has to consider his or her capacity and will tend to choose the most desirable partners. It is noteworthy that in a highly competitive grant-application system, there are always some researchers who have difficulty in obtaining grants, who may nevertheless become productive partners. On the one hand, researchers who have studied or worked overseas may be good partners, as they normally have good foreign language skills and better understanding of research norms and the current trends in their disciplinary areas, but, on the other hand, many of them are already established as the leaders or principal investigators in their institutions, and they also tend to be selective in agreeing to collaborate with overseas partners. To avoid a mismatch of collaborative partners due to asymmetric information and different expectations, it is advisable to pay a field visit or to engage in personal exchanges with the potential partners to understand their intent, their capacity, and the feasibility of collaboration.

Issues Related to Research Practices and Research Management

As mentioned above, many problems can emerge from differences in research-management practices. Attention should be paid to the following aspects and activities in collaboration processes in order to avoid potential problems.

The Sources of Research Funding

Since research funding available to researchers in developing countries is usually less than that available to their counterparts in developed countries, in terms of both sizes and numbers of grants awarded, these researchers often undertake commissioned research. Researchers from developing countries can use the funding to explore scientific problems and sharpen their research skills, but, as the research might be part of a larger project, it is usually not possible for them to act independently to design and implement research, and the benefits they receive can be limited. The contribution of research funding from all the parties involved in a research process will help to ensure that collaborations are equitable and linked to each party's particular strength.

Oversight of Research-Grant Management
In many other countries, research grants at an institution are administered by staff members instead of research investigators. In some Chinese universities or research institutions, the spending of grant money is typically approved by principal investigators, instead of administrative staff. It is advisable that all the parties should be required to follow strict regulations for grant management.

Research Management
The practices of research-facilities management and institutional management differ in general from country to country, and from one institution to another. Although management of research facilities in developing countries needs to be improved, it is also possible that the current management practices suit the local situation. In international research collaborations, concerns related to research management should be raised frankly, and usually collaborators will be willing to make appropriate arrangements or improvements.

Standards and Quality-Assurance of Research
There are differences in research standards and research quality among countries. Standards of peer review, for example, differ among national and disciplinary contexts. It is expected that successful international research collaborations will contribute to improving research behaviors worldwide through the introduction of globally accepted standards and norms, as well as procedures to ensure them.

Research Ethics and Other Norms
Some regulations and norms for research vary between national contexts. Some foreign researchers take advantage of the situation to collect data or carry out research in developing countries that would be impossible elsewhere. In the late 1990s, researchers from the Harvard School of Public Health undertook several research projects in Anhui Province, China, to seek the causes of certain common and lethal diseases such as asthma, pre-term birth, and hypertension. After receiving allegations from a complainant in China of fraud in informed consent, the U.S. Office for Human Research Protections carried out an investigation, and found that "there were weaknesses in some of the research procedures" (Harvard School of Public Health, 2003). With the increase in scientific and technological cooperation in biomedical research and research with human subjects, some universal norms and regulations should be developed and observed by researchers around the world.

Access and Confidentiality Problems
Access and confidentiality are universal problems in collaborations, not only among researchers from developed and developing countries. Regulations

concerning research access and confidentiality in a country should be followed carefully in order to avoid disputes or suspicions in the collaborative process that might have negative impacts on collaborations in the future.

Intellectual Property and Research Credit Issues

The ownership and protection of intellectual property are common concerns in international research collaborations. There are some incidents where researchers have published articles using data or information they obtained at international conferences or through personal academic exchanges, ignoring the propriety of such data or information transfer. The rise of such problems can be partly attributed to the researchers' lack of intellectual property awareness. It is believed that countries that are active in research and international research collaborations have been paying more attention to intellectual property protection. For example, in the regulations of the Chinese government and research-funding agencies, there are always sections highlighting the issue of intellectual property. In April 2008, the State Council of China approved *The Outlines on the National Strategy of Intellectual Property*, which indicates that by 2020, the degree of intellectual property creation, application, protection, and management in China will be raised to a relatively high level (Ministry of Science and Technology of China, 2009b, p. 373). As intellectual property issues are a major concern for all parties in international research collaborations, they should be carefully negotiated beforehand and formal agreements signed.

Benefits and Harm

Another issue is benefit distribution and harm prevention. There is a tendency in some international research collaborations for the distribution of benefits among the partners not to be proportional, due to variations in data-processing capacity and research-support systems. The reverse issue is that the negative impact of research on subjects or the local research community might be overlooked by researchers from another country. For example, in research projects involving blood samples or genetic material, the export of such research resources to another country will inevitably make domestic research more difficult, and the sharing of research benefits usually cannot be assured. Now, some developing countries have issued regulations protecting their research resources, such as *The Interim Measures for the Administration of Human Genetic Resources*, which was worked out by the Ministry of Science and Technology and the Ministry of Health, and promulgated by the General Office of the State Council of China (Ministry of Science and Technology & Ministry of Public Health, 1998). Such issues are associated with ethical and legal aspects of international research collaborations, and all the relevant parties should pay attention to them.

Responsibilities of Governments in Promoting International Research Collaborations

To avoid problems and disputes in international research collaborations, it is important to acknowledge and address differences in national laws, regulations, and practices. National governments and relevant international organizations should take action to promote the development and effectiveness of international research collaborations. Positive steps include: developing universal research norms and research regulations, making information relevant to international research collaborations readily available, disseminating experiences of international research collaborations, and dealing with research misconduct jointly and effectively

Some of the following additional suggestions have also been proposed at international conferences or appear among the best practices in some countries.

Promoting Solutions to Critical Problems

Many factors can affect international research collaborations. For example, during the current global economic downturn, both China and the United States have increased their investment in R&D. The competing interests of the two countries for attracting more talented researchers to undertake innovative research can be a challenge, but the challenge can also become an opportunity for more intensive international research collaborations, if the relevant governments provide a framework for jointly sponsoring large-scale research projects and sharing the benefits.

Different practices of research management and the levels of intellectual property protection in different countries may also affect the scope and depth of international research collaboration. The relevant countries should strive to improve their research management, institutions and practices, and to enhance intellectual-property protection systems in order to avoid conflicts or disputes. It is important for regulations related to international research collaborations to be agreed upon by relevant parties, and preferably drafted by relevant international professional organizations to avoid an imbalance of respective rights and obligations.

At the same time, relevant national institutions and international coordination mechanisms should be established or strengthened to facilitate international research collaborations. Some attempts have been made in this respect. For example, as research misconduct in international research collaborations can be difficult to identify and handle, the OECD Global Science Forum issued *Investigating Research Misconduct Allegations in International Collaborative Research Projects: A Practical Guide* in April 2009. Such documents, if adopted and implemented by all countries, will help to address common problems in international research collaborations.

Facilitating the Exchange and Sharing of Relevant Information

International collaborations need to focus on problems of global interest, at the frontiers of research knowledge. Collaborative work involves extra time, financial resources, and energy, and to make the extra investment worthwhile, all investigators involved need to know that their focus is on internationally important issues. Therefore, the adequate exchange and sharing of information on international research and on potential collaborative opportunities can benefit many stakeholders, including governments, research-funding agencies, research institutions, businesses, and researchers.

National governments and international organizations should cooperate in establishing a mechanism for information exchange beneficial to international research collaborations. For example, a mechanism for providing relevant and timely information will be very useful for universities or research institutions wishing to find a collaborative partner or to employ a researcher from another country. Efforts should also be made to help institutions and researchers with difficulties engaging in international research collaboration due to inadequate experience and communication.

Maintaining Research Integrity and Research Standards

The research integrity issue has become a hot topic around the world in recent years, especially after the scandals of South Korean stem cell scientist Hwang Woo-Suk and Chinese scientist Chen Jin, who faked research on the Hanxin digital signal processing chip in 2005. Many international organizations, government departments, and scientific communities have been working vigorously to promote the responsible conduct of research and research integrity. Governments should pay attention to research integrity issues and help to create a positive environment for scientists to follow ethical professional codes of conduct. Governments should also encourage the working out of widely accepted research norms and codes of conduct, establish or improve supervision and auditing mechanisms and educate scientists to follow the highest standards of research.

Notes

1. I am grateful to Mr. Wu Yishan, Chief Engineer, Institute of Scientific and Technical Information of China, Prof. Li Shuzhuo, Xi'an Jiaotong University, China, Prof. Cong Yali, Medical School, Peking University, China, and Prof. Qiu Renzong, the Chinese Academy of Social Sciences, for their thoughtful and valuable comments on the draft of this chapter.
2. Calculated as 1 U.S. dollar = 6.80 Chinese yuan.
3. Project 211 aims at cultivating high-level elite universities and some key disciplines for national economic and social development strategies. The project began in the mid-1990s, and the figures of 21 and 1 within 211 are from the abbreviation of the "21st century (oriented)" and approximately 100 universities and a number of key disciplines and fields respectively. Inclusion in the project means that universities have met scientific, technical, and human resource standards, and thus will obtain special support from the central and local governments.
4. Project 985 is a boosting project for promoting the Chinese higher education system under the framework of the *21st Century-Oriented Action Plan for Revitalizing Education*. The

objective is to support several top universities to be outstanding on a worldwide basis. The project was named from the time—May (5), 1998 (985)—when then Chinese President Jiang Zemin first made the announcement at the 100th anniversary of Peking University on May 4, 1998.

References

Department of Development Planning, Ministry of Science and Technology of China. (2009). 国家科技计划年度报告 [Annual report of the state programs of science and technology development 2009]. Retrieved September 28, 2009, from www.most.cn/ndbg/2009ndbg/200910/P020091028378516971836.pdf.

Harvard School of Public Health. (2003). *Conclusion of U.S. government's inquiry into HSPH genetic research in China*. Retrieved September 28, 2009, from www.hsph.harvard.edu/news/press-releases/archives/2003-releases/press05302003.html.

Ministry of Science and Technology, & Ministry of Public Health. (1998). Interim measures for the administration of human genetic resources. Retrieved September 28, 2009, from www.gdstc.gov.cn/HTML/zwgk/zcfg/zxzcfg/1222156320220-8502708574629089959.html.

Ministry of Science and Technology of China. (2007). 关于支持重点科研机构进一步扩大国际科技合作的意见 [Opinions on supporting key research institutions to expand international scientific and technological cooperation further]. Retrieved September 28, 2009, from www.most.gov.cn/fggw/zfwj/fwj2007/200711/t20071108_57066.htm.

Ministry of Science and Technology of China. (2008). 国际科技合作跨部门协调机制"启\动大会在京召开 [The starting-up meeting of "Inter-Departmental Coordination Mechanism for International Scientific and Technological Cooperation" was held in Beijing]. Retrieved September 28, 2009, from www.most.gov.cn/kjbgz/200801/t20080103_58199.htm.

Ministry of Science and Technology of China. (2009a). 科技部副部长曹健林就《国家科学技术奖励条例实施细则》修订答记者问 [Vice Science and Technology Minister Cao Jianlin answers correspondent's questions on the revision of Detailed rules for the implementation of the regulations on National Science and Technology Awards]. Retrieved October 10, 2009, from www.most.cn/fggw/zcjd/200901/t20090121_66928.htm.

Ministry of Science and Technology of China. (2009b). 中国科技发展60年 [The development of science and technology in China in 60 years]. Beijing: Scientific and Technological Documentation Publishing House.

National Bureau of Statistics, Ministry of Science and Technology, & Ministry of Finance of China. (2009). *Statistical communiqué on national expenditures on science and technology in 2007*. Retrieved October 20, 2009, from www.stats.gov.cn/english/newsandcomingevents/t20090108_402531578.htm.

NSFC (National Natural Science Foundation of China). (2009a). *NSFC2008年度报告* [Annual report 2008]. Retrieved September 28, 2009, from www.nsfc.gov.cn/nsfc/cen/ndbg/2008ndbg/05/index.htm.

NSFC (National Natural Science Foundation of China). (2009b). 国家自然科学基金国际（地区）合作研究项目管理办法 [Management measures on the international/regional research collaboration projects of the National Natural Science Fund]. Retrieved December 9, 2009, from www.nsfc.gov.cn/Portal0/InfoModule_514/28398.htm.

Perlin, R. (2008). *China and California: Clean energy comrades*. Retrieved October 10, 2009, from www.chinadialogue.net/article/show/single/en/2039.

Part III

Differences in Legal and Normative Environments

7

Legal and Regulatory Considerations in International Research Collaborations

Mark A. Bohnhorst, Meredith McQuaid, Stacey R. Bolton Tsantir, Donald M. Amundson, and Melissa S. Anderson[1]

Researchers who are involved in cross-national research collaborations need to be especially attentive to legal and regulatory aspects of their work. There may be no easier way to get into trouble in an international collaboration than running afoul of another country's laws, rules, policies or regulations. When a collaboration spans several countries, the sheer scope of legal and regulatory considerations can be staggering. Collaborating researchers must therefore rely on legal counsel, institutional officials, national offices and international organizations to help them avoid legal problems in multi-national projects. Those who do not can put themselves, their collaborators and their institutions at risk—often quite unintentionally and unnecessarily.

This chapter discusses an array of legal issues that may arise in collaborative contexts. The issues are intended to be illustrative, as no brief summary can fully capture the complexities of legal requirements for cross-national science. The chapter's attention to issues specific to the United States suggests the kinds of legal and regulatory issues that must be considered in any national context. It also, more specifically, draws attention to legal matters that non-U.S. scientists who collaborate with U.S. colleagues need to take into account, to avoid serious consequences for themselves as well as their U.S. counterparts.

Legal and Regulatory Environments of International Research Collaborations

An array of institutional offices and staff play important roles in supporting researchers who engage in international research collaborations. Particularly for complex transactions, the institution's legal counsel will be an integral part of that support team. The institution attorney represents the institution, not the researcher personally, and not any individual officer personally. The attorney's basic obligation is ensure that the client (and as a necessary result, the researcher) is complying with the law.

Most major research institutions have identified international research collaboration as a strong priority. It is the researcher who fulfills this mission, and as a general matter a researcher will find counsel to be a strong ally in trying to bring the proposed work to fruition. On occasion, an attorney may be required to advise that an activity simply cannot take place because of a legal prohibition or violation of institutional policy. Somewhat more frequently, the attorney will advise officials about potential risks that the officials should consider in deciding whether to pursue an activity that appears to be lawful.

The need for legal counsel is most obvious in large, complex programs funded by a national science agency, governed by the agency's detailed regulations or directives and often subject to a different regulatory regime in each of the countries in which the work is carried out. Legal review is needed both to understand what legal obligations the institution is taking on and to help minimize the risk of non-compliance with those obligations. Whether this involves a U.S. lawyer trying to understand a highly complex Australian system for organizing world-first work on controlling invasive species, or a Spanish lawyer trying to understand U.S. laws and regulations for conducting federally funded biomedical research, the challenge is fundamentally the same.

Legal Complexities in a Big Science Project: The Issue of Liability in the START Trial

For approximately 10 years, the University of Minnesota has served as the bio-statistical center and overall leader of a network for an international collaboration involving important clinical trials. The network is currently organized as the International Network for Strategic Initiatives in Global HIV Trials (INSIGHT). INSIGHT includes international-coordinating centers on three continents; it is supported primarily by the U.S. National Institutes of Health (NIH). A principal effort of INSIGHT at this time is the Strategic Timing of AntiRetroviral Treatment (START) trial, whose objective is to provide definitive data on the benefits and risks of beginning HIV treatment at CD4 cell counts of at least 500, rather than 350. The START study is designed to enroll 4,000 patients at almost 200 clinical sites, encompassing all continents but Antarctica; there is funding from other national governments as well as from multiple institutes within the NIH.

In the planning stages, it was anticipated that the NIH would serve as the sponsor of START. In the summer of 2008, however, as final preparations were being made to launch the study, developments in Europe resulted in the classification of START as a regulated trial in many E.U. jurisdictions.[2] The NIH concluded that, under European Union law,[3] a regulatory sponsor in Europe is subject to potentially unlimited liability. The NIH took the position that undertaking the sponsor role would violate U.S. statutes (primarily the Anti-Deficiency Act, 31 USC[4] Section 1341(a)(1)(A)(2000)) under which the federal government cannot accept an open-ended liability. The NIH's proposed resolution was that the University of Minnesota—as leader of INSIGHT and principal recipient of federal funding—take on the sponsor role, including the open-ended liability.

As one might expect, the idea that a state university should take on a liability that was "too big" for the United States was greeted with some incredulity by University of Minnesota officials.[5] The request seemed not only intuitively wrong, but legally illogical. Within the United States, states as well as the federal government enjoy protections of sovereign immunity. While most states have enacted partial waivers of immunity within their own courts, the waivers generally are rather limited, and the scope of insurance protection is correspondingly limited.[6] In addition, for most state entities in the United States, accepting an open-ended liability would violate the state constitution (an even more daunting obstacle than a mere statute, such as the federal Anti-Deficiency Act) and would be a legal impossibility.

Helping address this development became an immediate and major project for university counsel. The university needed to determine, among other things, (1) whether undertaking this role would be barred by Minnesota law; (2) the precise scope of obligations under E.U. law; (3) whether the view that the NIH could not act as sponsor in the European Union was correct under U.S. law and, if so, what alternatives might exist;[7] (4) whether the NIH had ever asked that a U.S. university assume regulatory sponsorship of an international trial (it had not); and (5) what risks were presented and what mitigation steps might be available. After long and careful deliberation, the university undertook this unexpected and unprecedented role. The university then had to renegotiate detailed clinical-trial supply agreements with pharmaceutical companies that supported the trial and enter into other arrangements to shift or cover potential liability.

Regrettably, working through these problems to ultimate conclusion took one year. Enrollment in a critically important HIV trial that was on the verge of being opened in summer 2008 was needlessly delayed. In addition, as the trial progresses, the University of Minnesota will have no choice but to expend its own resources on procuring additional insurance, at least until such time as issues relating to the European Union directive and/or the Anti-Deficiency Act can be resolved.[8]

The fact that the University of Minnesota accepted the sponsor role in the START trial under the circumstances described should leave no doubt about the genuineness and depth of the commitment to international research of major research institutions. The University of Minnesota was sorely tested; it passed the test. Many of the university's counterparts, both in the United States and abroad, would have passed as well.

An important lesson from START is that peculiarities of one's own country's laws, as well as of other countries' laws, can cause major problems. In this case, on one side of the Atlantic, a European Union directive that normalizes clinical-trial practice to commercial standards imposes an obligation of ultimate liability that, while appropriate for a commercial trial, is unnecessary and unreasonable when applied to a non-commercial trial such as START. The directive not only delayed the initiation of START by a year and imposed (and will continue to impose) needless costs on the University of Minnesota, it could also impede a range of potential E.U.–U.S. non-commercial collaborations, particularly when the U.S. party is a state university. On the other side of the Atlantic, the government that is largely funding the trial, that maintains significant involvement in the trial and de facto approval rights over much of what is done, that is running the data- and safety-monitoring board, that has an overriding public-health mission to be served by the trial, and whose expenditures of tens of billions of health-care dollars will be more effectively directed as a result of the trial, nonetheless backs away from its proper role as sponsor, for technical reasons grounded in arcane provisions of federal law.

When researchers and their counsel encounter obstacles such as these that unnecessarily interfere with international research collaborations, they should consider acting to resolve the problem. It would not be unreasonable for institutions and researchers to advocate for changes in relevant laws or directives, individually and through their professional and institutional organizations.

Alternatively (or simultaneously), the European Union and the United States could act on their own initiative—or following government-to-government consultation—to address such problems. Some efforts along these general lines appear to be under way.[9] Very recently, in an effort to enhance U.S. participation in the European Seventh Framework Programme for Research and Development, the E.U. delegation to the United States published a helpful booklet, *Transatlantic Cooperation in the European Seventh Framework Programme for Research and Development: A Guide for U.S. Users* (Delegation of the European Union to the USA, 2009) The booklet frames legal issues that can impede collaboration, identifies some solutions and special provisions that have been crafted to facilitate U.S. participation, and explains the reasons for the E.U. position on points where there is no flexibility.

The START trial is a vivid example of what can go wrong when there are differing expectations regarding liability. The E.U. Delegation's recent explanation of the E.U. position regarding liability under the Seventh Framework Programme is helpful: it explains that liability is limited to damages actually caused by the U.S. participant (Delegation of the European Union to the USA, 2009, p. 16). It would be very beneficial to non-commercial, clinical-trial collaborations if this same principle were extended to non-commercial trials under the E.U. clinical-trials directive.

The E.U. Delegation's booklet continues to state, however, that the European Union must be "indemnified," meaning that the liability is open-ended in amount (Delegation of the European Union to the USA, 2009, p. 16). Based on the position of the NIH in the START trial, it would appear to be a legal impossibility for an agency of the U.S. government to participate directly in Seventh Programme projects. Use of the term "indemnity" and the resulting implication of open-ended liability also might bar some U.S. state universities from participation in E.U.-funded collaborations. The U.S. government takes the position that it will self-insure for liabilities that might arise from research and that it does not require "indemnity"; it is not clear why the European Union would take a different position. Further work on bridging this legal/cultural gap is needed.

Other Recurring Issues

Differing expectations concerning intellectual property (IP) rights can also be a stumbling block to forming international research collaborations. The E.U. Delegation brochure discusses E.U. expectations in some detail (Delegation of the European Union to the USA, 2009, pp. 17–19). A core expectation is that all collaborators in a research program will be afforded reasonable "access" to other parties' IP—both the intellectual property that other parties bring into the collaboration, and new IP that the other parties develop. The minimum expected access is to assure the right of a party to commercialize IP that it develops in the collaboration: "access" includes the right to use enabling IP of other parties and the right not to be blocked by IP rights of other parties. The basic perspective is that, since the parties are collaborators, they will share and will not block one another from enjoying the fruits of the joint effort. On its face, this is quite reasonable.

A different set of expectations prevails in the United States. Under the Bayh–Dole Act and its implementing regulations (35 USC Sections 200–212; 37 CFR[10] Part 400), each party in a funded project is entitled to take title to what it creates, and no party is obligated to grant IP rights to other parties. The U.S. system has the virtue of not trying to "pick winners" at the beginning of a project. Research collaborators are chosen for many reasons, and the parties do not know in advance what IP will result. It is not necessarily true that members of a given team will be the optimal candidates to take an invention to the marketplace.

Indeed, the U.S. regulations explicitly prohibit a higher-level recipient from obtaining any rights in inventions from a sub-recipient under the sub-award (37 CFR 401.14(g)(1)). Furthermore, non-profit recipients of federal research funding are required to give small businesses preferential consideration in licensing IP for commercialization (37 CFR 401.14(k)(4)), which limits a university's ability to grant IP rights to any large-company collaborator, regardless of the contractual relationships. For all these reasons, U.S. universities expect not to have to grant IP rights at the outset of a collaboration and to retain the right to license discoveries on an exclusive basis if that is the best commercialization path.

There is logic and reason in both approaches and good cause to look for ways to accommodate expectations of other parties. On the E.U. side, alternative clauses concerning the right of non-E.U. participants to license IP rights exclusively (and outside the collaboration) have been issued (Delegation of the European Union to the USA, 2009, p. 18). On the U.S. side, the preference for small businesses is not absolute. Depending on the circumstances, a U.S. university might conclude that agreeing not to block a collaborator's right to practice its inventions does not prevent the university from licensing its inventions to small businesses, or it might determine that granting non-exclusive licenses is the norm in a particular industry and that granting such rights up-front to a collaborator is reasonable. A U.S. funding agency might support the university's position.

A recurring issue that can arise in any international contract, from a simple material transfer agreement to the most complex of collaborations, is: Whose law applies? This can be a surprisingly thorny issue, especially when each party is a governmental entity and asserts that it must be subject to its own laws. Where a national agency is providing funding for a project, it will insist that its laws apply, at least with respect to any dispute involving that agency and its funding. In other contexts, a preferred solution is to use accepted norms of international law, such as the International Institute for the Unification of Private Law (UNIDROIT), Principles of International Commercial Contracts (2004). The UNIDROIT principles have rather broad acceptance, were not drafted to benefit any particular country, and are straightforward, flexible and eminently fair.

Other common solutions to this problem are to remain silent (which actually is not very satisfactory, but is often a quick way to dispose of the issue), or to assign choice-of-law on the basis of the party against which a claim is brought. If UNIDROIT does not work, the latter should be considered the preferred solution. The split choice-of-law solution implicitly recognizes both that legal disputes involving research agreements are very rare and that relevant legal norms do not differ that much. The solution respects each party by assuring that, so long as a party follows its own legal norms and expectations, its conduct will be accepted by the other party. On a practical level this solution assures each party that, if need be, it will be able to defend itself on familiar legal turf, without expending undue resources learning an unfamiliar body of law.

Another recurring issue is: Where will a lawsuit or other legal proceeding be brought? Disputes over this issue are, in principle, rather high-stake. In an international collaboration, having to travel to the other party's home country and appear before the other party's home judges is likely to be expensive and disadvantageous. A common solution to this problem for international commercial agreements is arbitration on a written record before a neutral who is not a national of either party. Arbitration is frequently the agreed dispute-resolution system for international research collaborations.

Export-Control Laws and Regulations

International collaborations need to take account of each country's national security laws and regulations, as well as more ordinary questions of domestic law, such as those discussed above. There is one area of law, however, in which these normally separate domains intersect: export-control laws and regulations. Some unusual features of U.S. law may affect international research collaborations in unexpected ways, and it is important for both U.S. researchers and their non-U.S. counterparts to understand something of this complex area.

In general, export-control laws and regulations restrict export of certain items from one nation to another. The laws are similar to security classification: they affect items that are not classified, but that a national government has nonetheless determined should be restricted for various reasons, such as national security, economic security, compliance with treaty obligations, and foreign policy.

In the United States, there are two export-control regimes. One, the International Traffic in Arms Regulations (ITAR) (22 Code of Federal Regulation (CFR) Parts 120–130), regulates items with a uniquely military purpose.[11] If an item is controlled under ITAR, a license is required to export it to any other country. The second regime is the Export Administration Regulations (EAR) (15 CFR Parts 730–774). The EAR controls "dual-use" items—those that have mixed military and domestic uses.[12] The reasons for control under EAR are quite varied, from national security at one end of the spectrum to anti-terrorism at the other. If an item is controlled for national security purposes, licenses might be required for any exports. If an item is controlled only for anti-terrorism reasons, a license would be required only for exports to a country that is designated by the United States as a state sponsor of terrorism.

The obvious case of an export-control problem arises when a researcher wants to take or send a piece of equipment to another country. One well-known example that has affected international space research involved a re-classification of space-launch items from EAR to ITAR.[13] The ITAR controls affect many more nations than the previous EAR controls, and this change significantly complicated international collaborations involving scientific satellites. Other collaborations could run into unexpected problems with export controls. For example, the University of Minnesota needed to obtain an ITAR license to take a lakebed mapping instrument that it uses on Lake Superior to Iceland to do climate-change research. In addition to sonar and other instruments, the system incorporated an "inertial motion unit" to compensate for the movement of the boat. Inertial motion units are also used in missile guidance systems, and export from the United States requires an ITAR license.

International researchers and their collaborators should consider whether instrumentation to be taken from one country to another is of a type (or includes a component that is of a type) that might have a military use. If so, an inquiry should be initiated far in advance of the work to confirm whether the instrument is controlled and, if so, to allow time (which can be several months in the United States) for processing a license. Each country will have its own export-control rules; research that requires moving sensitive instrumentation between any nations could be held up for these reasons.

"Deemed Exports": A Unique and Problematic Feature of U.S. Law

The terms "export" and "item" have special and unexpected meanings under the U.S. export-control regimes. These special meanings are at the heart of the "deemed-export" rule, a unique feature of U.S. export-control law.

Under U.S. law, the term "item" includes certain "information."[14] In addition, the definition of "export" includes "any release" of controlled information to a "foreign national." Wherever the release occurs, it is "deemed to be an export to the home country or countries of the foreign national" (15 CFR 734.2(b)(1)(ii)).[15]

Thus, in contemplation of U.S. export-control law, the research conducted at any U.S. university laboratory staffed with any foreign students or postdoctoral fellows is an international collaboration. The information that is exchanged in the laboratory is "deemed" to be exported instantaneously to the home country or countries of the students. If that information is of the type that is controlled under EAR or ITAR (i.e., specific technical information needed to make, use or develop a controlled product), and if the student is from a country for which an EAR or ITAR license is required, and if a license was not obtained, then federal crimes may be taking place in the lab.

The potential gravity of violation of these rules has been driven home to the U.S. research community within the past two years. In 2008–2009, J. Reece Roth, a professor emeritus at the University of Tennessee (who has had a long-standing collaboration with Chinese colleagues), was indicted, tried and convicted on 15 counts of violation of ITAR regulations, and sentenced to four years in prison.[16] Of the 15 convictions, 12 were based on the ITAR deemed-export regulation—i.e., were for sharing ITAR-controlled information with graduate students from Professor Roth's lab (initially with a student from China, later with a student from Iran). One conviction was for taking the information on a trip to visit collaborators in China. The controlled information involved plasma physics research relevant to drones. Phase 1 of the research was open, unrestricted research, but the work transitioned into a Phase 2 that was subject to export controls. The evidence at the trial indicated that Professor Roth ignored contract restrictions and warnings of which he was aware. He has paid a heavy price.

The deemed-export rule would threaten much of U.S.-based university research, were it not for the Fundamental Research Exclusion[17] from that rule. "Fundamental research" means "basic and applied research in science and engineering, where the resulting information is ordinarily published and shared broadly within the scientific community" (15 CFR 734.8(a)). Thus, fundamental research is simply research carried out in accordance with the established norms of university work. So long as U.S. researchers adhere to these norms, the results of their research are not subject to export controls. The threat of the deemed-export rule, and the saving grace of the Fundamental Research Exclusion, create a legal imperative for U.S. researchers to conduct their work under the accepted paradigms of scientific inquiry.

These rules have a spill-over effect that limits the flexibility of U.S. institutions to negotiate IP and related terms. This lack of flexibility may be surprising to non-U.S. researchers, who do not labor under these difficulties.

For a U.S. university, a delay of publication for industry patent review, for patent filing, or for protection of unspecified proprietary interests raises an export-control issue, not just an academic issue. U.S. export-control regulations do allow publications to be withheld for review by a company or other sponsor to protect proprietary interests, but only for a limited time period, and only in order to file for patent protection prior to filing. The outer limits are generally considered to be in the range of six months.

U.S. universities also must consider the export-control implications of accepting confidential information from collaborators. The Fundamental Research Exclusion only protects the "results" of research, not the information that was contributed to the research. Proprietary information to be used in a research project may be subject to U.S. export controls; if it is, and if a university agrees to accept it, then the university recipient must implement rigorous controls.

This problem affects international collaborations to the same extent as collaborations with U.S. counterparts. Regardless of where the information was created, once the information is in the United States it can be subject to U.S. export controls.[18]

All U.S. universities will want to know if confidential information to be provided to them is export-controlled. In the absence of compelling circumstances, many U.S. universities will not accept such information. Some are a bit more willing to work with export-controlled information, but first they must set up special security plans for their laboratories to prevent prohibited nationals from accessing the information.

U.S. administrative team members generally will be familiar with these problems and with their own institution's methods of avoiding or managing them. Where the problem exists, those on the U.S. side should take the time to educate their non-U.S. partner about the problem and why the institution needs to solve it in a particular way.

In general, non-U.S. researchers and administrators should not be surprised if the U.S. side needs to be quite particular about the publication terms of the collaboration. Non-U.S. parties should also realize that confidentiality terms are very problematic on the U.S. side and should try to design their projects in a way that will obviate transferring confidential technical information that could have a military or other security application to a U.S. university. This prudent planning will help avoid delays in the project and help protect U.S. colleagues from potentially serious liabilities.

Foreign Corrupt Practices Act

Any researcher involved directly or indirectly with proposed payments of money or other consideration to foreign officials in an international research context should be aware of the U.S. Foreign Corrupt Practices Act (FCPA). The FCPA is a federal law that has been utilized with increasing frequency by the U.S. government in enforcement actions in cases of alleged international bribery and related accounting practices. The focus in this chapter is on prohibitions against bribery of foreign officials in connection with international activities of university researchers (see 15 USC § 78dd-2). The FCPA specifies that it is unlawful for any "domestic concern" (that is, a U.S. citizen, national or resident, or a company or organization with its principal place of business in the United States) or any officer, director, employee, or agent of a domestic concern to make or authorize a payment to a "foreign official" for the purposes of:

> (A) (i) influencing any act or decision of such foreign official in his official capacity, (ii) inducing such foreign official to do or omit to do any act in violation of the lawful duty of such official, or (iii) securing any improper advantage; or
> (B) inducing such foreign official to use his influence with a foreign government or instrumentality thereof to affect or influence any act or decision of such government or instrumentality,
>
> in order to assist such domestic concern in obtaining or retaining business for or with, or directing business to, any person.
> (15 USC § 78dd-2(a))

Thus the FCPA anti-bribery provisions apply to domestic concerns (such as U.S. universities) and their officers, agents and employees (including university staff and faculty members) when a payment or gift—or offer of a payment or gift—is made to a foreign official, directly or indirectly, for the purpose of influencing the official to obtain or retain business.

Who is considered a "foreign official"? Under the FCPA, a foreign official is an officer or employee of a foreign government or a public international organization, or "any person acting in an official capacity for or on behalf of any such government or department, agency, or instrumentality, or for or on behalf of any such public international organization" (15 USC § 78dd-1(h)2(A)).

The FCPA also has essentially parallel provisions (15 USC § 78dd-2(a)2 and § 78dd-2(a)3) that are applicable to payments to foreign political parties and their officials, or to any other person if all or a portion of such payments will be given directly or indirectly to a foreign official, foreign political party or party official, or any candidate for foreign political office. Thus, the payment need not be made or offered directly to a foreign official to be covered under the law, if there is knowledge or even some reason to know that the person receiving such payment or offer may forward it to a foreign official or other covered recipient.

The FCPA does, however, specifically permit or exempt certain activities that might otherwise seem to be prohibited under the law. For example, it is an acceptable defense to an alleged violation if the payment is lawful under the laws of the foreign country, or if it is a *bona fide* expense directly related to the promotion or demonstration of the domestic concern's service, or regarding the performance of a specific contract (15 USC § 78dd-2(c)). The FCPA also exempts facilitation payments if the purpose is to obtain the performance of routine governmental actions, such as the issuance of permits, licenses or other official documents (15 USC § 78dd-2(b)).

The challenge for a university official or researcher is how to determine whether such facilitation payments are, in fact, legitimate and allowed under the FCPA. The law does enumerate several examples of what could be considered routine governmental action, including actions ordinarily and commonly performed in obtaining permits or related documents to qualify to do business in that country, processing governmental papers such as visas, and providing certain basic utility services. But regardless of the specific circumstances, it would seem advisable to at least inquire as to the purpose of such payments and whether they are usual and customary in such a country for securing the non-discretionary performance of a routine governmental action. In addition, consultation with legal or other experts in the field should be considered, particularly with respect to larger proposed facilitation payments or payments not clearly within the acceptable parameters as set forth in the law. Finally, there is a mechanism under the FCPA by which a request for an opinion from the U.S. Department of Justice may be made as to whether certain proposed conduct would be lawful under the FCPA. This option could be especially important when either the amount of the proposed consideration or the scope of the research project is quite large.

Penalties for violation of the FCPA can be, and in many cases have been, significant. The FCPA specifies penalties up to $2,000,000 for domestic concerns that are not individuals, and up to $100,000 and/or up to five years of imprisonment for individuals (15 USC § 78dd-2(g)).

It should be noted that the FCPA specifically bars any domestic concern from either paying on behalf of or indemnifying an employee or the agent of the concern that may be fined (15 USC § 78dd-2(g)3). Thus, a university researcher who may otherwise be entitled to indemnification under his or her university's policies could not rely upon such policies in this case.

To help minimize the risk of alleged violations of the FCPA, researchers should, in addition to following the suggestions already discussed, consider adding language to the research contracts under which they will be working that addresses this risk. For example, a provision could be added that states that each party shall remain in compliance with all applicable laws and shall also take no action that would cause a violation of applicable law, including the FCPA and related foreign laws. The researcher's employer should also establish and implement appropriate legal compliance procedures and check-lists for all applicable laws and regulations, including the FCPA, relating to the proposed research activities.

Legal Presence and Tax Considerations

International research activities will by definition involve some degree of a "presence" in another country. While the laws of each country differ as to what such a presence may require from a legal and tax perspective, there are general categories that may apply to a researcher's activities in a foreign country. Such categories range from (1) no duty to register or account for income or taxes; to (2) a requirement to establish a branch or representative office there and inform the country of one's activities, with possible registration requirements and tax liabilities; to (3) a requirement to formally establish a legal entity in the country, with consequent registration, reporting and tax obligations. In some countries there may be additional categories with different requirements. Anyone planning to conduct more than *de minimus* activities in a foreign country should seek advice from legal and tax experts in this area before proceeding.

Prohibitions on Collaborations with Certain Countries

From time to time, the United States has imposed sanctions on certain countries; some of these sanctions can affect international research collaborations. The sanctions are subject to change (even frequent or sudden). Sanctions range from narrow restrictions prompted by a particularized foreign-policy concern to very broad, long-standing sanction regimes, such as those involving Cuba and Iran. Sanctions invariably include a financial component, and the U.S. sanctions regime is under the jurisdiction of the U.S. Treasury Department's Office of Foreign Assets Controls (OFAC).[19] If there is any question of whether a research activity involving a country subject to sanctions is appropriate, legal counsel should be contacted.

For countries such as Cuba and Iran, the OFAC sanctions can affect research because they extend to "services" provided for the benefit of persons in these countries. There are general exclusions for "informational materials," and certain editorial activities are allowed. However, as they currently exist, the sanctions appear to prohibit actual collaborative research with researchers in Cuba and Iran.

The OFAC sanctions are primarily of concern to U.S. researchers and to scientists in the countries that are subject to sanctions. Of course, researchers in all countries should be aware of any sanctions regimes that their governments have implemented and need to comply with those requirements.

Travel Regulations

In recent years it has become more difficult to keep up with changing immigration regulations of countries around the world. In some cases, rules for U.S. citizens traveling abroad may have been tightened in retaliation for the strict regulations of the U.S. Department of Homeland Security, which make it more difficult for international travelers to enter the United States.

The most basic travel requirements relate to passports and visas. The U.S. State Department provides passport and visa information on its website, whereas non-U.S. nationals can find information regarding passport requirements from their own government's equivalent. Entrance visas can be a complicated matter, as each country handles visa requirements differently. Academic travelers often take shortcuts by opting for basic tourist or holiday visas rather than work or research visas, which can require substantially more paperwork. It is strongly recommended that researchers follow visa regulations related to their international travel, as the penalties of not doing so can be quite high.

Further complicating international research efforts are increasingly stringent U.S. Customs and Border Protection limitations on items that can be brought or mailed to the United States. Specific restrictions apply, for example, to infectious agents and other bio-hazardous materials. Other countries also have limitations on materials that researchers might seek to bring in or remove from the country. These limitations should be considered very early in research planning to avoid costly fees and fines, or even the abandonment of a research project due to the inability to transport materials. Even where transport is allowed, the process that must be followed to release materials for transport can sometimes take months.

A recent case illustrates the risks of not following visa and permit regulations. A team of Brazilian and U.S. scientists were working on a climate-change project in southern Brazil. The U.S. researchers were in the country on tourist visas rather than the required scientific visas. In addition, the Brazilian research permit allowing the Brazilian scientist to take geological samples did not extend to the U.S. researchers, as it had been assumed. Both the Brazilian and U.S. scientists were arrested for suspected poaching, and the U.S. passports, computers and other personal belongings were confiscated. The Brazilian researchers were released the following day, but the U.S. researchers spent eight nights in jail before they were released on bail (Stone, 2009). Whether or not research data were accessed or compromised is unknown. The U.S. researchers' belongings were later returned and they were eventually allowed to return home; however, at the time of their departure from Brazil, charges were still pending.

Laptop Computers and Other Electronic Devices

There have been a number of reports of academics having their laptops confiscated at international airports and border crossings in recent years. In some cases the laptops were searched by officials concerned with export, and in others they were taken by officials concerned with import. In many cases, the laptops were taken for only a few minutes, but in others the scientists waited several hours before their laptops were returned, raising concerns about data corruption or release of sensitive information. Both the U.S. Department of Commerce and the Department of the Treasury have jurisdiction to search laptops, flash drives or personal digital assistants (PDAs) that are leaving or returning to the United States. As many countries have import and export regulations that include electronics, travelers could have their electronic materials searched and confiscated when entering or departing any country.

Due to export- and import-control laws and varying practices around the world, researchers should be very careful in deciding which electronic devices to take with them. As a general rule, items that are not necessary should be left at home. Travelers should remove all proprietary information, trade secrets, private student data, confidential research data, any research data that could not be easily replaced, and—most importantly—any export-controlled information. University technology staff can ensure that files are not only deleted but written over or electronically shredded.

Encryption software will not always protect sensitive data. Traveling with encrypted data on a computer is controlled in some countries, including Belarus, China, Hungary, Israel, Morocco, Russia, Tunisia and Ukraine, while in some instances a license to import and export encryption products can be obtained from government authorities. In other countries, including Saudi Arabia, encryption is prohibited (Koops, 2008). In the most extreme situations, travelers with encryption software could have laptops confiscated or even face imprisonment. For U.S. travelers, specific attention should be paid when traveling to the five Department of Commerce embargo countries— Cuba, Iran, North Korea, Sudan and Syria (U.S. Department of Treasury, 2009)—as encryption software must be removed and an export license from the Department of Commerce's Bureau of Industry and Security and the OFAC may be required. Traveling with a terminal laptop—that is, one that is stripped of information and is nothing more than a word processor with Internet capability—can avoid some problems related to encryption.

Recommendations and Best Practices

Complying with all the laws and regulations that apply to an international research project can be quite overwhelming, even for scientists with extensive international experience. It is critical that they take advantage of all available legal counsel, become familiar with online resources for updates on regulations and travel requirements, work with their collaborators to ensure compliance in the partnering country, and generally be aware of the legal and regulatory issues to which their work may be subject.

Research institutions likewise face a daunting task in keeping their researchers out of trouble in the international context. In large universities, merely tracking the international comings and goings of faculty is often beyond the capacities of administrative oversight. On any given day, a university's faculty, students and staff use planes, cabs, buses, ferries, and are in labs, hotels, factories and skyscrapers all over the world. They are renting property, hiring labor, signing agreements, sharing research, opening attachments to an email message, opening bank accounts, accepting cash payments for honorariums, and so on. Any of these tasks has the potential for a wide range of consequences for the university, as well as the researchers involved. Yet, universities generally do not know about all these activities or where they are taking place. Institutions are therefore limited in their ability to protect researchers from consequences, which range from embarrassing public relations problems to danger or harm, to a high-stakes security gamble.

For example, during the 2008 South Ossetia War, when in early August Russia and Georgia engaged in armed conflict, the University of Minnesota's Office of International Programs was surprised when local media reported that a university faculty member was "missing" in Georgia (Chang, 2008). After some investigation, the Office of International Programs learned that it was known within the professor's department that she was abroad, but there was no detailed itinerary indicating if she was meant to be in Georgia or Armenia during the days in question. No one from the professor's family had contacted the university. If the media had also reported that the university did not know that one of its own professors could not be located in Georgia, the result would have been embarrassing and a cause of reputation damage to the university. After the story ran, the Office of International Programs was able to put into motion efforts to locate the professor through academic and government channels, while also notifying the emergency evacuation service in case its services were needed.

It is important for universities and other research organizations to track not only their faculty's whereabouts, but also the areas of greatest potential risk and liability in the world. Fully monitoring global "hot spots" can be daunting.

In fact, the entire prospect of initiating and maintaining a productive research collaboration can be daunting to researchers, as they become aware of legal and regulatory issues, dangers related to travel in politically volatile areas, and the many details that can confound international research. Research collaborators, experienced or not, need ongoing support for their cross-national work.

Information and guidance can be offered through training, online sources, meetings and 24-hour telephone or web-based hotlines. Researchers may need to know about obtaining medical care in another country, health and life insurance while abroad, travel insurance, travel warnings issued by government bodies such as the U.S. Department of State, visa requirements, immunizations, first-aid supplies appropriate to a specific region, communications technology, emergency contacts, credit or debit card usage, and so on.

When researchers work internationally, it is often the non-research aspects of the collaboration that prove most problematic. Fluctuating currency rates can wreak havoc on research budgets. Research timelines and deadlines often do not anticipate the many delays that working internationally can introduce. Emergency evacuation can be a matter of life or death in the event of a bombing, natural disaster or epidemic. Loss or damage of equipment can halt a research project. Arrests and detentions can trump all other issues.

To handle the legal, regulatory and other issues that arise in international collaborations, researchers need to be well informed, well prepared and well supported by their home institutions, and—most importantly—they need to be careful. The benefits of global scientific collaboration are, in general, well worth the extra attention that these issues demand. Collaborations, however, may not be worth the consequences of breaking the law—intentionally or not—in one's own country or another.

Notes

1. The views and information set forth in this chapter are those of the authors and not those of the University of Minnesota. Contributions from Mr. Bohnhorst and Mr. Amundson are general legal commentary, not legal advice, and legal views expressed in this chapter may not be attributed to the University of Minnesota's Office of the General Counsel.
2. The START trial uses only previously approved drugs for their on-label uses, so this development was somewhat unexpected.
3. Directive 2001/20/EC of the European Parliament and the Council of April 4, 2001. The E.U. directive requires that the sponsor be a single entity and that it accept ultimate responsibility for the trial, including an obligation of indemnity. While the E.U. directive has brought a level of rigor to the conduct of clinical trials in the European Union that is generally compatible with drug companies' practices, it has had the unintended consequence of greatly complicating non-commercial research and has been quite controversial within the European Union (Flavell, Flavell & Sullivan, 2003; Williams, 2004; Baeyens, 2004; Hartmann & Hartmann-Vereilles, 2006; Hearn & Sullivan, 2007; Mitchell, 2007; Lambers Heerspink, Dobre, Hillege, Grobbee & Zeeuw, 2008; Pritchard-Jones, 2008).
4. "USC" refers to the codification of U.S. laws in the United States Code, U.S. Government Printing Office. The United States Code may be searched online at www.gpoaccess.gov/uscode (last accessed December 10, 2009).
5. It was a particular irony that this all played out while the U.S. government was bailing out Wall Street.
6. For example, Minnesota's waiver, which covers the University of Minnesota, is codified at Minnesota Statutes Section 3.736. The general waiver is set at levels below $1 million, but if an agency obtains valid insurance above the general waiver, it is subject to liability to the limits of its insurance. The University of Minnesota's general insurance limits are $1 million per claim/$3 million per occurrence with multiple claims. The university's coverage is far lower than is typical for private, non-profit entities. For example, an institute that

7.   counsel contacted in the course of resolving the START matter maintains $50 million limits.

7.   One possibility would have been for the NIH to cover costs of additional insurance for the trial. The NIH refused to do so, shifting these costs, as well as potential open-ended liability, to the University of Minnesota.

8.   The University of Minnesota agreed to serve as the sponsor of START for one year, with the explicit understanding that efforts to resolve the problem would be taken.

9.   For example, a legal discussion workshop, "E.U.–U.S. Research Information Day," was held in Washington, DC on December 9, 2009, at the offices of the Delegation of the European Commission to the USA. U.S. participation in the meeting was facilitated by a representative from the U.S. State Department; invited attendees were legal representatives of a few of the U.S. institutions that have raised concerns about legal terms in the E.U. Seventh Framework Programme that have impeded E.U.–U.S. research collaborations.

10.   "CFR" refers to the codification of U.S. regulations issues by U.S. government agencies in the Code of Federal Regulations, U.S. Government Printing Office. The Code of Federal Regulations may be searched online at http://ecfr.gpoaccess.gov/cgi/t/text/text-idx?c=ecfr&tpl=%2Findex.tpl (last accessed December 10, 2009).

11.   Items subject to ITAR control are described in the United States Munitions List, 22 CFR 121.1.

12.   Items subject to EAR control are described in the Commerce Control List, 15 CFR Part 774.

13.   The ITAR currently includes non-military scientific and research satellites within category XV of the United States Munitions List.

14.   Under 15 CFR 772.1 the definition of "item" includes "technology," and the definition of "technology" is "specific information" needed to make, use or develop a product. The ITAR definitions are to the same effect.

15.   "Foreign national" does not extend to permanent residents; however, it does encompass students, postdocs and visiting scientists.

16.   A Department of Justice FBI press release describing the case is available at http://knoxville.fbi.gov/dojpressrel/pressrel09/kx070109.html (last accessed December 4, 2009).

17.   The Fundamental Research Exclusion is a component of the more general principle that information in the public domain is not subject to export controls (15 CFR 734.3(b)(3)). There are other intuitively obvious exclusions, such as information that has already been published or is ordinarily taught in courses. The Fundamental Research Exclusion, however, is the most important component for university researchers.

18.   The EAR term defining the scope of the regulations is "subject to the EAR." Any non-excluded "item" that is "in the U.S." is "subject to the EAR" (15 CFR 734.3(a)(1)). "Item" includes "information," as per note 14.

19.   U.S. researchers and administrators can check the countries subject to sanctions by reviewing the OFAC website (U.S. Department of Treasury, 2009).

References

Baeyens, A. J. (2004). Impact of the European Clinical Trials Directive on academic clinical research. *Medicine and Law, 23*, 103–110.

Chang, B. (2008). Family awaits word from U of M anthropologist after cease-fire declared in Georgia. *Kare 11 News.* Retrieved August 13, 2008, from www.kare11.com/news/news_article.aspx?storyid=521558.

Delegation of the European Union to the USA. (2009). *Transatlantic cooperation in the European Seventh Framework Programme for Research and Development: A guide for US users.* Washington, DC: Delegation of the European Union to the USA, Science, Technology and Education Section. Retrieved from http://eurounion.org/policyareas/science.htm.

Flavell, D. J., Flavell, S. U., & Sullivan, R. (2003). European Clinical Trials Directive: responses made to MHRA consultation letter MLX 287. *Lancet, 362*, 1415.

Hartmann, M., & Hartmann-Vereilles, F. (2006) The Clinical Trials Directive: how is it affecting Europe's noncommercial research? *Public Library of Science Clinical Trials, 1*(2), e13. doi: 10.1371/journal.pctr.0010013.

Hearn, J., & Sullivan, R. (2007). The impact of the "Clinical Trials" directive on the cost and conduct of non-commercial trials in the UK. *European Journal of Cancer, 43*, 8–13.

International Institute for the Unification of Private Law (UNIDROIT). (2004). Principles of international commercial contracts. Retrieved December 10, 2009, from www.unidroit.org/english/principles/contracts/main.htm.

Koops, B. (2008). *Crypto law survey, version 25.2*. Retrieved December 1, 2009, from http://rechten.uvt.nl/koops/cryptolaw.

Lambers Heerspink, H. J., Dobre, D., Hillege, H. L., Grobbee, D. E., & de Zeeuw, D. (2008). Does the European Clinical Trials Directive really improve clinical trial approval time? *British Journal of Clinical Pharmacology, 66*, 546–550.

Mitchell, C. (2007). Clinical trials in paediatric haematology-oncology: Are future successes threatened by the E.U. directive on the conduct of clinical trials? *Archives of Disease in Childhood, 92*, 1024–1027.

Pritchard-Jones, K. (2008). Clinical trials for children with cancer in Europe—still a long way from harmonization: A report from SIOP Europe. *European Journal of Cancer, 44*, 2106–2111.

Stone, A. (2009, July 9). Accused Americans could be stuck in Brazil for months. *USA Today*. Retrieved December 2, 2009, from www.usatoday.com/news/world/2009-07-05-brazilstudents_ N.htm.

U.S. Department of Treasury. (2009). *Office of Foreign Assets Control: OFAC sanctions programs*. Retrieved December 3, 2009, from www.treas.gov/offices/enforcement/ofac/programs.

Williams, N. (2004). Breast cancer research and the European Union of Clinical Trials Directive. *Breast Cancer Research, 6*, 145–147.

8

The Governance of Scientific Collaborations

The International Reach of U.S. Law

Alexander M. Capron

Substantial differences exist among countries' legal and regulatory systems. The question is, to what extent are these cross-national differences relevant in scientific research ethics and, in particular, how do they affect the governance of research with human subjects globally? I argue that the answer to that question differs substantially between U.S. researchers and those from other countries, especially (but not exclusively) developing countries.

In brief, collaborating scientists' need to master other countries' laws and regulations is asymmetrical. U.S. researchers can generally rely on their non-U.S. collaborators to manage the legal and regulatory issues in their own countries; however, researchers from other countries who collaborate with U.S. colleagues or who undertake studies for sponsors in the United States need to know U.S. regulations on research with human subjects—and the research institutions where they work need to comply with the U.S. regulations—even when they differ significantly from their own. This imbalance is due to the dominant role the United States plays internationally in the governance of scientific research. I argue that this imbalance, though currently and unfortunately inescapable, is problematic for international scientific collaboration and is unjustifiable.

All U.S. recipients of federal grants know their obligations to comply with the so-called "Common Rule," the basic policy for the protection of human-research subjects of the Department of Health and Human Services (Federal Policy for the Protection of Human Subjects, 2005). The specific question here is, how does this set of regulations, which was developed for research in the United States, relate to the way research is governed around the world?

I first examine the governance situation in the context of international research. In considering the role that U.S. regulations play in global governance, it is important to note what is problematic about the current U.S.-centric system. To this end, we need to look at the origins of the U.S. rules, the difficulties that the United States actually faces in trying to exert oversight, and finally, what happens when U.S. regulators' attempts to oversee research institutions abroad lead to their ignoring important international issues. My views on this topic were greatly influenced by my four years as Director of

Ethics, Trade, Human Rights and Health Law at the World Health Organization (WHO) in Geneva, Switzerland, an organization that is increasingly concerned about governance in a number of areas of public health and health care.

What is Governance?

When we speak of "governance," what do we mean, and how does it differ from "government"? Both words come from the Latin root *gubernare*, meaning "to steer." When we talk about government, we're talking about something that has a formal structure and binding authority; that is to say, it has power to enforce its will. By contrast, governance includes less-formal means of directing action or regulating behavior, not necessarily through the law. Governments do exercise governance, but not all governance is through a government. Governance connotes steering an organization by setting goals and general directions. It may include some formal powers such as the authority a board of directors has to control an organization, but the term is used especially for situations that involve influence, direction and regulation through less-formal and binding means.

In fact, it is possible for governance to be achieved through means that have nothing to do with explicitly spelled-out rules. For example, what are elsewhere called "research ethics committees" are referred to as "institutional review boards" in the United States. The "institutional" part is largely a historical accident. When the first requirements for review of the ethics of research protocols were put into place in the 1960s, the National Institutes of Health were already using assurance mechanisms to achieve institutional accountability for compliance with federal financial rules on grants and contracts. They then simply chose to use the same model to require institutions to provide assurance that they were obeying rules on human subjects. To rationalize this institutional approach, however, some people argued that review boards at the institutional level, as opposed to the federal level, had two advantages in achieving good governance of research. First, members of institutional review boards knew the researchers within their own institution better than an external body could. Second, their influence would spread through contacts among colleagues, instead of just through formal meetings, thereby helping to develop an ethical climate. The justification for reviews at the institutional level thus recognized the power of informal means to ensure proper governance of research.

Global Governance

Global governance implicates four conditions: transnational problems; independent solutions; lack of existing over-arching authority; and independence of the actors (Rosenau, 1999). It involves the interaction of transnational actors and is aimed at solving problems that affect more than one state or region. The essential point here is that it denotes regulation directed at interdependent actions and interdependent relations among a group of free equals. Ideally, these would be independent states that need to form a regular, as opposed to ad hoc, relationship, in the absence of an over-arching political authority such as a United Nations body.

Such international arrangements can take four forms: formal or informal at either a governmental or non-governmental level. A prime example of a formal, governmental governance arrangement is the International Health Regulations (IHR) (WHO, 2005), the latest version of which was adopted by the World Health Assembly in 2005. The IHR is a binding document. The countries sign on and then have to fulfill the obligations established by the IHR. Similarly, when countries join the World Trade Organization, they subject themselves to obeying various trade agreements. Some formal international arrangements are non-governmental, such as the agreements set up by sports federations that conduct international competitions through agreements that bind the parties, even though the federations do not have governmental powers.

The second form of arrangement represents informal governance, where there is no power to enforce compliance. On the governmental side are instances of cooperative action, such as those set up among central bankers where they have a means of reaching collective, albeit non-binding, decisions. Likewise, there are many examples of informal governance arrangements in non-governmental realms. For example, the editors of scientific and medical journals have agreed to require authors to disclose conflicts of interest, to report information about institutional review board approval of research involving human subjects, and to have entered the study into a clinical trial registry prior to commencement of the project (Committee on Publication Ethics, 2009). These arrangements may be informal, but they constitute a form of governance not simply of the parties to the agreement, but also of those engaged in the underlying activity, such as carrying out and reporting on research. The governance arrangements control or steer what happens among independent actors so as to achieve a particular goal.

These four types of arrangement (formal or informal arrangements on a governmental or non-governmental basis) yield different sorts of actions: (1) formal/governmental: treaties; (2) formal/non-governmental: agreements; (3) informal/governmental: institutions; (4) informal/non-governmental: practices and understandings. There are also products of international governance that fall between informal and formal. For example, in the governmental realm, the declarations of the United Nations Educational, Scientific and Cultural Organization (UNESCO) have a certain formality, but they are not actually binding, even though they can—over time—become part of so-called "soft law." Likewise, standards established by various bodies amount to a non-governmental form of governance that crosses formal and informal lines.

The success of governance is dependent, of course, on characteristics beyond structural arrangements. The Integrated Project on New Modes of Governance, funded by the Sixth Framework Programme of the European Union, suggests that the hallmarks of successful governance are participation, capacity, legitimacy and effectiveness (European University Institute, 2008).

Global Governance for Research Ethics

Do we need a system of global governance for research ethics, and, if so, how might it fit within this analytic framework? The conditions for global governance are all present. Research with human beings is a transnational problem in need of interdependent solutions. Clinical trials and other forms of research are increasingly carried out around the world. Often the same or similar trials are being conducted simultaneously in multiple countries. Greater consistency in standards and regulation is highly desirable.

Further, at the moment no over-arching governance authority already exists. The World Medical Association, whose *Declaration of Helsinki* (World Medical Association, 2008) sets forth a set of ethical standards, has no enforcement authority. Likewise, the Council for International Organizations of Medical Sciences (CIOMS), whose ethical guidelines for biomedical research (CIOMS, 2002) are widely relied upon by research ethics committees outside the United States, particularly in developing countries, also lacks enforcement power. Thus far, the United Nations agencies have not exercised their standard-setting authority. UNESCO's bioethics declarations are just generalities, and its guidelines for formation and operation of ethics committees are merely advisory. Similarly, the guidance for research ethics committees provided by the Special Programme in Tropical Disease Research at the WHO (WHO, 2000) is basically procedural and technical, not a document approved by its governing bodies. In short, there is no organization with over-arching authority in the area of global research ethics.

Finally, the activities in question rest in the hands of independent actors: national governments; ministries of health or education or science and technology; the research institutions where trials are carried out; the institutions from which investigators come; private sponsors of research such as biotechnology and pharmaceutical companies; and non-governmental organizations including private foundations (such as the Wellcome Trust and the Bill and Melinda Gates Foundation).

The need and conditions for global governance of research ethics are clear. Any of the structural arrangements identified by the four combinations of formal/informal and governmental/non-governmental properties might be appropriate for some aspect of global governance. What is lacking is a governance system with the hallmarks of effective governance. Participation does not include all relevant stakeholders. Capacity for governance, where present, has not been exercised. Legitimacy is compromised when those bodies with the greatest relevant expertise lack the means of exercising authority and oversight. Effectiveness cannot be established when no organization or group has the ability to adopt and implement binding decisions and solve conflicts when they arise among the participants.

Current International Ethical Oversight of Research with Human Subjects

The lack of global governance of research ethics has produced something of a vacuum, which has been filled by a system dominated by U.S. regulation. The system has emerged in part because of the scope of U.S. scientific research, and in part because of the highly developed regulatory machinery to which U.S. science is subject. This system is both problematic and inappropriate in the context of worldwide scientific collaboration.

The U.S. regulations play a disproportionate role in the global governance of research ethics. Research ethics committees outside the United States have to apply to the U.S. Office for Human Research Protection (OHRP) for a "Federal-Wide Assurance." This office permits non-U.S. committees to use the *Declaration of Helsinki* (World Medical Association, 2008) as their guiding document, rather than the *Belmont Report* (Department of Health, Education and Welfare, 1979), which has been used as the touchstone document on basic ethical principles for human-subjects research since it was issued in 1978 by the U.S. National Commission for the Protection of Human Subjects of Biomedical and Behavioral Research. Otherwise, however, the requirements for international Federal-Wide Assurances are really no different than the requirements that apply to a U.S. organization. Any non-U.S. research ethics committee that will review research funded by the U.S. federal agencies must adhere to the Common Rule.

It doesn't have to be this way. Many countries currently have laws and regulations governing research ethics, standards and processes of review. The U.S. Department of Health and Human Services maintains an impressive online list of research standards and regulations in countries around the world (OHRP, 2010). Nevertheless, none of these are recognized by the U.S. government as providing human subjects with protection equivalent to that provided by the Common Rule.

In April 2001 the National Bioethics Advisory Commission, on which I served, in a report on ethical and policy issues in international clinical trials, recommended that the U.S. government identify a set of "procedural criteria and a process for determining" that a host country's system provides equivalent protection (National Bioethics Advisory Commission, 2001, p. 89). A few months later, the Office of the Inspector General for the Department of Health and Human Services (Rehnquist, 2001) urged the OHRP to address how it could "better assess whether other nations' laws and practices afford equivalent protection." After a brief flurry of bureaucratic activity when it appeared that Congress might force the OHRP to give substance to the regulatory promise that at least *some* countries' regulations might protect research subjects at least as well as the U.S. regulations, the threat of legislation abated and the OHRP reverted to that great temporizing stratagem of appointing another group to study the issue. In 2003 that working group concluded that the decision that a research institution was operating under rules equivalent to the Common Rule should rest on the finding that the institution had established norms of ethical conduct and due diligence at the institutional level, rather than adhering to national standards and requirements which had been found to offer "equivalent protection" (Department of Health and Human Services, 2003). They specified particular requirements of the regulation that would manifest compliance at an institutional level. For example, the institution would need to ensure initial and continuing review (§103(b)(4) of the Common Rule). It would also need written procedures for promptly reporting unanticipated problems or suspension or termination of the project to the review board, institutional officials and the head of the federal agency (§103(b)(5)). To ensure adequate authority and independence of the review board, it would have to meet specific provisions covering expedited review of proposals (§110(b)). To protect against biased and arbitrary decisions, the institution would have to meet conditions on the composition of the review board, such as gender balance, and the inclusion of at least one scientist, at least one non-scientist and at least one member not affiliated with the institution (§107(b)–(d)). Furthermore, institutions must also ensure sufficient quality and comprehensiveness of review, and ensure that review and oversight are commensurate with the risk of the research and the vulnerability of the study populations (§111(a)(2)–(3)).

These examples show just how procedurally obscure and specifically American are some of the requirements that the working group concluded must be part of any "equivalent" set of protections. Yet, as stated by Jordan Cohen, writing as the president of the Association of American Medical Colleges (Cohen, 2005), determinations of equivalence should not be equated with determinations of identity between the foreign rules and those in the United States. Rather, a determination of equivalence should be based on a finding that a national system—with its own, nationally appropriate counterpart to the Common Rule—achieves a level of protection of human subjects that is roughly the same as what the U.S. system achieves, not that individual institutions have adopted procedures that satisfy all the specific requirements of the Common Rule. According to the Department of Health and Human Services' interpretation of the Common Rule, assurance of meeting the Common Rule's specifications has nothing to do with "equivalent protection," but is rather just a determination that a particular foreign institution has met the requirements of the Common Rule, just as individual institutions in the United States must.

In sum, the current system is problematic in three ways. First, the U.S. rules have a particular form and substance because they evolved over time in light of specific events (typically, scandals in research) and institutional structures. As noted above, the system of assurance of compliance with ethical rules was grafted onto the existing system of assurance of compliance with rules for sound fiscal management of federal funding. Such a process is not aimed at the quality of research; indeed, it is not even aimed primarily at investigators, but at the institutions that employ them. Other, non-institution-based means of reviewing the ethical acceptability of research proposals are effectively placed out-of-bounds by the role that the U.S. regulations play in global governance of research with human subjects.

Second, and probably even more important, the content of the norms and standards in the Common Rule reflects a peculiarly U.S. set of views about what is important. It is unlikely that U.S. regulatory officials have sufficient understanding of how local cultural factors and institutional arrangements worldwide affect the appropriateness and adequacy of institutional oversight outside the United States. Many international issues were simply omitted from U.S. rules. For example, the European Group on Ethics, which advises the European Commission, has considered group benefit versus group risk, a trade-off that does not appear in the U.S. regulations (de Beaufort & Englert, 2003). They have also considered the importance of having a system of compensation for research injuries, which likewise is not addressed in the Common Rule.

Finally, the present arrangement is problematic because it is unseemly, to say the least, for researchers and their institutions from around the world to have to petition a bureau of the U.S. government for permission to conduct research and, in the process, to demonstrate that they meet U.S. standards rather than the standards that apply in their own jurisdiction. Moreover, reliance on the Common Rule discourages the development of strong domestic regulations that would be better adapted to each local situation. More significantly, it dampens the drive toward other, more effective and more responsive forms of global governance.

My conclusion is that the current system is likely to persist for some time. The goal, however, should be the establishment of truly global governance of research ethics. Expansion in international research collaborations will drive the push for effective governance systems that benefit from the best thinking and best experience worldwide, as well as attention to the specific features of local research circumstances, to ensure the proper, ethical conduct of scientific research.

References

Cohen, J. (2005). *"Comments on the Protection of Human Subjects, proposed criteria for determinations of equivalent protection,"* letter of May 24, 2005, to Ms. Gail Carter, Division of Policy and Assurances, Office for Human Research Protections [Response to a Notice published in the Federal Register on March 25, 2005] (70 *Fed. Register* 15322). Retrieved December 9, 2009, from www.aamc.org/advocacy/library/research/corres/2005/052405.pdf.

CIOMS. (2002). *International ethical guidelines for biomedical research involving human subjects.* Geneva: CIOMS.

Committee on Publication Ethics. (2009). *Guidance for editors: Research, audit and service evaluations.* Retrieved December 9, 2009, from http://publicationethics.org/files/u2/Audit_research_guidelines.pdf.

de Beaufort, I., & Englert, Y. (2003). *Ethical aspects of clinical research in developing countries* [Opinion No. 17]. Luxembourg: Office for Official Publications of the European Communities, European Group on Ethics in Science and New Technologies to the European Commission.

Department of Health and Human Services. (2003). *Report of the Equivalent Protections Working Group* [submitted to Dr. Bernard Schwetz, Director, Office for Human Research Protections]. Retrieved December 9, 2009, from www.hhs.gov/ohrp/international/EPWGReport2003.pdf.

Department of Health, Education and Welfare. (1979). *Belmont Report: Ethical principles and guidelines for the protection of human subjects of research, report of the National Commission for the Protection of Human Subjects of Biomedical and Behavioral Research* (44 Fed. Reg. 23192-97) (April 18).

European University Institute. (2008). *Integrated project on new modes of governance.* Retrieved December 9, 2009, from www.eu-newgov.org/public/Overview.asp.

Federal Policy for the Protection of Human Subjects. (2005). 45 Code of Federal Regulations, part 46, Subpart A ("The Common Rule"), revised June 23, 2005.

National Bioethics Advisory Commission. (2001). *Ethical and policy issues in international research: Clinical trials in developing countries.* Bethesda, MD: NBAC.

OHRP. (2010). *International compilation of human research protections* (2010 ed.). Retrieved September 9, 2009, from www.hhs.gov/ohrp/international/HSPCompilation.pdf.

Rehnquist, J. (2001). *The globalization of clinical trials: A growing challenge in protecting human subjects.* Washington, DC: Office of the Inspector General, Department of Health and Human Services.

Rosenau, J. (1999). Toward an ontology for global governance. In M. Hewson & T. J. Sinclair (Eds.), *Approaches to global governance theory* (pp. 287–302). Albany: State University of New York.

WHO. (2000). *Operational guidelines for ethics committees that review biomedical research* [TDR/PRD/ETHICS/2000.1]. Geneva: WHO Press.

WHO. (2005). *International health regulations* (2nd ed.). Geneva: WHO Press.

World Medical Association. (2008). *Declaration of Helsinki: Ethical principles for medical research involving human subjects* [1964, amended 2008]. December 9, 2009, from www.wma.net/en/30publications/10policies/b3/index.html.

9

Normative Environments of International Science

Raymond G. De Vries, Leslie M. Rott, and Yasaswi Paruchuri

Suppose that you are a Dutch academic working on a collaborative project with colleagues in Nigeria. Together with your Nigerian collaborators, you are assessing a program for delivering dental care to those with limited or no access to oral health services. While the subjects in this study will not be exposed to more than a minimal risk of harm, this is a research project, and as such it requires ethical oversight to ensure adequate protection for participants.

So far, so good. But the question arises: whose ethical standards should be applied to this research in Nigeria? In the Netherlands, there are regulations governing the conduct of research with human subjects. The Central Committee on Research Involving Human Subjects oversees research involving humans, supervising the work of the local medical research ethics committees that review and approve research protocols. Nigeria does have a system for the protection of human subjects of research; it is a system that uses Institutional Review Boards (IRBs), a model of research review developed in the United States in the late 1970s. While Nigerian IRBs are certified by the U.S. Office for Human Research Protections (OHRP, 2009), you know that in Nigeria it is not unusual for research to go ahead without IRB approval, and even when a research project is approved, the protocol submitted to the ethics board might not be followed in the field. You are also aware of the mixed motivation that lies behind the creation and use of IRBs in Nigeria (and elsewhere in Africa). It is true that the IRB mechanism—like your medical research ethics committee review—is intended to protect vulnerable research subjects. But the rush to win U.S. certification for IRBs in Africa is also linked to the need of North American and European researchers to obtain the imprimatur of an IRB in order to publish their findings or gain certification from the U.S. Food and Drug Administration for a new drug or medical device. The bottom line is that, when (and if) an IRB approves a research protocol in Nigeria, it is often the result of applying a set of standards based on an ethical tradition developed in a different culture, which is suited to the hypothesis-driven nature of most modern health science, but not to the values and urgent needs of the local population (Simon, Mosavel, & van Stade, 2007).

You—the Dutch researcher—understand the need for and value of ethical oversight of research on humans, but wonder about the use of Western ethical ideas as the basis for the protection of human subjects. There are those who argue that the ethical principles that guide IRB review are universal, that all cultures value "respect for autonomy," "beneficence," and "justice"—the principles described in the foundational document of North American research ethics, the *Belmont Report* (OHSR, 2009). But you are uncertain that this approach—known as principlism—can be applied in Nigeria. Indeed, in your own country, many have abandoned the principlist approach for an ethic guided by "care" (although the guidelines for medical research ethics committees—emphasizing informed consent and beneficence—are much like those in the United States). In the words of Shakespeare, "What's in a name?" Is Nigerian "autonomy" the same as North American "autonomy"? Is "care" in Nigeria defined in the same way as it is in the Netherlands? It is true that regardless of cultural differences, we can all agree that respect for autonomy is a good thing, but the way the citizens of Nigeria define autonomy is very different from the way you, a Netherlander, define that same principle. Conceptions of autonomy in Europe are colored by social and political traditions that emphasize individual liberty, whereas in African cultures autonomy must be understood in the context of family or community. In the more atomistic societies of Europe and North America, people believe that a free and independent individual should determine his or her care or decide to be a research subject, whereas members of more communal societies believe that decisions about these matters occur in consultation with or by the declaration of those with authority in the family, tribe, or clan. If autonomy can be defined in such different ways, the regulations created by the Dutch Central Committee on Research Involving Human Subjects, as well as the principles of the *Belmont Report*, become meaningless. Can you, as a European, speak of "respect for autonomy" if a treatment decision for an adult woman is taken by others?

How should the collaboration proceed? You have a set of values and a body of regulations that govern your attitudes and behavior. These values and regulations are the products of cultural ideas, ethical traditions, and structural conditions in the Netherlands. Your Nigerian collaborators have a different set of values and have adopted, but incompletely applied, regulations developed in your country. Furthermore, the structural conditions in Nigeria are an important part of the ethical landscape: access to any kind of health care is extremely limited and literacy rates are low. In the Netherlands, potential research subjects can find care outside of a research protocol; in these research sites in Nigeria, the only way to receive dental care is to "volunteer" to participate in this study.

This example, drawn from the work of Taiwo and Kass (2009), exemplifies the ethical tensions that arise in international collaboration. In their review of the situation, the researchers acknowledge the problems with application of Western ethical ideas and regulations in a non-Western setting:

- Of the three study sites for the dental health project, only one had IRB approval.
- The high degree of respect given to doctors by Nigerians led to "almost uniform agreement" to participate in research studies and an unwillingness to challenge medical directives.
- The idea of "voluntary withdrawal" from a study—part of a Western ethical framework—is "not rational" for those with no access to health care.
- Research-team members had little or no training in research ethics.
- The oral consent necessitated by low levels of literacy was nearly impossible to monitor.

Taiwo and Kass also admit that their own findings—about the ethical procedures used in the oral health research project they observed—may be skewed by the tool they used to gather their data: "[Our] findings could have been due to the survey instrument used which was largely adapted from those used in Western countries. It contained some words whose translations in the local languages may not have appropriately conveyed their intended meaning" (Taiwo & Kass, 2009, p. 6).

In this collaborative project the struggle is with incommensurable ideas about the protection of research participants. In other international projects, researchers labor to harmonize different ideas about how to interpret data, authorship, and the wisdom of data sharing. How might we make the incommensurable commensurable?

We approach the problem of incommensurable ethical concepts by looking closely at the way ideas about bioethics—in particular, ideas about the ethics of research that are crucial to international research—have traveled from North America and Europe to the rest of the world. We explore three ways in which Western bioethical ideas find their way into non-Western societies: (1) the ideas may be "adopted wholesale," borrowed directly and put into practice; (2) the ideas may be taken from the West, but molded and altered to fit local culture; and (3) Western ethical ideas may be used to open a conversation about moral standards and stimulate the search for applicable ethical ideas that are drawn from local culture and reflect local traditions.

The data that inform our discussion come from two sources: (1) close reading of the small but growing body of literature on Western bioethics in non-Western societies (e.g., Elsayed & Kass, 2007; Irabor, 2006; Manafa, Lindegger, & Ijsselmuiden, 2006, 2007; Marshall, Adebamowo, Adeyemo, Ogundiran, Vekich, Strenski et al., 2006; Marsh, Kamuya, Rowa, Gikonyo, & Molyneux, 2008; Mfutso-Bengo, Ndebele, Jumbe, Mkunthi, Masiye, Molyneux et al., 2008a; Mfutso-Bengo, Masiye, Molyneux, Ndebele & Chilungo, 2008b; Indian Council of Medical Research, 2006); and (2) a series of 21 interviews with trainees at a European-based bioethics program intended for those doing bioethics work in countries outside of the European Union.[1]

The Transport of Bioethical Ideas

The advent of international research has forced the question of "Whose ethics?"—reinvigorating the battle between universalists (those who believe in a universal ethical standard) and relativists (those who believe that ethical concepts can only be judged in terms of the society in which they appear).[2] Macklin (1999, 2004) argues "against relativism," contending that while we should avoid "ethical absolutism," there are universal ethical standards that can and should be applied across cultures. To accept anything less, according to Macklin, is to apply a double standard. Beauchamp (2003) agrees, asserting that there is a "common morality," committed to the "promotion of human flourishing" and against which the moral standards of particular societies can be judged.

In their discussion of bioethics "circling the globe," Fox and Swazey (2009, pp. 153–197) challenge the claims of universalists, calling on the work of two social scientists, Bourdieu and De Craemer. Bourdieu (2001) rejects universalism, noting the danger of "the imperialism of the universal," which occurs when a society universalizes "its own characteristics by tacitly establishing them in a universal model" (p. 3). Indeed, the principles that are often given the status of universals—autonomy, beneficence, non-maleficence, and justice—are inextricably linked to Western, individualistic notions of personhood. And as De Craemer (1983) reminds us:

> [O]ur modern Western and American outlook on the person tends to be culturally particularistic and inadvertently ethnocentric. To a significant degree, it rests on the implicit assumption that its ideas about personhood are common to many, if not most, other societies and cultures.
>
> (p. 21)

Fox and Swazey (2009, pp. 172–173) go on to point out that the Western, individualistic conception of the person that informs American bioethics is not the one that prevails globally. Most of the world sees the person not as an isolated individual, but embedded in kinship, group, and community.

The universal-versus-relative debate is theoretically interesting, but it tells us little about what actually happens when international collaborators must move forward with research and make decisions about the application of ethical standards. Our work examines the ethical problems of collaboration by looking at the way ethical ideas cross international and cultural borders. Our three "modes of ethical transport" offer a typology of the possibilities for exchanging ethical ideas and regulations. Our research suggests that one of these modes, "wholesale adoption," is by far the most common mode of transport; the other two are more nascent and suggest future strategies for ethical collaboration.

The Wholesale Adoption of Western Bioethics: Bioethics as Missionary Work

Writing about "the past, present, and future of a Latin American bioethics," Del Pozo and Mainetti (2009) observe that the new medical technologies introduced in Latin America in the 1980s created a number of new ethical questions "for which neither classical medical ethics nor the omnipresent but increasingly questioned teachings of the Catholic Church provided acceptable responses" (pp. 272–273). They continue:

> In this context, the new bioethical paradigm was rapidly embraced by Latin America. Taking the path of least resistance, countries *assimilated*, to a large extent, North American bioethics. At a fast pace, ethics committees, informed consent procedures, and legislation dealing with biomedical issues from organ transplantation to assisted reproduction flourished in the region.
>
> (p. 273, emphasis in the original)

The Latin American experience is typical. The export of new medicines, medical devices, and medical procedures to the developing world, together with the movement of clinical research from research-rich to resource-poor countries, created a need for new types of ethical advice (Petryna, 2005). Because the United States, Canada, and the countries of Western Europe had a head start in the development of medical technologies and the preparation of bioethical guidelines for implementing those technologies, it seemed only natural to import the bioethics along with the medicine and medical research. One of our interviewees told us that in India, her home country, medical ethics had long been a part of the medical school curriculum, but bioethics was new:

> Medical ethics was something like the ethics related to clinical care and the doctor, how we should be with patients and all that, that was what we were taught in medical school. But now because research is coming in a big way especially with a lot of international collaborations, the U.S. ethos of bioethics is coming in a big way.

The intent of the exporters and importers of ethics is noble—protection for those subjected to the new technologies—but wholesale adoption of ethical ideas and frameworks is not without problems.

Binyavanga Wainaina (2009), a young writer from Kenya, describes the general problem with the Western desire to help the people of Africa:

> A lot of people arrive in Africa to assume that it is a blank empty space and their good will and desire and guilt will fix it; and that to me is not any different from the first people who arrived and colonized us. This power, this power to help is just about as dangerous as hard power, because very often it arrives as a kind of zeal that is assuming, "I will do it, I will solve it for you, I will fix it for you," and it rides roughshod over your own best efforts.

In an earlier essay, we called attention to the remarkable similarities between Christian missionaries and those who bring the ideas of bioethics to the developing world (De Vries & Rott, 2010). Members of both groups care deeply about the plight of those in resource-poor countries and are interested in sharing the "gospel," be it the good news of the *Belmont Report* or that of the New Testament. And both missionaries and bioethicists realize that the best way to share the gospel is to "indigenize" the good news—that is, to train locals and send them back to their own countries as agents of change:

> Indigenization is a solution to … the "export problem," of Western bioethics—a problem that is unavoidable when bioethics, a creation of Western culture, collides with the systems of ethics found in local, non-Western cultures. Pursuing the indigenization solution, bioethicists from the developing world are currently being trained in the United States (via the National Institutes of Health Fogarty International Center), Europe (via the Erasmus Mundus Masters program in bioethics), and the United Kingdom (via The Wellcome Trust).[3] Having learned the language and logic of Western bioethics, trainees return to their home countries to spread the "gospel."
>
> (De Vries & Rott, 2009, pp. 2–3)

Unfortunately, the gospel of bioethics is often at odds with local cultural values. Several researchers have noticed this lack of fit when it comes to gaining informed consent from individuals in the developing world (Dawson & Kass, 2005; Ezeome & Marshall, 2008; Hyder & Wali, 2006; Molyneux, Wassenaar, Peshu, & Marsh, 2005). The Indian Council of Medical Research (2006) describes the problems associated with adopting the Western idea of informed consent:

> In the context of developing countries, obtaining informed consent has been considered many times as difficult/impractical/not meeting the purpose on various grounds such as incompetence to comprehend the meaning or relevance of the consent and culturally being dependent on the decision of the head of the family or village/community head.
>
> (p. 67)

Our interviews with bioethics students from the developing world revealed two dimensions to the "problem of fit": cultural and structural. Several students noticed that the bioethical principles they were learning were at odds with cultural values in their home countries. A student from China told us:

> If I want to accept all of the theologies and too the methods for the bioethics for Chinese people, it's a little bit difficult … in China, we have different religions … and very few people believe in God … they are not Christian … so they have no sort of knowledge about Christian history, about Jesus, so you know, a lot of bioethics, methods, and theories came from Jesus.

In particular, the concept of autonomy, rooted in Western ideas of individualism (Wolpe, 1998) did not translate well. One student commented:

> [In rural India] their idea of autonomy is totally different, like they're not, even for signing our hospital admission sheet, it is not a patient or immediate person, it is … the family [that] was signing for that patient, even for admission, even for taking out of the hospital, it's not the patient who is signing … we are not thinking the autonomy of the person, we are thinking about the collective autonomy of the whole family.

Another student called on his religious tradition to reject the idea of autonomy and defend the value of paternalism (a model of the patient–physician relationship rejected by most Western bioethicists, where the caregiver makes decisions for the patient): "In Buddhism you have no concept of autonomy…. So for myself, this is what I think for myself, compassionate paternalism, it's not that bad."

Beyond this cultural lack of fit, students also observed that the way healthcare delivery was structured in their home countries was at odds with Western ethical principles:

> Bioethics in [my South American country] is very influenced by bioethics in the U.S. mostly … we get taught mostly the four principles … [but] it's not exactly like the U.S. because we have a national health system which is parallel to a private system. So the idea of having a principle of autonomy that can overrule the other ones when they're in conflict doesn't exist.

Similarly, a student from India observed that autonomy can only be realized when people have the opportunity to make choices, a condition that does not exist for most people in India:

> Principlism did not answer many questions for me … [In India] people cannot exercise their autonomy … so what do you do with just giving them autonomy? … it's incomplete, yeah, it's a useful principle no doubt but it's not practical [in India] … unless you empower people to exercise their autonomy, autonomy has no meaning.

The "foreignness" of Western ethical thinking is also illustrated by students' comments on what they saw as the odd ethical problems associated with the structure of health care in the West. For example, a student from an Eastern European country was surprised by the market-based health-care system in the United States. As a physician, she had worked for a time in the United States:

> In the U.S. for me there was some strange things. Let's say insurance … I saw a patient and then my question was: why you are not doing [this] biopsy under … ultrasound … because it is the best way, I mean you

just can see ... that place and your needle would be right there ... Their answer was [that] insurance is not covering ultrasound exam, it's just covering that biopsy technique.... I was a little bit surprised, U.S., [the] richest country.

Other researchers confirm this lack of fit. Simpson (in press) describes the "growing disenchantment" that results from a "sense of mismatch between the ethical values that underpin the Western biomedical tradition and the reality of local circumstances" (p. 8). Chattopadhyay and De Vries (2008) go as far as suggesting that it is "*unethical* to impose, either consciously or unconsciously, the dominant Western socio-cultural-moral construct to ethnic minorities in the West and the vast non-Western world" (p. 108; emphasis in original).

The lack of fit that is associated with the "wholesale adoption" or "missionary" approach to the transport of ethical ideas brings with it the danger of harm. Ethical ideas that are imposed rather than indigenous can limit useful research by demanding that Western standards be met before research can begin. Furthermore, the imposition of ethical ideas can disrupt existing moral traditions, creating confusion and anomie.[4] The presence of representatives from resource-rich countries—be they missionaries, bioethicists, or colonial administrators—in resource-poor countries, creates opportunities for "cultural brokers." These brokers translate between cultures, gaining status in their local communities by associating with the agents from the developed world. In our interviews, students often talked about how the opportunity to be bioethical brokers would work to their advantage when they returned home. One student admitted that his first love was business, but: "In business ethics there are many experts already available [in India] but not in bioethics so if I do it in bioethics, I'll be more relevant."

Nearly 50 years ago, sociologist Howard Becker used the term "moral entrepreneur" to describe those who wrote the legislation that prohibited the use of alcohol and marijuana in the United States. According to Becker (1963, p. 148), the moral entrepreneur sees him- or herself as a reformer or crusader: "The crusader is not only interested in seeing to it that other people do what he thinks right. He believes that if they do what is right it will be good for them."

Moral crusaders typically want to help those beneath them to achieve a better status. That those beneath them do not always like the means proposed for their salvation is another matter. But this fact—that moral crusades are typically dominated by those in the upper levels of the social structure—means that they add to the power they derive from the legitimacy of their moral position, the power they derive from their superior position in society.

Although those who bring the gospel of bioethics to resource-poor countries would shrink from this definition of themselves, they are doing the work of a moral entrepreneur. The cost of this entrepreneurship is the loss of the possibility of mutual enrichment where those in the developed world and those in the developing world learn from each other.

Molding Western Ethical Ideas to Fit Local Culture

A second way that ethical ideas move between the West and the developing world is by adoption and reshaping. Western ethical concepts are imported but then reframed or molded to fit local circumstances. This mode of transport is illustrated by Siddiqui's (2009) description of an introductory bioethics class for medical technology students at Karachi University in Pakistan. The topics covered in the course are typically Western–informed consent, conflicts of interests, privacy and confidentiality, and patients' rights. However, Siddiqui points out that the instructors "decided to familiarize and educate students in basics of bioethics using practical examples and to highlight ethical issues keeping [the] cultural and social milieu of Pakistan in mind" (p. 4). He also notes that "students were also allowed to express their views in Urdu, as many were not fluent in English, and because we believe that ethics has no language barriers" (p. 7). The ideas are Western, but they are translated into the Pakistani context.

A similar process is visible in a bioethics curriculum developed by the Middle East Research Ethics Training Initiative (MERETI)—a research ethics training program involved in the career development of individuals from the Middle East and funded by the Fogarty International Center (FIC) of the National Institutes of Health. Members of MERETI formed a Workshop Development Team to create multi-day courses on research ethics targeted to investigators and members of research ethics committees. The course materials draw heavily upon Western sources, but are tailored for those working in the Middle East:

> Several of the articles chosen by the Workshop Development Team were co-authored by individuals from the Middle East and several documents are in Arabic. Many of the PowerPoint slide sets incorporate Arabic phrases, thereby enhancing their relevance to an Arabic audience. Finally, many of the informed consent exercises, case studies, and research protocols reflect researches performed in the Middle East.
>
> (Silverman et al., in press, p. 4)

Review of these materials reveals an emphasis on molding Western ideas to a Middle Eastern context. Assigned readings, for example, include an article by Professor Dr. G. I. Serour entitled "Islam and the four principles." This essay harmonizes the four principles of Beauchamp and Childress (2001) with the teachings of Islam, concluding: "Islam is a religion which has given great importance to what are known today as the ethical principles of autonomy, beneficence, non-maleficence, and justice" (Serour, 1994, p. 89). The effort in

Serour's essay is not to develop ethical ideas from the Islamic tradition, but rather it is to show that the Western ideas are supported by Islam.

In talking with bioethics students from the developing world, we heard many comments about the need to "translate" Western ideas for use in their home countries. When asked if the ethical ideas she was learning in her European classroom could be applied when she returned to India, one student replied:

> I don't think they [i.e., the ethical ideas] can go with our culture because it's totally different … you can "hire" the concepts but you have to always make changes into the cultural and religious whatever background that you have, you cannot apply them directly because it's entirely different, the situation here.… To apply [them] practically, in each situation is different because you have to take all the other things that are culturally, or religiously, or whatever is there in that particular situation, [so] you have to adopt a lot into that situation.

Notice that the idea is "adoption." She does not refute the Western ideas, nor does she argue for the need to apply moral ideas from the Indian tradition, but rather, she says Western ethical ideas must be molded to the local context.

Simpson (in press), an anthropologist who has looked closely at how the moral tradition of Sri Lanka is applied to the ethical questions of modern medicine, sees these efforts to mold Western bioethical ideas to developing world cultures and values as "largely rhetorical." The work of translating Western ethics into local idioms is a move in the right direction—a move toward recognizing the existence of moral traditions whose origins are not found in the Western Judeo-Christian society—but the act of molding or translating implies the priority of the imported ethical ideas. As Chattopadhyay and De Vries (2008) note:

> There is an interesting irony here: in order to make bioethics *global*, it must be *local*.… And yet today, most, if not all, of the efforts to make bioethics more "culturally appropriate" amount to little more than adapting Western bioethics to varied cultural settings.… Distinguished professors seek to train the future bioethicists of the (so-called) developing world in the acrobatic art of balancing the "principles" (in either their American or European version) to conquer the most troubling of ethical dilemmas. While the "principles" are often framed as meta-cultural, they derive from Western secular belief-systems that are not responsive to either the cultural ethos and moral sensibilities … or the emotional needs and religious/spiritual worldviews of people in the non-Western world … even when those principles are "adjusted" to the recipient culture.

(pp. 107–108)

Deriving Ethical Ideas from Local Culture

The final mode of transporting ethical ideas in our typology is more theoretical than empirical. While we have not seen this mode in practice, conversations going on in Pakistan lead us to believe it is the next logical step in the conversation about international ethical collaboration. This mode uses the knowledge of ethics developed in the West to encourage the ethicists of the developing world to generate their own culturally appropriate approaches to the ethical dilemmas that arise in their societies. Rather than importing ethical ideas wholesale, or modifying them to harmonize with existing moral traditions, this approach uses what ethicists in the West have learned about the process of articulating and applying moral ideas.

Unlike existing ethics training programs—funded by the FIC, the Wellcome Trust (2009), or the European Union—this approach is inductive. It begins with the solicitation of local moral ideas and uses the history of moral philosophy and bioethics in the West as an example of how moral ideas developed and were implemented. This model turns the existing mode of ethical transport on its head, asking what we in the West might learn from ethicists in the developing world. Ethicists from the West remain helpful, but not as the providers of moral maxims or principles. Their work is to explain how they reasoned from their Western traditions to bioethical guidelines.

Existing programs that fit into the second mode—molding Western ideas to local culture—can easily be adapted to this model. With some minor changes, the MERETI workshops, described above, can be used in this more inductive way. For example, the curriculum includes use of the movie, *Wit*, to exemplify aspects of informed consent (Silverman et al., in press). As such, it is a straightforward example of Western ideas informing Middle Eastern bioethics. But this movie—with its rich depiction of moral conflict, questionable researcher behavior, the clash of physician and nursing values, and patient stoicism—is better used as an example of moral values and moral transgressions, showing how people in Western societies deal with moral problems. It should not be used as a model—do this, just like they do in the United States!—but as the beginning of a discussion about the operationalization of moral values.

Bioethicists in the developing world are aware of the need for this way of creating ethical guidelines, but they lack the power to implement the model. The Centre of Biomedical Ethics and Culture in the Sindh Institute of Urology and Transplantation in Pakistan is one place where this approach is being developed. Shortly after the center was founded, its leaders organized a seminar, "Foundations of moral thought: From the Greeks to contemporary bioethics," intended to "introduce participants to the ways in which historically, religious, secular, and cultural values have been linked in the evolution of human ethical thought, and how these continue to shape and modulate moral comprehension" (Centre of Biomedical Ethics and Culture, 2005, p. 2). The center newsletter described the event:

> One of the distinctive features of the five-day event was a focus on the historical contributions of Muslim philosophers, theologians, fuqaha, and ulema to the human chain of moral thought. In current international bioethical seminars and conferences, whereas the role of secular Anglo-European and American thinkers is well documented, references to enduring religious moral traditions, especially those originating in Islam, receive insufficient attention. A second, and equally important, goal of the organizers was to offer a constructive critique of secular, philosophical bioethics, and to emphasize that one cannot dismiss the profound influence of indigenous values, cultural and religious norms, and socioeconomic realities on how individuals and communities arrive at decisions about ethical personal and professional relationships.
>
> (Centre of Biomedical Ethics and Culture, 2005, p. 2)

The center director, Dr. Farhart Moazam, continues to press for a local bioethics:

> It is necessary for us to evolve bioethics in a coherent way in this country, give it a form that resonates with our values. Otherwise bioethics in Pakistan will remain an academic exercise ... irrelevant to the needs of our population.
>
> (Cited in Fox and Swazey, 2009, p. 278)

If this approach flourishes in the developing world, it will generate a dialog about moral ideas that will enrich ethics both at home and abroad.

Conclusion

Finding an appropriate way to do science in different normative environments is one of the most difficult challenges facing those who collaborate with colleagues from other countries. This "normative challenge" is made more difficult when the collaboration is between scientists in resource-rich and resource-poor countries. A history of colonialism, fear of alienating a wealthy sponsor, and well-intended paternalism complicate the good intentions of collaborators.

Kempf (1996) offers a classic example of the ethical challenges of collaboration between the developing and developed world. In her work collecting medical specimens in South America, she observed several instances of inter-cultural misunderstanding. She recounts the story of an effort to inoculate members of an Ecuadorian lowland tribal population, the Awa. Members of the tribe, having seen the swollen arms and fevers that resulted from inoculations given to their children, refused to be injected. The physician, who had only the best of intentions, was perplexed. Threats of jail or confiscation of animals were used to coerce members into getting inoculated. Kempf observes:

> Paternalistic attitudes toward non-westerners most often arise in situations where the researcher or medical personnel view the end result of medical intervention as positive, but consent as not likely to be obtained or not worth the effort. In this case the population is viewed as incapable of making their own decisions.... Ironically, viewing the Awa as competent to give informed consent would have dramatically boosted the medical team's success rate. Had they treated the Awa with dignity, taken the time to explain what they were doing, and answered the questions they were being asked, they would have been able to inoculate many more people and had a lot less trouble. (An injection described as attacking illness-causing spirits would have been culturally appropriate and acceptable to the Awa.)
>
> (Kempf, 1996, p. 146)

She notes that researchers are often inclined to see people in developing countries as unsophisticated and unable to make competent decisions about their health care. In her experience, "it is often the medical or research team who are 'unsophisticated' about the appropriate ways to collaborate with members of non-western cultures" and therefore inclined to resort to paternalism (Kempf, 1996, p. 146).

We are aware that at first glance, our observations appear to be a critique of programs like those funded by the FIC, Wellcome, and the European Union. But in fact, listening to the voices of bioethicists from the developing world will make those programs more effective at protecting human subjects. The collaborative work of caregivers and researchers in rural Peru (Gabrysch, Lema, Bedriñana, Bautista, Malca, & Campbell, 2009) provides an excellent example of how listening and respect promote collaborative goals. Faced with the problem of high maternal mortality, health workers were perplexed when local women avoided the well-equipped local clinic in favor of birth at home. Rather than assuming that the local people were ignorant (and, as had been done, imposing de facto fines for providing birth certificates for children born at home), researchers asked women why they preferred birth at home over birth in a modern clinic. In the words of Grady:

> [The researchers] got an earful. Workers at the clinic did not speak the local language, Quechua. They treated patients brusquely, and barred husbands and other relatives from the delivery room. They forced women to wear hospital gowns instead of their own clothes, and made them give birth lying on a table instead of squatting. They threw away the placenta instead of giving it to the family to bury in a warm place.
>
> (Grady, 2009, p. D6)

Caregivers used this information to change their practices, not the beliefs and practices of the local women. The result? More women used the clinic and communication between local midwives and clinic staff improved. A little respect goes a long way.

The next step in training programs for research ethics is to find a way to continue the dialog that these programs have opened, to use the knowledge of ethics developed in the West to encourage the ethicists of the developing world to generate their own, culturally appropriate approaches to the ethical dilemmas that arise in their societies. This model of ethical collaboration will promote good research in both senses: research that is of high quality and that respects the moral traditions of all involved.

We see the following ethical challenges to international research collaboration:

- Whose ethics? It is difficult to decide whose ethical standards to apply in collaborative research, especially when researchers are responsible for adhering to guidelines developed in their home countries.
- The "golden rule" problem. Those who have the gold make the rules. This means that the researcher with the most resources often sets the ethical agenda and others must accommodate.
- Reliance on cultural brokers. International collaborations often rely on "cultural brokers" to translate language, customs, and values. Because these brokers gain status and wealth from their role, they are likely to accommodate the needs of the more powerful partner in the collaboration.

Our recommendations are as follows:

- Mutual respect. The ethical concepts that support guidelines should reflect local culture and traditions. Collaborators must recognize the legitimacy of their colleagues' moral traditions. Rather than assuming one tradition is superior to another, partners should explain how their norms fit with their culture and how these norms are realized in regulations and guidelines.
- Adopting an inductive approach. Use the knowledge of ethics developed in the West to encourage those in the developing world to generate their own, culturally appropriate approaches to the ethical dilemmas that arise in their societies.
- Talk. When a "moral impasse" is reached—when researchers' values collide—it is important that collaborators talk through the values in question and arrive at a solution that can be honored by all involved.

Notes

1. Nearly all of these students were from the developing world. Two students out of a cohort of 25 were from North America; one student was working in Africa, but was a citizen of an E.U. country. The interviews lasted between one and one-and-a-half hours each. The research was reviewed by the research ethics committee at the Katholiek Universiteit, Leuven, and deemed exempt.

2. See the *Kennedy Institute of Ethics Journal, 13*(3) for a series of articles on this theme.
3. According to The Wellcome Trust, "The focus of *the funding programme* is strengthening capacity for research into the ethical, legal, social, cultural and public policy aspects of biomedical research and health care in *developing and restructuring countries*" (2009, emphasis in original).
4. Literally, "without rules," anomie is a term used to describe the social instability that results from a breakdown of standards and values.

References

Beauchamp, T. (2003). A defense of the common morality. *Kennedy Institute of Ethics Journal, 13*(3), 259–274.

Beauchamp, T., & Childress, J. (2001). *Principles of biomedical ethics* (5th ed.). New York: Oxford University Press.

Becker, H. (1963). *Outsiders*. New York: Free Press.

Bourdieu, P. (2001). Uniting to better dominate. *Items and Issues, 2*(3–4), 1–6.

Centre of Biomedical Ethics and Culture. (2005). First international seminar and intensive course: Foundations of moral thought: From the Greeks to contemporary bioethics. *Bioethics Links, 1*(1), 2.

Chattopadhyay, S., & De Vries, R. (2008). Bioethical concerns are global, bioethics is Western. *Eubios Journal of Asian and International Bioethics, 18*(4), 106–109.

Dawson, L., & Kass, N. (2005). Views of U.S. researchers about informed consent in international collaborative research. *Social Science and Medicine, 61*(6), 1211–1222.

De Craemer, W. (1983). A cross-cultural perspective on personhood. *Milbank Memorial Fund Quarterly/Health and Society, 61*(1), 19–34.

Del Pozo, P., & Mainetti, J. (2009). Bioetica sin mas: The past, present, and future of a Latin American bioethics. *Cambridge Q Health Ethics, 18*(3), 270–279.

De Vries, R., & Rott, L. (2010). Bioethics as missionary work: The export of Western ethics to developing countries. In C. Myser (Ed.), *The social functions of bioethics around the globe* (in press). New York: Oxford University Press.

Elsayed, D., & Kass, N. (2007). Attitudes of Sudanese researchers on obtaining informed consent from study subjects involved in health research. *Sudanese Journal of Public Health, 2*(2), 95–102.

Ezeome, E., & Marshall, P. (2008). Informed consent practices in Nigeria. *Developing World Bioethics, 9*(3), 138–148.

Fox, R., & Swazey, J. (2009). *Observing bioethics*. New York: Oxford University Press.

Gabrysch, S., Lema, C., Bedriñana, E., Bautista, M. A., Malca, R., & Campbell, O. M. R. (2009). Cultural adaptation of birthing services in rural Ayacucho, Peru. *Bull: World Health Organization, 87*, 724–729.

Grady, D. (2009, September 8). Pregnancy: Clinic in rural Peru draws more women by following local childbirth traditions. *New York Times*, D6.

Hyder, A., & Wali, S. (2006). Informed consent and collaborative research: Perspectives from the developing world. *Developing World Bioethics, 6*(1): 33–40.

Indian Council of Medical Research, The. (2006). *Ethical guidelines for biomedical research on human participants*. Retrieved November 18, 2009, from http://icmr.nic.in/ethical_guidelines.pdf.

Irabor, D. (2006). Informed consent for surgery: A historical review. *West African Journal of Medicine, 25*(4), 301–304.

Kempf, J. (1996). Collecting medical specimens in South America: A dilemma in medical ethics. *Anthropological Quarterly, 69*(3), 142–148.

Macklin, R. (1999). *Against relativism: Cultural diversity and the search for ethical universals*. New York: Oxford University Press.

Macklin, R. (2004). *Double standards in medical research in developing countries*. Cambridge: Cambridge University Press.

Manafa, O., Lindegger, G., & Ijsselmuiden, C. (2006). Informed consent in a clinical trial: Participants' satisfaction of the consent process and voluntariness of participation. *Online Journal of Health Ethics, 1*(1). Retrieved from www.usm.edu/ethicsjournal/index.php/ojhe/article/view/48/55.

Manafa, O., Lindegger, G., & Ijsselmuiden, C. (2007). Informed consent in an antiretroviral trial in Nigeria. *Indian Journal of Medical Ethics, 4*(1), 26–30.

Marsh, V., Kamuya, D., Rowa, Y., Gikonyo, C., & Molyneux, S. (2008). Beginning community engagement at a busy biomedical research programme: Experiences from the KEMRI CGMRC–Wellcome Trust Research Programme, Kilifi, Kenya. *Social Science & Medicine*, 67(5), 721–733.

Marshall, P., Adebamowo, C., Adeyemo, A., Ogundiran, T., Vekich, M., Strenski, T., et al. (2006). Voluntary participation and informed consent to international genetic research. *American Journal of Public Health*, 96(11), 1989–1995.

Mfutso-Bengo, J., Ndebele, P., Jumbe, V., Mkunthi, M., Masiye, F., Molyneux, S., et al. (2008a). Why do individuals agree to enroll in clinical trials? A qualitative study of health research participants in Blantyre, Malawi. *Malawi Medical Journal*, 20(2), 37–41.

Mfutso-Bengo, J., Masiye, F., Molyneux, M., Ndebele, N., & Chilungo, A. (2008b). Why do people refuse to take part in biomedical research studies? Evidence from a resource-poor area. *Malawi Medical Journal*, 20(2), 57–63.

Molyneux, C., Wassenaar, D. R., Peshu, N., & Marsh, K. (2005). "Even if they ask you to stand by a tree all day, you will have to do it (laughter)…!": Community voices on the notion and practice of informed consent for biomedical research in developing countries. *Social Science and Medicine*, 61(2), 443–454.

OHRP (Office for Human Research Protection). (2009, November 18). Retrieved November 18, 2009, from www.hhs.gov/ohrp.

OHSR (Office of Human Subjects Research, National Institutes of Health). (November 23, 2009). *The Belmont report: Ethical principles and guidelines for the protection of human subjects of research.* Retrieved November 23, 2009, from http://ohsr.od.nih.gov/guidelines/belmont. html.

Petryna, A. (2005). Ethical variability: Drug development and globalizing clinical trials. *American Ethnologist*, 32(2), 183–197.

Serour, G. I. (1994). Islam and the four principles. In R. Gillon (Ed.), *Principles of health care ethics* (pp. 75–91). New York: John Wiley & Sons.

Siddiqui, M. (2009). PGD alumni bring bioethics to medical technologists in Karachi. *Bioethics Links*, 5(1), 4, 7, and 8.

Silverman, H., Ahmed, B., Ajeilet, S., Al-Fadil, S., Al-Amad, S., El-Dessouky, H., et al. (in press). Curriculum guide for research ethics workshops for countries in the Middle East. *Developing World Bioethics*.

Simon, C., Mosavel, M., & van Stade, D. (2007). Ethical challenges in the design and conduct of locally relevant international health research. *Social Science and Medicine*, 64(9), 1960–1969.

Simpson, R. (in press). Capacity building in developing world bioethics: Perspectives on biomedicine and biomedical ethics in contemporary Sri Lanka. In C. Myser (Ed.), *The social functions of bioethics around the globe*. Oxford University Press.

Taiwo, O., & Kass, N. (2009). Post-consent assessment of dental subjects' understanding of informed consent in oral health research in Nigeria. *BMC Medical Ethics*, 10, 11–17.

Wellcome Trust, The. (2009). *Bioethical grant schemes: Biomedical ethics in developing countries grant schemes: Call for applications.* Retrieved from www.wellcome.ac.uk/Funding/Medical-humanities/Grants/Biomedical-ethics/eveloping-countries-schemes.

Wolpe, P. (1998). The triumph of autonomy in American boethics: A sociological view. In R. De Vries & J. Subedi (Eds.), *Bioethics and Society: Constructing the Ethical Enterprise* (pp. 38–59). Upper Saddle River, NJ: Prentice-Hall.

Part IV

Differences in Regulatory and Publication Oversight

10

International Cooperation to Ensure Research Integrity

Christine C. Boesz and Peggy L. Fischer

How would one handle an investigation into an incident like the following? A student trained in one country went to another for graduate school. After a short period of time, he returned to his home country and published a paper based on the data allegedly stolen from the other country's laboratories. The student included as authors some scientists from the home-country laboratory, who were allegedly unaware of the theft but presumed instead that the data were generated in the home-country laboratory. How would one coordinate the investigation, gather documents and make sound decisions, despite conflicting national systems, an inability to conduct face-to-face interviews, and language and customs barriers (Office of the Inspector General (OIG), 2008, 2009)?

Or how would one investigate the following situation? A scientist reviewed a grant proposal submitted to a funding agency by a researcher from another country. He gave it a low score but then submitted part of the proposal's text into his own grant proposal to another country's agency. How would one obtain the relevant information from the two grant proposals—information that the funding agency considers confidential—and then take effective action against the individual (OIG, 1994, 1995, 2003, 2004)?

Dilemmas like these actual cases are complicated by the increasingly international nature of scientific research. Academic research has undergone a transition from separate national efforts into complex collaborative and international efforts. Research projects and administration must now interweave international policies, rules, and regulations governing the use of public, private, and commercial funds. Coordination presents significant challenges for ensuring the integrity of scientific data, methods, and findings.

The most critical issue in addressing misconduct in the cross-national context is that there is no international body with the authority and legitimacy to provide consultation in cases of suspected misconduct or to handle allegations and investigations arising out of international collaborations. There are no internationally accepted standards or procedures to assure consistent and fair investigation into matters of research misconduct. Further, there is no cross-national consistency in expectations for training on principles of responsible research.

Policy Development

Over the past 20 years, researchers in the United States have engaged in a vigorous debate about research misconduct and resulting declines in the public's trust in researchers. Several policies were formulated in an attempt to bolster research integrity (Commission on Research Integrity, 1995; Federation of American Societies for Experimental Biology, 1996; Panel on Scientific Responsibility and the Conduct of Research, National Academy of Sciences, National Academy of Engineering and Institute of Medicine, 1992). In 2000, the White House's Office of Science and Technology Policy (OSTP) developed what is now the U.S. federal government's policy for handling allegations of research misconduct. The OSTP policy describes procedures that are to be followed by federal agencies and local institutions in evaluating allegations. The common use of these procedures has resulted in considerable consistency of investigations across types of institutions and types of allegations.

In the United States, federal OIGs are charged with preventing and detecting fraud, waste, and abuse, and ensuring economic, efficient, and effective operations of federal agency operations. At the National Science Foundation, for example, the OIG conducts audits of academic systems and investigates allegations of fraud and violations of regulations, rules, and policies. This latter responsibility prominently includes investigating allegations of research misconduct.[1] Many, but not all, federal agencies identify their inspector general as responsible for the federal research misconduct investigations. In the Department of Health and Human Services, by contrast, a separate office (the Office of Research Integrity (ORI)) bears this responsibility. In any case, the investigating agency usually refers allegations to the academic institution where the accused is employed. These institutions then complete investigations and impose institutional sanctions, where appropriate. The federal role, then, is to review the institution's report of its investigation, assessing the procedures and final decision for fairness and completeness, and conducting any additional investigation needed to support action to protect the federal interest.

The OSTP policy has produced some uniformity in investigations within the United States, but the situation is far more complicated in the international context. International collaborations are on the rise, as are multinational disputes about authorship, intellectual property, and patent claims (National Science Board, 2006). These collaborations bring together researchers with different practices and customs that are bound to create tensions and misunderstandings, resulting in more allegations. As research becomes increasingly global, there is greater urgency in the need to develop an international consensus on how allegations and investigations will be handled.

The Need for Attention to Research Integrity

A number of studies have attempted to assess the prevalence of research misconduct and other behaviors that can compromise the integrity of research, often referred to as questionable research practices. The overall conclusion seems to be that they are both more prevalent than the number reported to oversight bodies would suggest. In the past 10 years, the National Science Foundation has seen a doubling in the number of research misconduct allegations received, and the amount of research misconduct has increased dramatically, suggesting that the allegations arising involve more serious matters. The ORI, within the Department of Health and Human Services, has also observed an increase in the number of allegations reviewed (ORI, 2007a, 2007b). Overall, estimates of the percentage of researchers who engage in questionable research practices are much higher than estimates of those who commit actionable research misconduct (Martinson, Anderson, & De Vries 2005; National Science Foundation, 1990). Whereas egregious research misconduct tends to be exposed over time, questionable research practices tend to go undetected or uncorrected, posing a potentially greater threat to research integrity. The science literature now contains more reports of serious misconduct cases internationally (Giles, 2005; Steneck, 2000; Yidong, 2005).

Given the increasing number of scientists, the intermixing of ethical and regulatory regimes, tighter funding, and the potential for an erosion of ethics, it is reasonable to assume that the number of allegations and also the number of confirmed cases of research misconduct or questionable research practices will increase (Altman & Broad, 2005).[2] In addition, erosion of integrity can be detected in large numbers of students, well before they chose to become researchers (McCabe, 1997). One survey found that 75 percent of high-school students had engaged in "serious cheating," another found that 53 percent of undergraduates had cheated on written work, and yet another found that students find it acceptable to do anything to win (McCabe, Butterfield, & Trevino, 2006; Morin, 2006; Slobogin, 2002; Tanner, 2002). A recent study concluded that early- and mid-career scientists are more likely to commit acts that create ethical, legal, or regulatory issues when they perceive that they are treated unfairly in organizational decision-making (with respect to funding, peer review, and advancement) (Martinson, Anderson, Crain, & De Vries 2006; see also Giles, 2007).

Finally, the increasing sophistication of electronic resources and availability of data have made it easier to commit research misconduct. Scientists intent on plagiarism can easily search and find the precise text they desire on the Internet (Cook, 2007). Plagiarists have claimed that, when working in a digital environment and cutting and pasting text, they "lost" or "misplaced" the citations. Effectively, they claim that they were the victims of the technologies they were exploiting to commit misconduct. Over 10 years ago, concerns about digital technology's capacity to facilitate inappropriate manipulation of figures were just beginning to surface (Anderson, 1994; Mitchell, 1994; Vogel, 2005). Now, data and figure manipulation are quite easy with commonly available software. There are confirmed cases of individuals who have simply expanded a given dataset by a selected multiplier to create new datasets (OIG, 2004), who have "erased" background data points or inverted figures (OIG, 2005), or who have simply adjusted the gain on data-gathering equipment to create data logs (Katsnelson, 2007). All are examples of research misconduct facilitated by modern technologies.

The Challenge

Our experience suggests that research misconduct in the international context has become easier to perpetrate, because it is both harder for authorities to investigate and to take appropriate action in the global arena.[3] Institutional investigating committees find pursuing cases that cross international boundaries particularly difficult and have, in some cases, declined to investigate matters. Among cases with international threads have been instances where:

- international collaborators have published research without each other's knowledge;
- international collaborators have expended funds because the partner has no financial control;
- international collaborators have inappropriately sought duplicate funding using the ideas or text of the partner without permission;
- international students have run afoul of rules, regulations, and expectations because they were not carefully trained or mentored;
- physical or genetic samples or native knowledge have been obtained without permission of the scientist or the proper export/import permits and transported across international borders (Steghaus-Kovac, 2002);[4] or
- researchers have submitted to another country's funding entity ideas stolen from proposals shared internationally for merit review.

Investigations into these cases are made more complex because:

- subjects, complainants, or witnesses depart for their home countries, thereby making it difficult to obtain responses to questions, gather evidence, or identify institutional officials to assist in these efforts;
- systems and customs are poorly understood, training is inconsistent and conflicting, and spoken and written language skills are found wanting (Demaine & Fellmeth, 2003; Gibbons, 2002; Marshall, 1997);
- collaborations and collaborators cross borders; and
- original or confidential documents are difficult to obtain (OIG, 1994, 1995, 2003, 2004).

Addressing Allegations of Wrongdoing in International Collaborations

International collaborations bring with them exciting opportunities to link ideas and advance knowledge. Research support systems must include policies and procedures to support this work in ways that appropriately address potential wrongdoing.

As yet, there is no organization or treaty agreement that handles allegations of research misconduct for international collaborations. The task of investigation therefore falls to existing, locally based structures. These structures vary by country and often by funding source. The challenge of defining internationally acceptable definitions and procedures was taken up by the Global Science Forum (GSF) in 2006. The GSF operates under the authority of the Organisation for Economic Co-operation and Development (OECD), established by treaty with a current membership of 30 nations. The initial question posed to the GSF by the Japanese delegation focused on how nations could quickly and fairly address growing concerns about research misconduct. The query came on the heels of several highly publicized cases of research misbehavior in Japan (Normile, 2006a, 2006b, 2007).

The GSF accepted the challenge and established a committee of experts nominated by national delegations to the OECD GSF. The committee, chaired by representatives from Japan and Canada, was established to study the scope of the problem and formulate recommendations. The committee quickly acknowledged several fundamental complications. First, there is no common agreement on what behavior constitutes research misconduct. Second, there is substantial diversity among nations in the legal structures that address misconduct. Third, there are strong and conflicting views on who should handle allegations and how they should be handled. Although the committee believed that focusing on responsible conduct of research would be productive and instructional, it decided that defining the scope of behavior that constitutes research misconduct and developing relevant definitions would be useful and a welcome contribution to the research community. The 2007 report of this committee defines research misconduct as fabrication of data, falsification of data, and plagiarism, commonly referred to as FFP (OECD GSF, 2007). The GSF recommended that OECD-member nations adopt this definition within the contexts of their respective research cultures and legal structures.

While this step of establishing common definitions was important, the challenge of how to address allegations of research misconduct in international collaborations remained. At the suggestion of the U.S. delegation to the GSF, a second committee was established, called the Co-ordinating Committee for Facilitating International Research Misconduct Investigations. Its membership consisted of experts nominated by GSF delegations, and it was chaired by representatives of the United States and Canada.[5] As the committee's name clearly indicates, the focus was on the practical challenges of how to conduct investigations of possible research misconduct in international research collaborations. While harmonization of national procedure would be useful and perhaps even desirable from the point of view of individuals responsible for investigating allegations, the committee realized that such a goal was unlikely to be reached and could even be undesirable in the context of diverse research systems. This committee therefore turned its attention to developing the definitions of core principles that are needed in international research misconduct investigations. It also recognized the importance of promoting awareness of the issues among researchers engaged in international collaborations. It recommended that networks of experts and institutions be developed and maintained—a formidable challenge on its own. A final report (OECD GSF, 2009a) summarized the work of the committee and appended a *Practical Guide for Investigating Research Misconduct Allegations in International Collaborative Research Projects*. The guide includes boilerplate text that could be inserted into international collaborative research project agreements. This boilerplate text can establish a common ground upon which research misconduct allegations can be resolved fairly and equitably.

The remainder of this chapter discusses the committee's findings and their relevance to the research community. It is useful to keep in mind that our focus here is on the investigation of wrongdoing, that is, fraud and the use of other people's work or ideas without appropriate attribution. It is not about research itself; rather, it is about investigating allegations of research misconduct and coming to conclusions based on the facts.

Research investigators rush to explain that science knows no political or geographical boundaries. Criminal investigators of wrongdoing point out, with equal adamancy, that neither do deception or fraud. The consequences of misconduct can be dire for the individual researcher, including loss of vital research data, loss of funding, loss of reputation, and possibly loss of a career.

Investigative Challenges Addressed by the GSF

Given the complex nature of multi-national research and its inherent challenges, the focus of the committee was on developing recommendations and tools that would facilitate investigations of alleged research misconduct. Again, the committee's recommendations do not address specifics of the responsible conduct of research or accompanying standards and codes. These were left for others to consider. In fact, many organizations such as research-support organizations and professional societies have done so.[6] Given the lack of international standards or agreement on desirable behaviors in the research environment, the challenge of handling allegations of wrongdoing is daunting. The committee decided to develop principles for conducting investigations in international settings, because researchers need to be aware of how to handle the issues that will inevitably arise. Also, researchers need to establish rules and procedures for handling investigations before something goes awry. It makes good sense to do so. Once a problem surfaces, the environment is not optimal for such discussions. Advance agreements will help expedite the investigative process and help protect the rights of the researchers involved. Often, an individual researcher does not appreciate the complexities of attempting to establish facts to support an allegation in the international arena. The collaborative research agreement should therefore establish, at a minimum and preferably in writing, rules and procedures that would implement the general principles recommended by the committee for handling investigations. The principles are discussed below.

Promoting Responsible Research Practices

The promotion of responsible research practices should be addressed to ensure that all researchers are cognizant of and operating within the same framework of rules and research customs. The collaborating researchers should identify and agree to any existing standards that may exist in their disciplines or fields of expertise. This step is critical, because it establishes a framework for how investigations of wrongdoing may be structured. Just as auditors need standards in order to assess compliance, investigators rely on standards. Where standards simply do not exist, the investigators must establish such benchmarks. Anyone subject to an investigation or audit should know the ground rules in advance.

Compliance with National Laws

Compliance with national laws is critical. Investigations must adhere to the parameters of a legal structure in order to be credible and enforceable. Under what laws will the investigators operate? How will jurisdiction be determined? Who determines it? What investigative body has the legal authority to conduct an investigation? Who must cooperate with requests? What recourse does an investigator have, if the researchers or other parties are not cooperative? These are some of the questions that may arise when an allegation of misconduct arises. Agreements for collaborative research projects must therefore recognize the authorities of the nations involved in the research and the requirements with which researchers—both organizations and individuals— must comply. Factors that determine which national legal requirements may apply are: where researchers and their support staffs are employed; where a researcher is based for the study; where the fieldwork takes place; and where facilities and infrastructure for the research project are located. Obviously, in a multi-national collaboration, the laws of two or more countries may govern the research. All parties need to agree in advance how compliance with national laws and rules will be assured. Collaborative agreements should specify who is responsible for determining compliance requirements, who disseminates to the team the information necessary to maintain compliance, and who assures compliance.

Procedures for Investigating Allegations

If there are no specific requirements governing investigations, the collaborators should agree what investigative standards will be used. Procedures should identify the party or parties to whom allegations should be reported and in what form. For example, should the allegation be in writing? Can it be anonymous?

Experienced investigators know the importance of establishing facts. They will want to have as much information as possible to perform an inquiry, a precursor to launching a full investigation. This step is very common in a wide range of investigative matters in order to determine whether an investigation is even necessary, that is, to answer the question of whether there is any merit to the allegation and, if there is, to assess the scope of the issues and the resources needed. Funding organizations may have very specific procedures for handling such allegations. The researcher should be aware of what the sponsor may require. It is important to note that investigations have many costs. In addition to the stress on the researchers involved, there is a need for real money to conduct an investigation. How these resources are made available should be identified.

The purpose of an investigation is to establish facts. An investigation should be timely. It should be conducted by unbiased, competent individuals who are experienced in handling such procedures. All parties in the collaboration should assist with the investigation. Even if the allegations involve researchers in other nations, the entire collaboration may be open to examination during the investigative process. The parties in the collaboration should agree in advance of beginning the research on procedures for conducting an inquiry and an investigation. If an allegation is made about research conducted in a nation that is not a party to the collaborative agreement and that has no researchers involved in the collaboration, the laws and rules of this nation should nonetheless be considered.

In pursuing its activities, the investigative team may need to examine the research record, laboratory notes, and original data. They may need access to laboratory instruments, computers, and other equipment used in the research. In carrying out these functions, the investigative team will need to ensure that it is preserving a chain of custody that meets the highest standard of all nations involved. The investigative team should have clear, written procedures on how to handle evidence in order to comply with adjudication processes within the nations involved in, or affected by, the collaboration.

Overarching Principles for Investigations

Unless a nation has an established system for investigating allegations of research misconduct, the challenge of doing an investigation can be intimidating to the inexperienced. To assist people who will be responsible for establishing investigative policy and procedures, the GSF developed a set of principles that provide guidance (OECD GSF, 2009b). In general, investigations should adhere to written, clearly defined procedures. They should be conducted with appropriate transparency, yet protect the rights and reputations of those under investigation. They must adhere to the highest standards of integrity, fairness, and confidentiality.

Integrity

While investigations must be fair, comprehensive, and timely, they must also be objective and thorough and produce accurate results. Any member of the investigation team who may have a conflict of interest in the case must disclose the conflict and provide a plan for how the conflict will be managed. In order for the investigation itself to sustain any challenge of integrity, the investigative record must be detailed and backed by evidence. If records are confidential, the investigative team must ensure that all records are maintained in a manner that will protect confidentiality over time.

Fairness

Fairness is another standard that is critical in conducting an investigation. All relevant laws should be identified. Compliance with these laws is a mandatory expectation, with no exceptions. Persons accused of research misconduct must be given full, written details of the allegations. The investigative process must allow the accused person to ask questions, present evidence, produce relevant witnesses and expert testimony, and provide a written response to the written allegations. Relevant witness information and expert testimony may be gathered in writing or orally. If provided orally, however, there should be an accurate, written record that becomes an integral part of the investigative record. If a subject of an investigation wants to have legal or other counsel, such representation or assistance should be permitted.

Confidentiality

Although confidentiality has already been addressed above, it is such an important factor in investigations that it merits additional attention. An investigation should always be conducted with as much confidentiality as possible, in order to protect the rights of all subjects of the investigation. An exception may occur if the health or safety of research participants is at risk. If third parties are needed in the investigation process, then these individuals should adhere to the rules of confidentiality that have been established by the investigation team. Also, funding organizations or legal structures may have confidentiality policies that need to be built into the investigation process. One of the most difficult situations in investigations involving multiple nations is that different confidentiality rules may apply. In some nations, full disclosure of the allegations and names of accused parties is expected at the outset of an investigation. In other countries, the investigative record may be kept confidential until the case is adjudicated.[7] In short, the general rule operating within an investigation is that only those with a need to know should be given information. There should be no release of investigation findings to the public until the case is closed. The results of investigations should only be released to those organizations or individuals who are responsible for adjudication, to those who were the subjects of investigations, and to organizations that are funding the research.

No Detriment

All investigations should start with a presumption of innocence. Subjects of investigations should not suffer penalties until such time as the allegations are found to be true and appropriate adjudication has taken place. Persons making the allegations should also not suffer any harm. Often there is concern that the allegations are brought by individuals with malicious intent or by a competing researcher in an effort to thwart progress. It is sad to note that such allegations do occur; however, an experienced investigator or investigative research team can quickly identify the flaws in allegations not brought in good faith. One important reason for the inquiry stage is to determine whether or not the allegations have merit before a full investigation is launched.

Although investigations do not have appeal procedures, the adjudication process should. The adjudicator must have the full investigative record, including all written responses by the subjects and their representatives. To ensure fairness and integrity in the process, the procedures to be used upon appeal should be made clear in writing. The procedures should state to whom an appeal is to be made, on what basis an appeal may be made, and in what time frame.

Balance

The GSF report calls for balance as a guiding principle (OECD GSF, 2009a). Balance is an abstract notion that recognizes the enormous challenges that investigators have. For example, the investigators may need to weigh the disclosure of identities to facilitate the investigation and confidentiality to protect the individual. The reputation of the accused may need to be balanced against the interests of the research community or society in health or safety. During any investigation many tensions will confront the investigators. In the end, experienced investigators will balance their obligations against individuals' rights and desires. The likely reality is that not all people will be happy.

Applying the Recommendations

Using the guiding principles and the practical guide and incorporating the boilerplate language (OECD GSF, 2009b) into international agreements for research collaborations will go a long way toward heightening awareness among collaborators and institutions about their respective responsibilities. If there is an allegation of wrongdoing, these provisions and guidance will help set the stage for a timely investigation and resolution of the matter that will be perceived as fair and balanced by all parties.

Still, however, there is no internationally recognized organization charged with reviewing and handling integrity issues that arise in cross-national collaborative science. There remains a crucial need, therefore, for continued work and international attention in this area. The GSF's approach has advantages because it is not proscriptive. Its flexibility allows for easy implementation within different national systems and laws. The disadvantage of the approach is that it is not sufficiently detailed to help newcomers handle a complex investigation. Ongoing exchanges of information and ideas for ensuring fair and equitable investigations would continue the process started by the GSF.

Notes

1. For case summaries of research misconduct findings and discussions of issues in ethics see the OIG's *Semiannual Report to the Congress* at: www.nsf.gov/oig/pubs.jsp.
2. See also discussions on access to data in Arzberger, Schroeder, Beaulieu, Bowker, Casey, Laaksonen et al. (2004).
3. This observation is also supported by KPMG (2007) and Olsen (2007).
4. For a discussion of the history of this issue, see Mauro and Hardison (2002).
5. The U.S. representative was Christine C. Boesz, Dr.P.H. She was assisted by Peggy Fischer, PhD. They are the co-authors of this chapter. Nigel Lloyd, PhD. was the Canadian representative.
6. Just a few of the many societies and programs are at: www.cgsnet.org; http://publicationethics.org; www.aaas.org; www.nap.edu/catalog.php?record_id=12192; and www.sigmaxi.org.
7. In the United States, when an investigation is conducted by a federal entity, such as an OIG, then all records may be held confidential until the case is closed. The records are protected by the Freedom of Information Act. Also, certain information about an individual may be protected by the Privacy Act.

References

Altman, L. K., & Broad, W. J. (2005, December 20). Global trend: More science, more fraud. *New York Times*. Retrieved from www.nytimes.com/2005/12/20/science/20rese.html.

Anderson, C. (1994). Easy-to-alter digital images raise fears of tampering. *Science, 263*, 317–318.

Arzberger, P., Schroeder, P., Beaulieu, A., Bowker, G., Casey, K., Laaksonen, L., et al. (2004). Science and government: An international framework to promote access to data. *Science, 303*, 1777–1778.

Commission on Research Integrity. (1995). *Integrity and misconduct in research.* Washington, DC: U.S. Department of Health and Human Services. Retrieved from http://ori.dhhs.gov/documents/report_commission.pdf.

Cook, G. (2007). From the editor: When words aren't yours. *American School Board Journal, 194*(8), 4.

Demaine, L. J., & Fellmeth, A. X. (2003). Natural substances and patentable inventions. *Science, 300*, 1375–1376.

Federation of American Societies for Experimental Biology. (1996). *Implementation proposals on recommendation by the commission on research integrity.* Bethesda, MD: Federation of American Societies for Experimental Biology. Retrieved from http://opa.faseb.org/pdf/raub.pdf.

Gibbons, A. (2002). Glasnost for hominids: Seeking access to fossils. *Science, 297*, 1464–1468.

Giles, J. (2005). Special report: Taking on the cheats. *Nature, 435*, 258–259.

Giles, J. (2007). Breeding cheats. *Nature, 445*, 242–243.

Katsnelson, A. (2007, August 20). Neuroscientist censured for misconduct. *TheScientist.com.* Retrieved from www.the-scientist.com/news/home/53493.

KPMG (2007). *Cross-border investigations: Effectively meeting the challenge.* Retrieved from www.kpmg.ie/DestinationIndia/pubs/Cross-Border%20Investigations.pdf.

McCabe, D. L. (1997). Classroom cheating among natural science and engineering majors. *Science and Engineering Ethics*, *3*(4), 433–445.

McCabe, D. L., Butterfield, K. D., & Trevino, L. K. (2006). Academic dishonesty in graduate business programs: Prevalence, causes, and proposed action. *Academy of Management Learning and Education*, *5*(3), 294–305.

Marshall, E. (1997). Whose DNA is it anyway? *Science, 278*, 564–567.

Martinson, B. C., Anderson, M. S., Crain, A. L., & De Vries, R. (2006). Scientists' perceptions of organizational justice and self-reported misbehaviors. *Journal of Empirical Research on Human Research Ethics*, *1*(1), 51–66.

Martinson, B. C., Anderson, M. S., & De Vries, R. (2005). Scientists behaving badly. *Nature, 435*, 737–738.

Mauro, F., & Hardison, P. D. (2002). Traditional knowledge of indigenous and local communities: international debate and policy initiatives. *Ecological Applications*, *10*(5), 1263–1269.

Mitchell, W. J. (1994). When is seeing believing? *Scientific American*, *270*(2), 68–73.

Morin, R. (2006, September 27). Captains of industry, masters of cheating. *Washington Post*. Retrieved from www.washingtonpost.com/wp-dyn/content/article/2006/09/26/AR200609 2601742.html.

National Science Board. (2006). *Science and engineering indicators 2006*. Arlington, VA: National Science Board. Retrieved from www.nsf.gov/statistics/seind06/c5/c5s3.htm.

National Science Foundation. (1990). *Survey data on the extent of misconduct in science and engineering*. OIG-90-3214. Washington, DC: National Science Foundation.

Normile, D. (2006a). Panel discredits findings of Tokyo University team. *Science, 311*, 595.

Normile, D. (2006b). Top chemist accused of funds misuse. *Science, 313*, 31.

Normile, D (2007). Japan's universities take action. *Science, 315*, 26.

OECD GSF. (2007). *Best practices for ensuring scientific integrity and preventing misconduct*. Retrieved from www.oecd.org/dataoecd/37/17/40188303.pdf.

OECD GSF. (2009a). *Final report*. Retrieved from www.oecd.org/dataoecd/29/4/42713295.pdf.

OECD GSF. (2009b). *Investigating research misconduct allegations in international collaborative research projects: A practical guide*. Retrieved from www.oecd.org/dataoecd/42/34/42770261.pdf.

OIG. (1994). *Semiannual report to the Congress*, April 1, 1994–September 30, 1994. Arlington, VA: National Science Foundation. Retrieved from www.nsf.gov/pubs/stis1995/oig11/oig11.txt.

OIG. (1995). *Semiannual report to the Congress*, October 1, 1994–March 31, 1995. Arlington, VA: National Science Foundation. Retrieved from www.nsf.gov/pubs/stis1995/oig12/oig12.txt.

OIG. (2003). *Semiannual report to the Congress*, April 1, 2003–September 30, 2003. Arlington, VA: National Science Foundation. Retrieved from www.nsf.gov/pubs/2003/oigsept2003/start.htm.

OIG. (2004). *Semiannual report to the Congress*, April 1, 2004–September 30, 2004. Arlington, VA: National Science Foundation. Retrieved from www.nsf.gov/pubs/2004/oigsept2004/start.htm.

OIG. (2005). *Semiannual report to the Congress*, October 1, 2004–March 31, 2005. Arlington, VA: National Science Foundation. Retrieved from www.nsf.gov/pubs/2005/oigmarch2005/start.htm?org=NSF.

OIG. (2008). *Semiannual report to the Congress*, April 1, 2008–September 30, 2008. Arlington, VA: National Science Foundation. Retrieved from www.nsf.gov/pubs/2009/oig0901/index.jsp.

OIG. (2009). *Semiannual report to the Congress*, October 1, 2008–March 31, 2009. Arlington, VA: National Science Foundation. Retrieved from www.nsf.gov/pubs/2009/oig0902.

Olsen, W. (2007). Don't let US focus crimp oversight abroad. *Financial Executive*, *23*, 24–27.

ORI. (2007a, March). 15 misconduct findings, 35 cases closed in 2006. *Office of Research Integrity Newsletter*, *15*(2), 1. Retrieved from http://ori.dhhs.gov/documents/newsletters/vol. 15_no2.pdf.

ORI. (2007b, June). Research misconduct activity sets no records in 2006. *Office of Research Integrity Newsletter*, *15*(3), 3. Retrieved from http://ori.dhhs.gov/documents/newsletters/vol. 15_no3.pdf.

Panel on Scientific Responsibility and the Conduct of Research, National Academy of Sciences, National Academy of Engineering and Institute of Medicine. (1992). *Responsible science, Volume I: Ensuring the integrity of the research process*. Washington, DC: National Academies Press.

Slobogin, K. (2002, April 5). Survey: Many students say cheating's OK. *CNN*. Retrieved from http://archives.cnn.com/2002/fyi/teachers.ednews/04/05/highschool.cheating.

Steghaus-Kovac, S. (2002). Tug-of-war over fossil. *Science, 295*, 1212–1213.

Steneck, N. H. (2000). Assessing the integrity of publicly funded research. *Proceedings of the First ORI Research Conference on Research Integrity* (pp. 1–16). Washington, DC: Office of Research Integrity. Retrieved from http://ori.hhs.gov/documents/proceedings_rri.pdf.

Tanner, A. (2002, March 8). Educating the University of Iowa on the challenges of plagiarism. *FYI Faculty & Staff News, 39*(12). Retrieved from www.uiowa.edu/~fyi/issues/issues2001_v39/03082002/plagiarism.html.

Vogel, G. (2005). Landmark paper has an image problem. *Science, 310*, 1595.

Yidong, G. (2005). China science foundation takes action against 60 grantees. *Science, 309*, 1798–1799.

11

Scientific Integrity in the Context of Pan-European Cooperation

Andrew C. Stainthorpe

Many aspects of scientific research systems worldwide trace their origins to Europe. European diversity, culture and competition were key components in the evolution of the research practices now in place across the globe. In particular, the foundations of research integrity are rooted in the standards and practices of many European institutions. However, the development of these standards and practices into a system for promoting integrity in research has taken place without systematic planning or regulation.

The recent development of European research includes some high-profile cases of poor practice (Edwards, 1986; Horton, 2006; Lucent Technologies, 2002; Smith, 2006). These cases of misconduct raise questions as to whether current mechanisms and safeguards are sufficient to: (1) prevent misconduct in research projects in the European context; (2) detect any occurrence of such behaviour; and (3) investigate and apply appropriate sanctions to those perpetrating such behaviours.

The problems are particularly acute in the context of cross-national collaboration. Although Europe, in global terms, is often treated as a single entity with respect to research, there remain many differences both within and between countries in the norms for and approaches to research. Such differences can contribute to difficulties in the area of research integrity. A number of European and international organizations have been established to further cooperation in research and the sharing of research results. These organizations have engaged in a debate over standards and integrity in research, a process that has gathered pace in recent years.

European Structures Supporting Integrity in Research

Europe, depending upon which grouping is used, is a continent of some 50 countries and states, many of which have active research programmes resourced by organizations internal or external to their borders. European research is predominantly supported by government, commercial and charitable sources, and increasingly by partnerships involving all three. Research takes place in universities, research institutes, industry facilities, health- and social-care facilities, and a range of other public and private organizations.

Many funding organizations have issued statements and guidance on research integrity for the research communities they support. Some have also issued requirements for organizations to self-report compliance with research integrity as a condition for receiving funding.

When high-profile allegations of misconduct in research have surfaced, governments have responded by establishing mechanisms to investigate the allegations and providing guidance for research integrity or codes of good practice for research. The European response to misconduct has, however, varied considerably from country to country. The responsibility resides variously with the individual, the employer, the research funder, or the countries hosting or sponsoring the activity. It is often the national government that, through the department responsible for the research budget, initiates steps to establish systems to address research misconduct and promote good conduct in research. Some countries have set up national offices with responsibilities for the investigation of misconduct on projects involving government funding; some of these offices advise employers on the best approach to take. In some countries, research integrity and research ethics are handled together; in others countries, they are addressed as related issues, but managed independently (European Science Foundation (ESF), 2008).

Although many European countries have taken steps to promote good research practice, and have put in place policies for research and mechanisms to handle allegations of misconduct, others have taken little or no action. There are countries in Europe that leave the handling of research misconduct to the individuals and organizations that do the research. Approximately half of the countries in Europe do not have national offices with responsibilities in research integrity. This includes countries with significant portfolios of research. Few European countries make any information on research integrity investigations available, unless cases are already in the public domain (ESF, 2008).

Examples of the variety of approaches across Europe are outlined below.

Germany

Serious cases brought to light in Germany (Lucent Technologies, 2002) led the Deutsche Forchungsgemeinschaft (DFG) to invite an international commission to consider the causes of misconduct in research and advise on measures to prevent dishonesty. The commission published *Recommendations for Safeguarding Good Scientific Practice* in 1998 (Commission on Professional Self-Regulation in Science, 1998), which complemented existing guidance. The recommendations included appointment of an independent authority to advise on issues of research conduct. The DFG created the ombudsman service, whose roles include the provision of advice to researchers and employers, mediation, and, where appropriate, referral to an authority such as a DFG Committee of Inquiry. A further recommendation was that all German universities put in place guidelines for handling research misconduct.

Croatia

Croatia set up the National Committee for Ethics in Science and Higher Education, an independent body reporting to the Croatian Parliament. The committee has roles in the promotion of ethical standards in research and education and in the investigation of allegations of research misconduct. Applicants for research funding from the Ministry of Science, Education and Sports must sign to ensure responsible conduct of the research supported.

The Netherlands

In the Netherlands, the Academy of Arts and Sciences, the Organization for Scientific Research, and the Association of Universities came together to promote research integrity. This involved the publication of a *Memorandum on Scientific Integrity* (ALL European Academies, Royal Netherlands Academy of Arts and Sciences, Netherlands Organization for Scientific Research, & Association of Universities in the Netherlands, 2003), which outlines the general standards for research with attention to how infringements need to be handled. The National Committee for Scientific Integrity was established to facilitate the proper investigation of allegations. The National Board for Scientific Integrity was also set up to advise universities and the Academy of Arts and Sciences and the Organization for Scientific Research "regarding violations of scientific norms" ("National Board", n.d., para. 2). The latter also provides a post-investigation appeals-mechanism and can require institutions to re-investigate.

Denmark

The Danish Ministry of Science and Technology and Innovation set up Committees on Scientific Dishonesty (Danish Agency for Science, Technology, and Innovation, 2009) to investigate dishonesty with an impact on Danish research. Set up by national executive order and presided over by a high court judge, the Danish committees can take forward investigations independently of the employing organization. Similar national judicial committee-based systems are in place in other Nordic countries.

Norway

In Norway, the Act of 30 June 2006 No. 56 on Ethics and Integrity in Research (2009) facilitated the setting up of the National Commission for the Investigation of Scientific Misconduct and other structures supporting research integrity. The responsibility of the commission covers all areas of research and allows investigation of allegations relating to cases overseas where Norway has responsibility through funding or employment contracts. Universities in Norway still have the primary responsibility to investigate allegations, but can refer cases to the National Commission (Vinther, 2009).

United Kingdom

The United Kingdom is currently in the process of developing a national policy on research misconduct. The national research-funding organizations, through Research Councils UK, issued a Policy and Code of Conduct on the Governance of Good Research Conduct in 2009. This policy supports the use of a national system for the investigation of research misconduct such as that developed by the UK Research Integrity Office (2008). The Research Councils have the option to investigate allegations that have been raised within research organizations in receipt of funding from a council, but the United Kingdom does not have a national body tasked with investigating allegations.

Independent Organizations

There are other independent organizations within Europe that provide guidance to researchers about the proper conduct of research. The Wellcome Trust, a major funder of international research and supporter of ethical practices, has issued guidelines for researchers (Wellcome Trust, 2005). The ALL European Academies has produced a memorandum to promote the application of general standards of scientific conduct and ways in which infringements of those standards should be handled (ALL European Academies et al., 2003). The Committee for Publication Ethics provides guidance on handling allegations of research misconduct identified through the publication process (Committee on Publication Ethics, n.d.).

The diversity of approaches taken, the range of organizations involved, and differences in national policy and positions on research misconduct complicate efforts to develop agreement on standards across Europe. Steps taken by global and pan-European organizations, such as the Organisation for Economic Cooperation and Development (OECD) (Boesz & Lloyd, 2008; OECD Global Science Forum, 2007), the European Commission (European Commission Expert Group of Research Integrity, 2007), the ESF (n.d.) and the European Network of Research Integrity Offices ("The UK Research Integrity Office", n.d.), may facilitate progress towards harmonization of standards for research integrity on international joint projects, but at present there is no consistency in misconduct policies across Europe.

Mechanisms for Defining and Promoting Research Integrity

Many research institutions have identified the need to have fair and rigorous policies for handling research misconduct and most have developed policies to meet their circumstances. Researchers, as employees, commit to the standards of behaviour laid down by employing organizations, as well as the national laws that apply to their field of research. Some researchers have contracts with the state, and work to national terms and conditions. Others work to contracts agreed upon with the funding organization. Variations also exist according to partners in a study and according to the country in which the research might take place.

In many European countries, universities and organizations are in competition for research grants and other forms of sponsorship, which can lead to the development of local standards for research and other arrangements aimed to give an organization a competitive advantage. University researchers in some countries have national government contracts, which should facilitate greater harmonization of standards for research and for the investigation of allegations of misconduct within the country. In some countries funding for research is held by employers, whereas in others it can be held by the researcher. Student researchers are also subject to different rules and regulations to those of their salaried and tenured colleagues.

Such diversity in the management of research and researchers might be of little consequence if all researchers were required to abide by an agreed-upon code of practice, as applies in regulated professions, such as medicine. However, in research there are no universally accepted standards regulating research conduct. To the contrary, there is a wide variety of standards, codes of practice, regulations and requirements that apply to researchers. The definition of misconduct in research also varies from country to country and institution to institution. Poor practice in one situation can lead to career-ending sanctions for one individual, but the same practice might lead to no sanctions in another situation. This level of variation can occur locally, nationally and internationally, and undermines procedures for the fair investigation of allegations.

Many organizations have developed codes of practice for research. Approaches vary from the comprehensive—which define all aspects of required behaviour, norms and standards to which researchers are expected to adhere—to the advisory, which offer general guidance. Such codes can be contradictory and confusing. Organizations that fund research can also set requirements for the conduct of research, with which eligible organizations must agree to comply. Such requirements apply to the organization in receipt of the funding, and sanctions for non-compliance with the requirements can include withdrawal of eligibility to receive funding. Sanctions for misconduct in research are typically applied to the researcher. National laws also regulate certain areas of research, particularly those concerning research involving humans, animals and human artefacts.

The European Dimension

Cooperation and competition in research have brought together many fruitful partnerships in research both nationally and internationally (European Commission, CORDIS, 2008). In Europe, cooperation in research, whether bilateral or multilateral, has been highly successful. Whether the focus is on a large capital infrastructure project or a clinical trial, the benefits of conducting research on a pan-European basis are widely recognized.

The Role of the European Union

The European Union defined the European Research Area in 2000 to inspire investment of talent and resources in European research (European Commission, n.d.). In 2007 the European Research Council (ERC) was set up to support "investigator-driven frontier research" (ERC, 2008, para. 1). The ERC aims to "strengthen and shape the European research system ... through high quality peer review, the establishment of international benchmarks of success, and the provision of up-to-date information on who is succeeding and why" (ERC, 2008, para. 6).

Many organizations have active programmes that facilitate pan-European research, among which the European Commission has played a leading role in promoting and funding research across Europe. The commission's Framework Programmes (FP1, 1984–1987 to FP7, 2007–2013), have facilitated many pan-European research projects. The current programme (FP7) invests approximately €70 billion (European Commission, CORDIS, 2007). Allocation of commission funding follows stringent multi-stage peer review and includes steps to monitor progress and audit use of funding. Recipient organizations are required to agree that they will comply with agreed-upon national standards of behaviour and achieve the stated objectives of the research following the specific protocol. However, the commission does not set specific requirements relating to investigations of misconduct in research. The commission currently does not employ a mechanism to monitor or investigate poor conduct, or require organizations that have investigated an allegation of misconduct in research to report the outcome to the commission. The commission has taken steps to gauge community views, support research and promote debate relating to integrity in research (European Commission Expert Group on Research Integrity, 2007; "FP7 Capacities", 2007), but has not developed Europe-wide policies for promoting integrity or investigating misconduct in research.

Relevant European Legislation

In 1997 the European Union included an obligation to implement European research programmes in the Amsterdam Treaty, which includes a chapter on research and technological development. The European Union also introduced Directive 2001/20/EC, which relates to the implementation of good clinical practice in the conduct of clinical trials on medicinal products for human use (EUR-Lex, 2001). Member states implemented laws to comply with the directive. This directive set basic standards for the conduct, management and review of research involving humans.

Behaviour in Pan-European Research Cooperation

Does research misconduct occur in cooperative European research? The question is almost impossible to answer. There is a lack of hard evidence on the occurrence of misconduct in research. Few funders of international projects require research organizations to inform them of allegations or investigations that have taken place or of the outcome.

However, absence of evidence is not evidence of absence. Research suggests that in many fields of research, there occurs a certain level of misconduct (Martinson, Anderson & De Vries, 2005). There is no evidence to suggest that researchers participating in international projects behave any differently to those in the groups studied. Factors that might prevent research misconduct in international projects from being more widely exposed include failures to detect (no audits or checks of work), investigate (uncertain organizational responsibilities for detected misconduct), gather evidence (which is necessary to support an investigation) and disclose (that is, share the details of prima facie research misconduct).

Cross-National Devices for Research Integrity in Europe

Many international and European organizations and instruments require and serve to promote good conduct in research. These organizations include the European Commission, the ESF, the ALL European Academies, the European University Association and the League of European Research Universities. These organizations are mostly large and complex, and are viewed as remote by researchers. The aims of these organizations include supporting the wider development of research, facilitating links and relationships involving researchers based in many different organizations, and involving the public and private sectors. They can also have roles in the development of common approaches and benchmarking for research. Such organizations contribute to the health of research across Europe.

Organizations that fund research, including those supporting pan-European research, assess research through a rigorous peer-review process. It is often the case, however, that, aside from fiscal audit and reporting requirements, post-award monitoring and audit are devolved to recipient institutions. That key funders of pan-European research do not place conditions for accountability in research integrity on all award recipients could be considered a missed opportunity. Such a requirement would further the development and promulgation of standards and systems for research integrity across Europe. Through this route the wider acceptance of standards and a degree of European harmonization might be achieved. Conditions on research awards might also provide opportunities for improved education and training in accepted standards and principles for research.

Several initiatives noted here illustrate recent progress in promoting and facilitating pan-European research integrity. The ESF, an association of organizations in Europe involved in scientific research, is committed to facilitating cooperation and collaboration in science on behalf of its members and the science community of Europe. In recognition of the need to show leadership in research integrity, the ESF published a policy briefing on the topic of good scientific practice (ESF, 2000). This included reference to policies and practices already in place in Europe and the United States. In partnership with the U.S. Office of Research Integrity, the ESF initiated the First World Conference on Research Integrity, which took place in Lisbon, Portugal in September 2007. An ESF policy briefing (ESF & Office of Research Integrity, 2007), *Research integrity: Global responsibility to foster common standards*, provided updated advice to member organizations and included recommendations from the conference and the OECD. Working in partnership with the ALL European Academies, the ESF has also convened a members' forum to take forward the development of specific guidance on the following: promoting activities to continue raising awareness and sharing information on good practices to promote research integrity; developing a code of conduct that can be used as a template for national codes; investigating what might be involved in setting up national and institutional structures to promote good research practice and handle research misconduct; and developing and promoting research on research integrity.

The Committee for Publication Ethics also provides guidance and support in research integrity by providing a forum for publishers and editors of peer-reviewed journals to discuss issues related to the integrity of work submitted for publication. The committee recently set up an ombudsman service to assist with disputes (Green, 2008).

In 2007 representatives of the Research Integrity Offices in Europe set up the European Network of Research Integrity Offices to explore issues raised and share best practices ("The UK Research Integrity Office", n.d.). The network has raised awareness of the various approaches to research integrity in European countries and facilitates dialogue between offices on pan-European issues.

The European Network for Ombudsmen in Higher Education is an informal network that was established in 2003 to enable academic ombudsmen to learn from each other and share best practices in ombudsman functions in Europe ("The European Network", n.d.). Issues in the educational field include research and forms of misconduct such as plagiarism and misrepresentation.

Challenges and Problems Related to Initiating and Maintaining Successful Research Collaborations

Europe has a long and successful track record in collaborative research. This includes partnerships in large research facilities and programmes, as well as small-scale projects. The European Commission research programmes (Framework Programmes) have been a major driving force facilitating cooperation and wider inclusion of European partners. Other funders and agencies also contribute and have assisted in creating a dynamic European research community of academic and commercial partners capable of leading and contributing to research innovation and development of the highest standards.

One of the greatest challenges to continuation and growth of collaborative research might come from the loss of public support and trust in research. Loss of public faith in research would have negative impacts on funding for research, education and infrastructure support. Talented individuals might be less willing to enter a profession with a lower public status than current researchers enjoy.

Research credibility and the development of new avenues of enquiry are of considerable importance in initiating and maintaining cooperative research. Researchers would not wish to work in partnerships with those of poor or tainted reputations or on research projects of little or no merit. Credibility and reputation should be enhanced by overt compliance with research integrity standards. Currently, credibility and standing in research are most strongly influenced by innovation in the field, publication and citation indices and grant income. However, concerns arise when such markers are not robustly linked to high integrity. Very high rates of innovation and publication can point to fabrication or superficial engagement in activities, as in the case of Jan Hendrik Schön (Lucent Technologies, 2002).

Europe has a strong tradition of tolerance and respect for research and academic endeavour. The systems in place across Europe are typically based on self-regulation by individuals and organizations. In many of Europe's older universities and in some countries, such principles are part of the constitution. Changing such systems can be challenging. However, more dynamic institutions are able to accommodate such requirements as a necessary part of remaining competitive in research. Achieving acceptance of change in systems—towards more overt oversight of research integrity—across European universities and institutions may be a slow process. An external driver, such as an eligibility requirement for funding of research, might accelerate acceptance and adoption of such systems. Compliance with a pan-European requirement might also facilitate moves towards the harmonization of standards for research integrity.

Steps to Improve Pan-European Cooperation in Research

Broadening cooperation in research may involve extending existing networks to involve more researchers or setting up new networks. Either approach involves quality checks and agreements with new partner organizations, which could target best practices in research integrity. Funder requirements might include evidence of institutional commitment to research integrity.

Opening more funding to pan-European cooperative projects will also support increased participation. National funding could further international projects through bilateral or multilateral matched funding agreements. Such agreements could include statements on research standards and integrity.

Improving the mobility of the research workforce will serve to enhance skills and build networks across Europe and elsewhere. Training in core skills of research integrity will enable researchers to demonstrate that they have the necessary awareness of research integrity issues to work in research anywhere in Europe. Researchers might be registered as able to demonstrate a commitment to and education in standards for research. Researchers sanctioned by employers following investigations into research misconduct might have this registration withdrawn for a period of time or limitations placed on their work.

Industry is a leading sponsor of research and employer of university-trained researchers. Industries and commercial organizations are active partners in and sponsors of many pan-European projects. Many industries, notably the pharmaceutical industry, have extensive research programmes and work closely with clinical and academic partners in global trials of new drugs and interventions. The pharmaceutical industry has developed effective means to conduct high-quality research around the globe and support many effective partnerships for research. Support from industry for agreed standards in research integrity might facilitate greater cooperation and support for industrially sponsored research.

What might further cooperation on research integrity throughout Europe and bring greater acceptance of the benefits of effective oversight of research and openness?

Research-funding organizations have a key role in bringing about acceptance of more effective oversight in research. All funders of pan-European research could require organizations receiving funding to take steps to demonstrate their commitment to research integrity through overt implementation of policies and procedures, reports on integrity-monitoring initiatives, education and training in research integrity, and reports of allegations, investigations and findings.

Through the wider introduction of education and training in standards and principles of research, organizations within Europe could strengthen the research-skills base. Education in research integrity should be continuous, and organizations should ensure that new researchers and those recruited from overseas are trained in organizational and national practices. This should be supported by appropriate mentoring and continuing professional development for all active researchers, to ensure they keep their knowledge up to date.

To provide a basis for education and training in research integrity, an agreed code of conduct in research for Europe should be adopted by representative national organizations. This should include principles and standards for research, and definitions of research misconduct that all countries can agree upon. The systems developed by a number of countries, such as Australia (National Health and Medical Research Council, 2007), and the work of the OECD Global Science Forum (2007), could form the basis for such a code, as might the code currently being developed through the ESF Members Forum on Research Integrity (ESF, n.d.).

Publishers and conference organizers based in Europe should be vigilant and take steps to identify and investigate poor practice in the dissemination of the outcomes of research. Where appropriate they should liaise with the researcher's employing organization over concerns with respect to work presented. National boundaries and differences in language should not be a barrier to such steps. The peer-review process could be strengthened by improved training and more effective editorial and managerial oversight. Peer review in assessment of research proposals might be strengthened in a similar way, to identify and act on any misconduct in the process of research review.

All parties and leaders in research should take a firm stance on research integrity. Evidence suggests a passive acceptance of misconduct and questionable research conduct (Fanelli, 2009). This should be replaced with a zero-tolerance approach to all forms of misconduct in research, with all researchers supporting colleagues in meeting appropriate standards in research (Titus, Wells & Rhoades, 2008). The job descriptions of senior researchers and research facility managers of European research projects should include a requirement to monitor and report on compliance with prescribed standards in research.

There is a lack of available information about researchers who have been sanctioned for misconduct and about research findings that are therefore questionable. Although such information may be in the public domain through, for example, retracted publications, there is little national availability or formal sharing of such findings. Disclosure of information on matters related to research integrity needs to be actively debated. Information related to an investigation should, of course, be shared with partner organizations, including organizations in other countries. In the case of a finding of research misconduct, information might be shared with the individual's national research integrity office or even with the national integrity offices of other countries. Effective liaison among the coordinated national offices for research integrity has already proved an effective route to facilitating an investigation of an international case in Europe.

The development of Directive 2001/20/EC, the clinical trials directive (EUR-Lex, 2001), led many European countries to harmonize mechanisms for reviewing and monitoring health-research projects. Such mechanisms might be extended to ensure that effective oversight of research integrity is facilitated within health research and in other research disciplines.

Research misconduct is not overtly addressed in many European countries. More open attention to the subject and research into the causes of misbehaviour may facilitate greater awareness of misconduct and willingness to take early actions to address poor conduct. Studies suggest that there is a general awareness that colleagues in the research community do not always adhere to the principles of good conduct of research (Martinson et al., 2005; Titus et al., 2008). By acknowledging that such practices do take place, the European research community should be able to take steps to facilitate greater oversight to prevent misbehaviour and enable those who witness such behaviour to have a more straightforward means of reporting their concerns.

References

Act of 30 June 2006 No. 56 on Ethics and Integrity in Research. (2009). Retrieved from www.etik-kom.no/no/In-English/Act-on-ethics-and-integrity-in-research.

ALL European Academies, Royal Netherlands Academy of Arts and Sciences, Netherlands Organisation for Scientific Research, & Association of Universities in the Netherlands. (2003). *Memorandum on scientific integrity*. Retrieved from www.allea.org/Content/ALLEA/Themes/Scientific%20Integrity/Memorandum_Scientific_Integrity.pdf.

Boesz, C., & Lloyd, N. (2008). Collaborations: Investigating international misconduct. *Nature, 452*, 686–687.

Commission on Professional Self Regulation in Science. (1998). *Recommendation of the Commission on Professional Self Regulation in Science: Proposals for safeguarding good scientific practice*. Bonn, Germany: Deutsche Forschungsgemeinschaft. Retrieved from www.dfg.de/en/dfg_profile/structure/statutory_bodies/ombudsman/index.html.

Committee on Publication Ethics. (n.d.). *About COPE*. Retrieved from http://publicationethics.org/about.

Danish Agency for Science, Technology, and Innovation. (2009). *The Danish committees on scientific dishonesty*. Retrieved from http://en.fi.dk/councils-commissions/the-danish-committees-on-scientific-dishonesty.

Edwards, A. W. F. (1986). Are Mendel's results really too close? *Biological Reviews, 61*, 295–312.

ERC. (2008). *Mission: What is the ERC?* Retrieved from http://erc.europa.eu/index.cfm?fuseaction=page.display&topicID=12.

ESF. (n.d.). *ESF member organisation forum on research integrity*. Retrieved from www.esf.org/activities/mo-fora/research-integrity.html.

ESF. (2000). *Policy briefing: Good scientific practice in research and scholarship* (ESPB 10). Retrieved from www.esf.org/publications/science-policy-briefings.html.

ESF. (2008). *Stewards of Integrity: Institutional approaches to promote and safeguard good research practice in Europe*. Strasbourg: European Science Foundation.

ESF, & Office of Research Integrity. (2007). *Research integrity: Global responsibility to foster common standards* (ESPB 30). Report of the First World conference, Lisbon, Portugal in September 2007. Retrieved from www.esf.org/publications/science-policy-briefings.html.

EUR-Lex. (2001). *32001L0020: Directive 2001/20/EC of the European Parliament*. Retrieved from http://eur-lex.europa.eu/LexUriServ/LexUriServ.do?uri=CELEX:32001L0020:EN:HTML.

European Commission. (n.d.). *What is the European Research Area?* Retrieved from http://ec.europa.eu/research/era/index_en.html.

European Commission, CORDIS (2007). *Seventh Framework Programme: Understand FP7*. Retrieved from http://cordis.europa.eu/fp7/budget_en.html.

European Commission, CORDIS (2008). *Seventh Framework Programme: Cooperation*. Retrieved from http://cordis.europa.eu/fp7/cooperation/home_en.html.

European Commission Expert Group of Research Integrity. (2007). *Integrity in research: A rationale for community action*. Retrieved from http://ec.europa.eu/research/science-society/document_library/pdf_06/integrity-in-research-ec-expert-group-final-report_en.pdf.

European Network for Ombudsmen in Higher Education. (n.d.). Retrieved from www.english.uva.nl/enohe/enohe_network.cfm.

Fanelli, D. (2009). How many scientists fabricate and falsify research? A systematic review and meta-analysis of survey data. *PLoS ONE, 4*(5), e5738.

FP7 capacities work programme: Part 5 – science in society. (2007). Retrieved from www.madri-masd.org/proyectoseuropeos/documentos/doc/FP7-SCIENCE-IN-SOCIETY-2008-1.pdf.

Green, R. (2008). *Richard Green: Ombudsman*. Committee on Publication Ethics. Retrieved from http://publicationethics.org/about/council/richard-green-md-jd.

Horton, R. (2006). Retraction. Non-steroidal anti-inflammatory drugs and the risk of oral cancer: A nested case-control study. *The Lancet, 367*(9508), 382.

Lucent Technologies. (2002). *Report of the investigation committee on the possibility of scientific misconduct in the work of Hendrik Schön and coauthors.* Retrieved from http://publish.aps. org/reports/lucentrep.pdf.

Martinson, B. C., Anderson, M. S., & De Vries, R. (2005). Scientists behaving badly. *Nature, 435,* 737–738.

National Board for Scientific Integrity. (n.d.). Retrieved from www.knaw.nl/cfdata/advisory/advisory_detail.cfm?orgid=690.

National Health and Medical Research Council. (2007). *Australian code for the responsible conduct of research.* Retrieved from www.nhmrc.gov.au/publications/synopses/r39syn.htm.

OECD Global Science Forum. (2007). *Best practices for ensuring scientific integrity and preventing misconduct.* Retrieved from www.oecd.org/dataoecd/37/17/40188303.pdf.

Research Councils UK. (2009). *RCUK policy and code of conduct on the governance of good research conduct: Integrity, clarity and good management.* Retrieved from www.rcuk.ac.uk/ cmsweb/downloads/rcuk/reviews/grc/goodresearchconductcode.pdf.

Smith, R. (2006). Research misconduct: The poisoning of the well. *Journal of the Royal Society of Medicine, 99,* 232–237.

Titus, S. L., Wells, J. A., & Rhoades, L. J. (2008). Repairing research integrity. *Nature, 453,* 980–982.

UK Research Integrity Office. (n.d.). Retrieved from www.ukrio.org/sites/ukrio2/uk_research_ integrity_office__ukrio_/index.cfm.

UK Research Integrity Office. (2008). *Procedure for the investigation of misconduct in research.* Retrieved from www.ukrio.org/resources/UKRIO%20Procedure%20for%20the%20Investigation%20of%20Misconduct%20in%20Research.pdf.

Vinther, T. (2009). *The National Commission for the Investigation of Scientific Misconduct.* Retrieved from www.etikkom.no/no/In-English/Scientific-Misconduct.

Wellcome Trust. (2005). *Guidelines on good research practice: Including statement on the handling of allegations of research misconduct.* Retrieved from www.wellcome.ac.uk/stellent/groups/ corporatesite/@policy_communications/documents/web_document/wtd002754.pdf.

12

Collaborating with Colleagues in Latin America

Publication Issues

Herbert Stegemann, Juan Miyahira, Sergio Alvarado-Menacho, and Reyna M. Durón

Research in the Latin American region can be characterized in many ways. Some countries, such as Argentina, Brazil and Mexico, have relatively large, well-funded programs, in comparison to the smaller, less-well funded programs in most other countries. The imbalances here have been well known at least since the early 1990s (Organización Panamericana de la Salud, 1992) and are likely to continue in the near future. There are also language differences, with most researchers speaking and writing in Spanish, though Latin America also includes the English- and French-speaking Caribbean islands and Portuguese-speakers in Brazil.

Latin America in general follows the same international codes, regulations and guidelines as other countries and regions of the world, such as the World Medical Association's *Declaration of Helsinki* (World Medical Association, 2008). Most Latin American journals also subscribe to the ICMJE uniform requirements (International Committee of Medical Journal Editors, 2008), even though there is no official Spanish translation on the ICMJE web page (unofficial translations can be found on the Internet, but most have not been updated). Latin American researchers are also beginning to work more with global pharmaceutical industries. The International Federation of Pharmaceutical Manufacturers and Associations (2008) have shown interest in participating in an organized manner in research in developing countries particularly. Likewise, there are also research ties developing through the World Health Organization (WHO), which is also active in promoting discussions of research ethics through publications and international conferences. At this general level, working with colleagues in Latin America is similar to working with colleagues elsewhere in the world.

This overview of issues that arise in collaboration with Latin American researchers is written from the perspective of three researchers located in Central America (Honduras), Venezuela and Peru, but takes into consideration developments and problems that can arise more generally. It begins with an overview of trends in collaborative publications, then turns to challenges in the three regions.

Research in Latin America

Per-capita investment in research varies between countries in Latin America. According to the United Nations Educational, Scientific and Cultural Organization (UNESCO), despite efforts to increase investments in research and development, expenditure remains low in developing countries (UNESCO, 2001, 2004). In 2000 developing countries spent 0.9 percent of their gross domestic product on research and development, still falling short of the minimum target of 1.0 percent proposed in international policies and declarations for over 30 years. In Latin America, investment in research remained stable from 1990 to 2000, reaching 2.9 percent of the world total in 2000. In absolute terms, Latin American expenditure almost doubled during this period, but its gross domestic expenditure in research and development:gross domestic product ratio improved only slightly from 0.5 percent to 0.6 percent. Newly industrialized economies in South East Asia and China have achieved higher profiles. At the same time, there is a slight decline in participation of the United States and the European Union in the world total investment in research, but they still keep their leadership in research funding.

A careful review of journal databases shows that there is an increasing number of research projects being developed as international collaborations between researchers in the United States, Europe, Mexico, Central America and South American countries. In the five-year period of 2004–2008, at least 100,000 original reports resulting from international collaborations by authors from the American continents were indexed in the PubMed database. The production of Latin American articles concentrates in five countries (Brazil, Mexico, Argentina, Chile and Colombia), which generated 88 percent of the region's articles. These countries show higher per capita output of scientific publications per million inhabitants of the region, ranging from 22.5 papers to 38.8 papers (World Bank, 2002; National Science Foundation, 2004). An analysis of author affiliations in papers from this sample showed that research collaborations are more common between Latin American countries and the United States. However, there is a tendency toward an increase in collaborations with European countries, and a modest but growing number of collaborations with Japan and India. On the other hand, there are some multi-national projects between Latin American countries, but they are fewer in number. The level of participation of local researchers as first authors varies between countries.

According to the same sample from PubMed, most collaborative research projects being developed in Latin America are related to: several public health issues (29 percent); infectious diseases (27 percent); maternal/child health (18 percent); genetics (10 percent); psychiatry/psychology (8 percent); and other (8 percent). This shows that there is demand-driven collaborative research, and the access to new technologies is helping to reach important levels of development in basic sciences.

Other reported results of these collaborations are: more research personnel training; additional incentive for research careers in new investigators; technology transfer and better understanding; and new strategies to solve health problems affecting the Latin American populations. Together with these advantages from international collaborations, there are parallel challenges and problems related to differences in research regulations, availability of resources, incentives for research, and ethics. Incentives for research are important. In some universities in developed countries, researchers are required to have high indexed-publication rates, but in Central America, as in most Latin American countries, research and publication are more vocation-driven than institutionally promoted.

Central America

Human- and Animal-Subjects Research

Despite improvements, there is still quite a bit of flexibility and variation in the regulations that govern human- and animal-subjects research in Latin American countries. This can be explained in part by the small number of oversight committees working in institutions where research is developed. In general, animal-subject research is less regulated than human-subject research in many undeveloped countries.

The growth in human- and animal-subject research in Central America has increased the need to create new local institutional review boards and to train board members to oversee international, as well as local, research (Lescano, Blazes, Montano, Kochel, Moran & Lescano, et al. 2008). Most Central American countries have started ethics committees in some universities and hospitals. Researchers outside these institutions have to seek oversight from the directors of medical or university departments. This practice slows research and does not ensure that all the international ethics standards are met.

Sponsoring institutions from the United States can require that local IRBs obtain a U.S. Federal-Wide Assurance as a prerequisite for funding of collaborative projects. Imposing U.S. regulations does, however, raise concerns. Local ethics committees sometimes see foreign requirements as a burden, a situation that could be improved through better communication and understanding of cultural and even legal differences between countries.

Developing consent forms accepted both by the foreign and the local institutions can also be a challenge. Some protocols—for example, in genetics studies—can involve complex methodologies. Explaining the methods can result in long and detailed consent forms. The experience of several groups working with Latin American populations is that some participants will not sign long consent forms that, for them, resemble a legal contract. They raise false suspicions and discourage participation. Training researchers on the consent process is therefore essential. Subjects should have places where they can get second opinions and advice on their participation in research projects.

Availability of Resources for Research

External funds are needed to develop high-quality research in Latin American countries, resulting in financial dependence. Governments and universities have become more conscious about the need to fund research over the last decade. However, some universities in Central America invest less than 5 percent of their budgets in research, since most of their budgets must be used to support salaries. Honduras has adopted legislation requiring that at least 6 percent of the national budget should be used to support public universities, but this is not done in practice. Since research is not a top priority, researchers cannot be assured of sustained funding, either to support their participation in international collaborations or to support their own short- and long-term international projects.

Central American countries need to build research capacities that will support long-term commitments to fundamental projects (Lansang & Olveda, 1994; Olliaro & Smith, 2004). Raising funds from sources other than the government could help accomplish this objective. Researchers in Central American countries therefore need to develop fund-raising strategies that will reduce dependence on other countries. This will require more work, some training and, perhaps, some overtime.

Due to the lack of institutional funds, it is common for some dedicated Central American researchers to use personal funds to support their research. How much international collaboration is supported in this way is not known. More support should also be provided by the international collaborators, who benefit by gaining access to large datasets and populations, sometimes not available in developed countries. In these collaborations, Central American researchers should be more than peripheral or occasional collaborators for foreign researchers that come and take data and samples out of the Central American country. Local researchers should benefit from the exchange and get training to continue research within their institutions. More and better training is needed to help Central American researchers become active and equal partners in international collaborations.

Patents and Ownership

As their participation in international collaborations grows, Central American researchers in particular, and Latin American researchers more generally, are beginning to discuss patenting and ownership issues. The voice they bring to international collaborations will not necessarily agree with decisions already made in more-developed countries. Some feel that current patenting and ownership policies already run counter to fundamental human rights and the principles of the freedom, autonomy and dignity of each human being (Terragni, 1993).

Despite the ongoing controversies, patent offices worldwide have issued thousands of patents on human DNA sequences. In 2000 the U.S. Patent and

Trademark Office issued about 2,000 patents on full-length genes for all species. Reportedly, more than 3,000,000 genome sequences have pending patent applications in the United States, a country where there are more filings for patent applications for human DNA sequences every year (NSB, 2002). Whether human DNA sequences should be patentable has been strongly debated for many years. Arguments in favor state that patents on human DNA sequences should be provided to promote diagnostic and therapeutic products that can be commercialized. Others argue that giving companies monopoly rights over specific DNA sequences will hinder scientific progress.

An increasing number of collaborative projects in genetics are being developed using Latin American researchers and families, and result in reports of discoveries of new mutated genes every year. Unfortunately, too often, researchers or universities from developed countries patent and claim exclusive ownership of the discoveries. In addition to the credit, developing countries also should benefit from spin-off technologies or products resulting from the discoveries. Local institutions from Latin American countries will likely, in the future, ask for more credit and, eventually, financial benefits from research products. One example of advances toward improving this process has been reported in Brazil (Xavier, Capanema, Ruiz, Oliveira, Meyer, D'Afonseca, et al., 2008). As education on patenting and ownership is improved in Latin American, the terms established for collaborations with colleagues in developed countries will need to change.

Clinical Trials

International clinical trials sometimes raise particularly knotty ethical issues that can be difficult to resolve, such as the 1996 study of antiretroviral treatment of HIV-positive women in African and Asian countries through a protocol developed with North American funding. Women were randomized into treatment groups receiving either half-doses of antiretroviral medication or placebo. At the time, there was a standard of treatment that combined several antiretroviral and other drugs to prevent vertical HIV transmission. This standard contraindicated the use of placebo. Critics argued that the principle of justice and equity was violated by this protocol. The researchers justified their approach by alleging that poor and more vulnerable populations who do not have access to good health care could try risky treatments that "are better than nothing."

To avoid similar problems in clinical research conduct in Central America, the oversight of human ethics regulations needs to be reviewed. The new registries of clinical trials should help evaluate trials, but they are not sufficient. Multi-national collaborations should be developed through multi-country consensuses that take into account local needs and local culture. Full and balanced international collaborations, appropriate networking, adequate support for the trials, support for research capacity building, advocacy and fund raising, management and information management (Matee, Manyando, Ndumbe, Corrah, Jaoko, Kitua, et al., 2009). Besides strengthening and increasing the number of ethics committees, there is a need for: local and international policies and laws to protect research subjects; the existence of governmental and non-governmental organizations to protect the rights of subjects and patients; subjects' access to the benefits that result from the research; and return of the benefits to the community where the study was carried out (Zoboli, 2007). These are global needs, but they are particularly apparent in the countries of Central America.

Rules for Authorship

As multi-national research partnerships with Central American countries have been improving and growing between developed and developing countries, attention to authorship issues is essential. Some initiatives are starting to address this subject in order to develop long-term successful partnerships (Matee et al., 2009). A sample of the last 50 papers indexed in PubMed resulting from international collaborative research in five Central American countries shows that first authors come from the country where research was done in less than one-third of publications. These papers are mostly published in journals from the United States and Europe. Most first authors are researchers from the United States (46 percent). This predominance of non-local first authors can be explained by the source of funding and planning of research, the ability of local researchers to write in English or the level of training of these researchers for developing high-quality manuscripts for medical publication.

More data are needed to determine whether the figures above have changed over time, perhaps showing that local authors are getting more chances to be first authors. The apparent higher first-author rate for Costa Rican researchers may be related to more research opportunities and capability in that country.

There is a question as to whether international collaborative research between developed and developing countries meet rigid criteria as applied in developed countries. Misconduct could occur when local researchers are not given the opportunity to write first-author papers even when they do the work and collect or produce the data. This challenges local authors from developing countries to develop high-level skills in writing research papers in order to be able to compete for the available opportunities.

Venezuela

Researchers who are working or may want to work with colleagues in Venezuela or other countries in Latin America need to be aware of the fact that the standards and practices of the institutions and journals in the area do not match standards and practices followed elsewhere in the world. Research behavior in Venezuela is unevenly regulated.

Anyone doing clinical research in Venezuela must comply with three human-subjects regulations: (1) Ley de Ejercicio de la Medicina (1982) (The Law of Exercise of Medicine); (2) Federación Médica Venezolana Código de Deontología Médica (n.d.) (The Medical Deontology Code). This is the principle regulatory document for the practice of medicine in Venezuela. It is based on another document known as the "Moral Médica," which was authored by Dr. Luis Razetti and which has served as a model in medical education for several decades in many Latin American countries (Martín, 2005); (3) Código de Bioética y Seguridad (The Bioethics and Biosafety Code (FONACIT, 2008)). This code is already in its third edition. It is broad but practical. Compliance is required by any investigator or institutions that receive funds from the Fondo Nacional de Ciencia, Tecnología e Investigación.

Institutions that conduct clinical research must, as a requirement of the national health system, have Ethics Committees. In health centers where these committees have not been established, it is required that someone in higher authority reviews and approves the research protocol. However, the principles that should be used for making decisions about the ethics of particular projects are not well developed or widely known. More needs to be done to publicize basic rules and procedures. In addition, a lack of language skills presents a major problem. The so-called universal language of science, English, still has not been widely adopted in different circles, including academic ones, and at times there is even opposition to its use. Spanish is the official legal language and every document must be translated into Spanish.

Research in Venezuela is also unofficially "governed" or "influenced" by politics. Disagreement can arise over the objectives of an investigation, plotting the interests of the investigator against the interests of the institution or nation. These disagreements can have a serious impact on the chances of receiving funding.

The unevenness of the rules and practices in Venezuela is particularly evident in the area of publication. The following brief analysis of some of the major problems and shortcomings is based on many years of experience involving publications committees, editorial associations of biomedical journals (ASEREME, 2009) and work with the pharmaceutical industry, academic institutes and scientific societies. The experiences and observations summarized below do not necessarily coincide with what one would expect in developed countries. They do seem to be in agreement with experiences with other countries of the region and therefore are probably applicable to Latin America more generally.

Looking specifically at biomedical publications, Venezuela has about 60 registered journals, which publish 600 copies for each issue. Journals publish either two or three issues annually, with issues typically running to about 80 pages and containing one or two original research or primary articles (based on the definition of the Council of Science Editors (2009)). Most medical journals are sponsored by their respective scientific society and are not academic. Most of their funding comes from advertisements, principally taken out by the pharmaceutical industry. Distribution is free and often informal. Punctuality is not uniform, largely as a result of financing problems and the ability of the editors to get authors to write papers regularly. The Vancouver standards for authorship are widely acknowledged in instructions to authors, but often not followed in practice. This divergence between ideal and practice is common in Venezuelan research publications, although this should not detract from the fact that there are important contributions to research in Venezuelan journals, which can unfortunately sometimes be overlooked by the English-speaking world.

Authorship

Using the ICMJE standard for authorship as a reference, it is frequent to see unqualified authors listed in Venezuelan publications. The most common violation is by superiors and laboratory chiefs, who use their position to demand authorship credit without having participated in the research. The justification for listing these individuals is the fact that they made the research possible by raising funds and supporting a laboratory. In many academic environments this justification is still accepted for being listed as an author.

Duplicate Publication

Duplication of the same research article in another periodical without mention of the original publication is also found in Venezuelan journals. Sometimes, efforts are made to disguise the duplication by altering the names of the co-authors or dropping or adding some co-authors. This problem is aggravated by the delay in publishing journals, which prompts authors to send their manuscript to another journal in hope of seeing it published sooner.

Plagiarism

Plagiarism is probably more frequent than recognized, particularly in what is called "gray literature." Technological advances will, in the future, allow detection of this kind of fraud more easily, as it even has international implications.

Poor-Quality Manuscripts Submitted to Journals

Authors too frequently submit poor-quality manuscripts to a journal, with the expectation that the editors, who are often in need of publications, will do the editing and polishing needed to get the work ready for publication.

Not all of the problems with research publications in Venezuela stem only from the authors. Editors often fail to:

- develop clear policies for the publications they are charged with directing, particularly for improving the distribution of their journal and signing up to databases for the purpose of improving their visibility;
- meet editorial and publication deadlines;
- train new editorial staff;
- expand referee pools;
- keep up-to-date with compliance rules and guidelines for authors and referees;
- keep current with new editorial and technological developments;
- take advantage of national and regional literature;
- use cover letters as a way of facilitating communication between the authors and the editor; and
- publish errata and retraction notes.

Referees fail to:

- meet review deadlines;
- respect manuscript confidentiality;
- refrain from using information in the articles they review before it is published; and
- take responsibility for improving the quality of publications.

Advertisers fail to:

- develop regulations to ensure that their significant financial influence does not compromise the quality of the research published. The regulations that exist to control advertising in Latin America are weak and lack consistency in comparison to the countries where the most prestigious pharmaceutical companies are located. Advertisers should consider following the regulations of well-established journals, such as the *British Medical Journal* (2009), in Latin American countries.

Publishers fail to:

- follow well-established standards for research publications, such as those proposed by Blackwell Publishing (2009);
- improve technological capabilities;
- guarantee confidentiality;
- follow schedules; and
- take into account the important financial differences between developed countries and developing countries.

Putting these pieces together, it should be apparent that collaborators need to be aware of the weaknesses and shortcomings of Venezuelan—and probably many Latin American—research publications. There are, of course, many good and reliable journals in Latin America, and to further collaboration, researchers outside Latin America should consider publishing in these journals. In doing so, they should set the same standards and exercise the same vigilance as they would in any other publication.

Peru

In Peru, as in many other countries, situations arise that present challenges to the integrity of research and scientific publications. The experience of the Peruvian Association of Scientific Editors (APECi, as it is known in Spanish) suggests that these situations often result from a lack of knowledge. Most universities have no courses at the undergraduate level on publication and good research practice. This problem can be compounded by a culture that does not stimulate interest in research and results in students taking the easiest route to complete assignments, such as copying work from each other, or from the Internet. The new accreditation process has encouraged universities to increase the pressure on faculties to publish. This section discusses two areas where the problems seem to be particularly apparent: clinical trials and research that can lead to patents.

Clinical Trials

Peruvian convention requires that clinical trials be registered and authorized by the National Health Institute (Instituto Nacional de Salud—INS (www.ins. gob.pe/registroEC)). In trials financed by an international pharmaceutical company, the study protocols are developed by company's researchers, but the Peruvian researchers have to comply with INS rules, including listing the study in the INS registry, following the Peruvian Clinical Trial Regulations and getting approval through an accredited and registered Ethics Committee.

Peruvian researchers are personally responsible for work done under their supervision in Peru if they are registered as the primary researcher. Article 26 of the Peruvian Clinical Trial Regulations states that:

> A clinical trial may only be carried out when the main researcher and sponsor sign a sworn declaration by which: a) free medical attention and treatment is provided to subjects of an investigation should they be injured as a direct result of the clinical trial; b) they are forced to give adequate compensation for the damage any research subject could suffer as a result of the use of a product in the research or by a procedure or intervention performed with the purpose of the investigation (non-therapeutical procedures).
>
> (Ministerio de Salud del Perú, 2007)

This may mean that they are liable for any damages or injury that may occur to patients that are research subjects, despite the fact that the Peruvian Clinical Trial Regulations require the sponsor of the study to have health insurance coverage in the country to cover any damages the study subjects could incur.

Article 28 indicates that compensation will cover all the costs of damage to the health or physical state of the research subject, as well as economic loss arising directly from such harm that is not inherent to the pathology under study, or the evolution of the disease itself (Ministerio de Salud del Perú, 2007).

Even with all of this responsibility, Peruvian researchers often do not participate in the analysis or interpretation of the trial due to the fact that the final report is made by company researchers. In some studies, all participating researchers are included as authors when the study is published, but in most cases they are not. This technically follows the conventions established by the ICMJE: researchers who do not participate in the interpretation of data and draft of an article should not be listed as authors (ICMJE, 2008). But at the same time, is it reasonable to exclude a person who is legally responsible for a study from authorship? Conflicts such as these can seriously undermine a researcher's respect for systems that regulate research and publication.

Another situation that erodes confidence in rules, although with decreasing frequency, is sponsors blocking publication of trials that are not favorable to the medication being studied. At the same time, the Peruvian Clinical Trial Regulations require the sponsor to provide a report at the end of the investigation. What should researchers to do when caught in this situation?

A researcher's responsibilities can be further complicated when they conduct trials on patients with chronic illnesses within a vulnerable population. Some pharmaceutical companies will continue to supply the medication after the study has finished until the product is launched into the market, but in most cases this does not happen. Instead, patients are forced to return to their prior, now-shown-to-be-less-effective treatments. If the medication is shown to have clear benefits, should the patients subject to a study not continue with the treatment? Who should provide it? What responsibilities does the researcher who conducted the study have? In Peru, a research group managed to have a pharmaceutical company continue the supply of antiretroviral medication to patients that participated in the study until the government decided to provide the treatment free of charge (J. Echevarría, personal communication, August 7, 2009). When such support is not available, researchers are put in the difficult position of being part of a project that many see as failing to meet basic responsibilities toward research subjects.

Patents and Ownership

Peruvian legislation does not protect ideas. Article 9 of Law Decree 822 of the Copyright Law (Presidencia de la República del Perú, 1996) states that "Copyright shall not protect: a) Ideas contained in literary or artistic works, procedures, operation methods or mathematical concepts in themselves, systems or the ideological or technical contents of scientific works, nor their industrial or commercial use."

This has created problems with the research on plants that have medicinal properties. It is recognized that Peru's diverse plant population includes many with nutritional and medicinal properties; products such as Cat's Claw (*Uncaria tomentosa*), Andean Maca (*Lepidium peruvianum*) and the wild Yacon (*Smallanthus sonchifolius*) are currently traded all over the world. However, this has not benefited the indigenous populations that had knowledge of the uses of these plants. They remain as poor as they were before. For this reason, the process of researching medicinal products extracted from plants is now slower and more complex due to the lack of trust of the indigenous communities, preventing them from revealing their ancestral customs. Also, patents for natural products may not be obtained.

Publications

The Peruvian experience with publication is similar to the Venezuelan one, and the experience with patents similar to the Central American one. Honorary and ghost authorship are common practices. Service managers or department heads often demand that they be included as authors on research studies without ever having participated in them. Laboratory heads have been known to present an investigation at congresses as the sole author, without including the actual authors.

Problems also arise when the thesis work of a student needed to complete degree requirements is also submitted to a scientific journal for publication. Disputes frequently arise over whether the student or advisor should be the primary author, and over how and when authorship agreements should be worked out. Can the professor negotiate with the student over authorship before the start of a thesis, considering the difference in status? Should the advisor of a thesis only be acknowledged when it is published?

Incomplete publication is also a serious problem in Peru. Congresses and sessions at scientific meetings often include research studies presented only in summaries, with a few tables or graphs, but very few are published afterwards as a full study in a scientific journal. Why does this happen? The presentations increase the publication list of the presenter and are considered when she or he is being promoted. The value of a study presented at a congress is equal to publication of an original investigation in a scientific journal in many institutions in Peru. Similar pressures seem to be leading to an increase in duplicate or redundant publications.

Finally, with the increased use of computers, copying and pasting has increased the likelihood of plagiarism in Peru, and presumably elsewhere. The most frequent form of plagiarism that we have observed is in the unreferenced used of ideas published by others; but direct copying of paragraphs and sections also happens. These violations go undetected because many studies remain in a library archive in a thesis or a similar format and are not published in scientific journals. Also, many journals do not have the proper tools or resources to discover plagiarism or duplicate publication.

APECi (2006) believes that the best way to improve scientific integrity and the ethics of the scientific publication is to develop strategies for training students and researchers. For publication problems specifically, the creation of an online review—such as the open journal system (Public Knowledge System, n.d.) available through some SciELO portals—could reduce the number of duplicate publications. But for other publication problems, the problems identified with patents and clinical trials, and the other issues highlighted in this chapter, increased awareness and better training would seem to be the best option.

Conclusions

If Latin American countries are to increase their participation in research on an international level and to enter more aggressively into collaborations with colleagues from around the world, they need to address the problems identified above. This is essential for the improvement of the quality of Latin American research for its own sake and to inspire the confidence needed by others to enter into collaborations with their Latin American colleagues.

We see the major challenges as follows: (1) work to reduce technological barriers; (2) accept that English is not the "universal language of science" in many regions of Latin America, including academia; (3) recognize the costs involved in attending international meetings, access to books, journals and scientific documents; (4) foster research projects that can be applied to the region; and (5) accept socio-cultural differences in the scientific environment. Instead of stimulating brain drain, stimulate international exchange.

Our recommendations for change are: (1) develop international exchange of experiences in research, publishing and scientific editing, particularly through attendance at international meetings to allow more personal contact; (2) given their scarce distribution and knowledge, include these topics in the discussions about superior academic studies; (3) for the Latin American collaborations, reconsidering the rigid use of English as a language and at least add summaries in Spanish and Portuguese in the English texts; (4) reduce the elitist structure of international groups by publicizing their existence and working to include more Latin American institutions and individuals; and (5) foster the development of agreements to redress developed/non-developed research networking imbalances, support clinical trials relevant to Latin America and enhance research capacity building in developing countries.

Overall, and based on experience, we feel it is necessary to incorporate authors, reviewers and editors from Latin America into international meetings related to scientific publication. As many—or most of them—work on a purely honorific basis, they often work in isolation from the international journal mainstream. Many journals from the region are totally unknown internationally. Emphasis needs to be placed on encouraging more international cooperation and collaboration in research as an essential ingredient in successful collaboration itself.

References

Asociación de Editores de Revistas Biomédicas Venezolanas (ASEREME). (2009). Retrieved September 10, 2009, from www.asereme.org.ve.

Asociación Peruana de Editores Científicos (APECi). (2006). Retrieved September 5, 2009, from www.freewebs.com/apeci.

Blackwell Publishing. (2009). *Best practice guidelines on publication ethics: A publisher's perspective.* Retrieved September 23, 2009, from www.blackwellpublishing.com/Publicationethics.

BMJ Group. (2009). *Advertising and sponsorship policy.* Retrieved September 23, 2003, from http://group.bmj.com/group/advertising/policy.

Council of Science Editors. (2009). *What constitutes primary publication?* Retrieved September 8, 2009, from www.councilscienceeditors.org/members/securedDocuments/v32n2p057-058.pdf.

Federación Médica Venezolana (n.d.). *Código de Deontología Médica.* Retrieved September 8, 2009, from www.saludfmv.org/archivos/deontologia.pdf.

FONACIT. (2008). *Código de Bioética y Bioseguridad* (3rd ed.). Retrieved September 8, 2009, from www.fonacit.gov.ve/bioetica.asp.

International Committee of Medical Journal Editors (ICMJE). (2008). *Uniform requirements for manuscripts submitted to biomedical journals: Writing and editing for biomedical publications.* Retrieved August 4, 2009, from www.icmje.org/urm_full.pdf.

International Federation of Pharmaceutical Manufacturers & Associations. (2008). *IFPMA health partnerships 2009 database.* Retrieved September 7, 2009, from www.ifpma.org/healthpartnerships.

Lansang, M. A., & Olveda, R. O. (1994). Institutional links: Strategic bridges for research capacity strengthening. *Acta Tropica, 57,* 139–145.

Lescano, A. R., Blazes, D. L., Montano, S. M., Kochel, T., Moran, Z., Lescano, A. G., et al. (2008). Supporting the creation of new institutional review boards in developing countries: The U.S. Naval Medical Research Center Detachment Experience. *Military Medicine, 173*(10), 975–977.

Ley de Ejercicio de la Medicina. (1982). *Gaceta Oficial de la República de Venezuela.* Número 3002 Extraordinario.

Martín, P. F. (2005) *Contribuciones humanísticas. De Razetti a Porter.* Retrieved September 8, 2009, from www.scielo.org.ve/scielo.php?pid=S0367-47622005000400007&script=sci_arttext.

Matee, M. I., Manyando, C., Ndumbe, P. M., Corrah, T., Jaoko, W. G., Kitua, A. Y., et al. (2009). European and Developing Countries Clinical Trials Partnership (EDCTP): The path towards a true partnership. *BMC Public Health, 9*(249).

Ministerio de Salud del Perú (2007). *Modificatoria del Reglamento de Ensayos Clínicos en el Perú, Decreto Supremo N° 006-2007 SA.* Retrieved August 4, 2009, from www.ins.gob.pe/registroEC/reglamentoEnsayosclinicos.asp?fpt=1.

National Science Board (NSB). (2002). *Science & engineering indicators 2002.* Washington, DC: U.S. Government Printing Office.

National Science Foundation. (2004). *Latin America shows rapid rise in science and engineering articles. Info brief. Science resources statistics.* Arlington, VA: National Science Foundation. Retrieved December 5, 2009, from www.nsf.gov/statistics/infbrief/nsf04336/nsf04336.pdf.

Olliaro, P., & Smith, P. G. (2004). The European and Developing Countries Clinical Trials Partnership. *Journal of HIV Therapy, 9,* 53–56.

Organización Panamericana de la Salud. (1992). La Investigación en Salud en América Latina. *Publicación Científica, 543.*

Presidencia de la República del Perú (1996). *Ley sobre el Derecho de Autor (DL N°822).* Retrieved August 4, 2009, from www.indecopi.gob.pe/repositorioaps/0/9/par/leyesdda/dl822.pdf.

Public Knowledge System. (n.d.). *Open journal system.* Retrieved September 5, 2009, from, http://pkp.sfu.ca/?q=ojs.

Terragni, F. (1993). Biotechnology patents and ethical aspects. *Cancer Detection and Prevention, 17*(2), 317–321.

UNESCO Institute for Statistics. (2001). *World science report.* Paris: UNESCO.

UNESCO Institute for Statistics. (2004). *A decade of investment in research and development (R&D): 1990–2000. UIS bulletin on science and technology statistics, 1.* Paris: UNESCO.

World Bank. (2002). *World development indicators 2002.* Washington, DC: World Bank. Retrieved November 21, 2009, from www.worldbank.org/data/wdi2002/index.htm.

World Medical Association. (2008). *Declaration of Helsinki.* Retrieved September 7, 2009, from www.wma.net/e/policy/c8.htm.

Xavier, E. R., Capanema, B. P., Ruiz, J. C., Oliveira, G., Meyer, R., D'Afonseca, V., et al. (2008). Brazilian genome sequencing projects: State of the art. *Recent patents on DNA & gene sequences, 2*(2), 111–132.

Zoboli, E. L. (2007). Vulnerability in biomedical research: A framework for analysis. In M. Häyry, T. Takala, P. Herissone-Kelly & A. M. Capron (Eds.), *Ethics in biomedical research: International perspectives* (pp. 167–180). Rodopi: Amsterdam and New York.

Part V

Differences in Graduate Education and Postdoctoral Training

13

Differences in National Approaches to Doctoral Education

Implications for International Research Collaborations

Melissa S. Anderson, Felly Chiteng Kot, Yiyun Jie, Takehito Kamata,
Aliya Kuzhabekova, Christine C. Lepkowski, Marta A. Shaw,
Martha M. Sorenson, and Sonia M. R. Vasconcelos[1]

Students currently in doctoral programs worldwide have, in general, grown up with a global perspective on their lives and careers. Ease of communication and travel have opened the world to them in ways that they simply take for granted. As a group, they have a kind of global citizenship that bodes well for expanding international research collaborations.

At the same time, of course, they are still newcomers to the scientific community, in need of training and socialization if they are to take their places as full-fledged researchers. Their experiences are shaped by the systems of doctoral education, both formal and informal, in their own countries. Some aspects of these systems are virtually universal; others are distinctive features that differ by national, regional or historical context. How do these distinctive features of national systems of doctoral education affect international research collaborations—those in which doctoral students participate as students and those they will join later as mature researchers?

This question is addressed here by doctoral students (and one postdoctoral fellow) from seven different countries. Their task is two-fold: to describe some of the distinctive characteristics of doctoral education in their home country, and to consider how these features might influence cross-national research collaborations involving doctoral students from that country or scientists who likewise were trained under that system. For example, international research collaborations are likely to be affected by differences such as group (Japan) versus individual (Poland) orientation to work and achievement; ample resources and up-to-date facilities (China) versus a significantly challenged research infrastructure (Congo); research training largely independent of course structures (Kazakhstan) versus structured curricula offered by departments within graduate schools (United States); and federally mandated training in the responsible conduct of research (United States) versus little attention to research ethics in graduate programs (Brazil).

The authors of this chapter have drawn on their personal familiarity with their own national systems, their current study of systems of higher education in their doctoral programs, and their special interest in international issues in higher education.

China (Yiyun Jie)

Chinese higher education has gone through enormous change, restructuring and development. With the founding of the new People's Republic of China in 1949, China switched to the former Soviet Union's model to build up its higher education system (Ministry of Education China, 2002a). Since the mid-1980s, higher education has experienced over two decades of various reforms. Reintegration of higher education brought it more closely inline with Western education. The previously highly centralized administering authority at the Ministry of Education has been partially decentralized to the provincial educational bureaus and institutions. Tuition and fees were introduced to the traditionally government-subsidized system.

Finally, there has been a dramatic expansion in Chinese higher education (Ministry of Education China, 2002b, 2002c). As of 2007, there were 1,908 regular higher-education institutions, the majority of which (1,480) are administered by local authorities. The Chinese government has been very strategic in allocating research funding and other resources, targeting a handful of flagship universities as well as disciplinary areas that are deemed to be important for the nation's development. Unbalanced development and significant variations are widely observed among universities and across disciplines.

Modern doctoral education in China has a short history of only 20 years. As of 2007, 795 institutions (479 universities and 316 research institutes) offer graduate education programs in China. With a new cohort of 58,000 in 2007, over 2,000,000 doctoral students were enrolled in the system (Ministry of Education China, 2008). Chinese doctoral education is in a transition stage, and there is strong government input, aimed at enhancing the innovativeness of Chinese graduate education. However, these reformative strategies are highly concentrated on a small number of prestigious universities, while broader changes may take longer to take place.

A professional doctoral degree is not differentiated from a research doctoral degree. Until recently, many university employees had, at most, a Master's degree; now, many are enrolled in doctoral programs on a part-time basis, with a professional development purpose. Doing research is not the primary interest for many of these students.

In China, most doctoral students work with a single advisor in an apprentice-style relationship; course-taking has not been considered a major part of doctoral-level education. The advisor has a significant influence on Chinese doctoral students' training and development in such areas as the students' research directions, projects, doctoral courses, dissertations and other academic publications, and research ethics. Doctoral students typically work on their advisor's research projects and are therefore not challenged to explore their own research interests during doctoral study. They work on sub-topics handed over from their advisor. Ironically, many doctoral students report low levels of contact with their advisor, and communication tends to occur in group meetings rather than in individual session (Wang, 2008; Zhao, 2008). Some advisors have so many students that they do not have enough time to advise every one of them closely. This might be a result of the recent expansion in Chinese graduate education.

Doctoral students work as research and teaching assistants, but these positions are not institutionalized, though there have been efforts by the Ministry of Education to establish a system of assistantships. Doctoral students work on their advisor's research projects and receive various types and amounts of rewards that usually depend on the advisor's personal preference. Sometimes doctoral students' contributions to a research project are not appropriately rewarded, either through authorship or financial payment (Wang, 2008).

The majority of doctoral programs require doctoral students to have at least one publication in the core journals or higher before they can apply for the final dissertation defense. Doctoral degrees are not granted until students get published, and usually students must publish at least one first-author research article in a national core journal or Science Citation Index (SCI) journal. Chinese universities and research institutions have "adopted the SCI as the main indicator for research evaluation, and simply equate SCI-CP [SCI, Chinese Paper] with high quality papers" (Jin & Rousseau, 2005, p. 4). The requirements as to the number of publications and type of journal to publish in differ across universities and programs, but in general programs require at least one journal publication.

The pressure for publication is so overwhelming that publishing is often more important to students than finishing the dissertation. Various incentives for publication in SCI-indexed journals have been built into the reward and promotion systems (Jin & Rousseau, 2005; Wang, 2005). Other pressures for getting published come from the student's doctoral advisor and institutions, since publication is an influential measure for them as well. A direct result is that the number of publications from China in SCI journals has been increasing significantly (Zhou & Leydesdorff, 2006).

Such strong emphasis on publication provides room for unethical practices, especially when systematic training in academic ethics is not provided. The Chinese higher-education system has no well-developed ethics-oversight procedure. Recently, the Ministry of Education has started to guide universities and institutions in setting up ethics committees, workshops and courses; however, the effectiveness of these top-down efforts may not be revealed for a long time (Wilsdon & Keeley, 2007).

The distinctive characteristics of Chinese doctoral education have implications for researchers' participation in international research collaborations. In general, new initiatives aimed at establishing a more comprehensive and internationally connected system of graduate education tend to collide with out-dated organizational settings and institutional norms. Four more-specific implications are worth noting.

First, a strong emphasis on theoretical foundations in doctoral education means that Chinese researchers tend to have a strong theoretical foundation, typically without an applied orientation (Li, 2008). Scholars are often hesitant to adopt cross-disciplinary approaches.

Second, some junior scholars may not be comfortable taking the initiative in collaborations. Chinese doctoral students are trained through a "well-planned" research path that does not emphasize leadership skills, taking initiative in research or developing one's own research agenda. The advisor (commonly called "boss") is responsible for all aspects of a doctoral student's development, including funding for his or her study. Such a situation implies an extremely unbalanced power relationship. There is little cultivation of a colleague relationship between an advisor and doctoral student.

Third, most research funding comes through central government, and international research collaborations are often part of major, top-down, government-funded projects. The Chinese government is heavily involved in determining which institutions get funding and for what areas of work (Wilsdon & Keeley, 2007). Moreover, even for researcher-initiated projects, researchers have to add another layer of government expectation to their own research agenda: international collaborators may be surprised to find out that there is an implicit political agenda that Chinese scholars have to respond to, in addition to their research agenda. Chinese researchers are also likely to bring their pressures for more publication in internationally recognized journals into their collaboration.

Finally, Chinese researchers may be more prepared for international collaboration than their collaborators expect. The strong focus on English proficiency throughout the doctoral-training process eliminates language barriers for Chinese researchers in international collaborations. Chinese researchers are also at least aware of, if not personally experienced in, the Western research-training process. Chinese returnees with overseas education experience are taking prominent positions in the education and science sectors (Ministry of Education China, 2009). They have brought back not only knowledge and research experience, but also the connections they have established with the international community. These returnees are gradually developing new norms in graduate education in China.

Kazakhstan (Aliya Kuzhabekova)

As in the rest of the former Soviet Union, graduate education has been reshaped during almost two decades of educational reform in Kazakhstan.

The main task for reformers was to retain—during economic decline—the research training capacity built in Kazakhstan over the Soviet era, and to adapt the Soviet model to an open, knowledge-driven, market economy during the more recent economic revival.

By 1991, when Kazakhstan became an independent state, it had the best system of graduate training and the strongest research capacity in Central Asia (Organization for Economic Co-operation and Development [OECD] & The European Bank for Reconstruction and Development [EBRD]/The World Bank, 2007). The Soviet government invested heavily in building a strong graduate training and research system in Kazakhstan because local research-ers were needed to industrialize the country in order to exploit its rich natural resources, to develop agriculture to benefit from its vast territories and favo-rable climate, and to build nuclear- and biological-weapons testing and space-craft launching facilities, which were possible in the sparsely populated region.

In Soviet Kazakhstan, the system of research training had two degrees—Candidate of Science and Doctor of Science, both offered by higher-education institutions, as well as research institutes. The Candidate degree was very sim-ilar to the U.S. Doctor of Philosophy (De Witt, 1961). Admission to the Can-didate degree program (aspirantura) required a Specialist diploma, an equivalent of the U.S. Bachelors with an undergraduate thesis written during an additional year. Competitively selected applicants were required to have demonstrated ability to do scientific research and two years of practical experience. Aspirantura training could be completed within three years of full-time study or four years of part-time study, but typically took longer (De Witt, 1961). The program included optional attendance of seminars in the field of specialization and in communism theory; independent study in the field of specialization; preparation for foreign-language examinations; and experimental work for the dissertation (De Witt, 1961). To be awarded the Candidate degree, aspirants were required to pass a qualifying exam, includ-ing exams in their major, in communist theory and in a foreign language. They were also required to write, defend and publish a research dissertation. The Soviet Doctor of Science degree was awarded either after receiving a Can-didate degree upon successful defense of an additional dissertation of a very high quality, or as an honorary degree (Lindquist & Rokitiansky, 1963). Writ-ing such a dissertation required 12 years on average, and the degree was awarded to a very small number of people (Lindquist & Rokitiansky, 1963).

Certain characteristics of the system of graduate training in the Soviet Union (De Witt, 1961; Lindquist & Rokitiansky, 1963; Smolentseva, 2003) are worth noting due to their continued influence on the nature of graduate train-ing and research in modern Kazakhstan. The Soviet system of education and research was characterized by a high degree of centralization in decision-making. Such centralization destroyed the commercialization stage of scientific production and entrepreneurship. Academic freedom was significantly undermined by the ideological control of the Communist party, with a resulting self-censorship affecting the quality of research and graduate training, and resulting in an almost complete extermination of the social sciences. Soviet researchers were largely isolated from the global research community, with limited opportunities for international travel, research collaboration or access to ideas via outside publications.

Finally, the institutional structure for research and graduate training was hierarchical. Most prestigious research was conducted at the well-staffed and equipped research institutes under various ministries and academies of science, and most of the funding was channeled to the European part of the Soviet Union. As a result, at the dawn of Kazakhstan's independence, many researchers had been trained outside the republic.

All these features made the system of research and graduate training in Soviet Kazakhstan very vulnerable and led to a significant decline during a decade of economic turmoil following independence. Many talented researchers, especially ethnic minorities, left for better prospects in Russia, Ukraine and the West. Others chose to start their own businesses, abandoning the research career that barely made ends meet financially. Those who persevered faced difficulties in conducting quality research due to the decreasing quality of library holdings, research facilities and equipment. Though the country's borders opened, few had the financial resources to travel or to participate in international collaborations.

Graduate programs had difficulty attracting students, who were diverted from graduate education due to insufficient financial support from the government, high levels of unemployment, low salaries in research careers and negative experiences during undergraduate study. The quality of graduate training within Kazakhstan declined due to the loss of talented faculty, lower research productivity among the remaining faculty and lack of access to library resources and modern research facilities. Nepotism in faculty hiring and promotion, as well as corruption in admission and educational progress, also contributed to the decline in the quality of research training. In the context of declining quality, the Kazakhstani government created the "Bolashak" scholarship for graduate study abroad. However, in the early years, the scholarship was given mostly for studies in business, economics and public policy.

From 2001 onwards, Kazakhstan has been experiencing economic revival. Innovation capacity building has become the strategic focus of economic and institutional reforms. An earlier preoccupation with merely structural changes to comply with the Bologna process requirements has been replaced with greater attention to educational quality at all levels, as well as with commitment to foster research, development and commercialization capacities. Higher education has been somewhat decentralized; public universities have greater freedom in deciding how to spend centrally allocated budgets, but at the same time, basic faculty salaries, program offerings and curricular standards are determined by the Ministry of Education. A large number of private universities have emerged. All universities are charging tuition and fees as an important revenue source. There are no longer serious restrictions on academic freedom in research and teaching.

The Soviet degree sequence has been replaced with a Bachelor–Master–PhD sequence in all higher-education institutions in Kazakhstan. Admission to graduate study, however, is still based solely on the admission committee's subjective evaluation of an applicant's competence based on oral or written exams. The majority of students study independently and do not take the formal course sequence. The main elements of the curriculum (not actual courses) are determined by the Ministry of Education and include a mandatory internship. The qualifying exams and dissertation defense are evaluated by an external committee of 12, appointed by the Ministry of Education (Ministry of Education and Science of the Republic of Kazakhstan, 2008). Students are required to publish several articles in recognized journals in order to graduate (Ministry of Education and Science of the Republic of Kazakhstan, 2008). Graduate programs are encouraged to incorporate international partners in training and dissertation work.

Although graduate programs are offered by many public and private universities, research-oriented programs tend to be concentrated in public universities because they receive subsidies for maintaining their historically stronger research facilities and equipment, as well as government research grants. The private institutions support graduate study only in areas such as business and public administration, which are in high demand among employers and do not require many resources. Among graduate institutions there is also a certain sub-type of what could be called pseudo-private institutions (the Kazakh–British Technical University and a newly established university in Astana) that were intentionally created by the government to serve as a model for reform. These institutions enjoy the freedom of private institutions and the benefit of subsidization from the government. They offer the best salaries in the country and are able to attract leading researchers from Kazakhstan and from abroad. These institutions are anticipated to be actively involved in international collaborations in graduate training and research and have the capacity to do so.

Although funding has not increased to a level comparable to that in advanced economies (OECD & IBRD/The World Bank, 2007), universities have better access to research databases and the Internet and are able to pay sufficient salaries for faculty to stay in academia and even to participate in international conferences and workshops. Leading universities are also able to hire permanent or visiting foreign professors. Indirectly, the government is paying for improving the quality of faculty and internationalization of higher education in Kazakhstan by expanding the "Bolashak" program and making it available for graduate study in sciences and engineering. Many graduates of the program work as faculty at leading universities in Kazakhstan and serve as the point of contact for international collaborations.

A substantial portion of oil revenue is expended on research incubators, university-affiliated techno-parks, well-equipped shared-use research facilities and research and training projects in areas of strategic interest for Kazakhstan. These initiatives, however, enjoy only limited success, due largely to the over-complicated institutional structure for distribution of funds and for management of the facilities. In a sense, the initiatives continue to exist, at best, in the form of blueprints and, at worst, mostly in the imagination of policy-makers.

Although the Kazakhstani government and universities have a very strong motivation and make major efforts to establish international research ties with other countries, some characteristics of the system create complications for successful collaborative research. First, the Kazakhstani system of education and research is much less stable than those in the West due to continuing reform. Second, the existing pool of researchers includes some trained in the Soviet system, others educated under the new system in Kazakhstan, and still others with degrees from contemporary Russia, the West and non-Soviet Asia. These different groups have different understandings of the process of scientific inquiry, somewhat different motivations, as well as varying types of expertise and methodological skills in their fields. Third, regardless of their training, Kazakhstani researchers are highly motivated to participate in international partnerships, but often have less access to information technology, equipment and research databases, and have to carry greater teaching loads. Potential collaborative partners should also be prepared to deal with a high level of bureaucracy, lack of project management skills among counterparts in Kazakhstan and the challenges of conducting research in a culture of corruption with a poorly enforced intellectual property regime.

Democratic Republic of Congo (Felly Chiteng Kot)

Since the founding of its first university in 1954, the Democratic Republic of Congo (DRC) has made significant progress with respect to higher education access and attainment. When the country achieved independence in 1960, it had fewer than 10 college graduates, due to the Belgian colonial policy that restricted access to postsecondary education, and the academic staff in its institutions was almost entirely European.

Today, Congolese institutions produce thousands of graduates yearly, and their academic staff are almost entirely made up of Congolese people. However, despite its growth, the higher-education system has been confronted with unprecedented financial, political, social, academic and organizational challenges in the last two or three decades because of the country's political and economic instability. Although postgraduate education has not yet been at the center of much public debate, it is unequivocally one of the greatest challenges confronting the higher-education system in the nation.

In the last few years, there has been an increasing concern that postgraduate training in African institutions of higher education is in crisis (Tettey, 2009). This crisis has several dimensions: the small size of the postgraduate training sector, lack of resources for training the next generation of academics, shortage of qualified academic staff in African institutions, low postgraduate completion rates, and the overall erosion of the quality of higher education, among others. The DRC's postgraduate education sector faces these issues and more, given the severe political and economic situations that have crippled academic institutions for many years.

The DRC has a small postgraduate education system. (The term "postgraduate" is used to designate education beyond the undergraduate level.) Historically, postgraduate training has been organized by the country's three main public universities (the University of Kinshasa, the University of Lubumbashi and the University of Kisangani), where about 10 percent of the students are enrolled at the postgraduate level, with the University of Kinshasa alone accounting for over 90 percent of postgraduate students (computed from SARUA, 2009).

Lack of capacity, specifically the small number of faculty members who are qualified to train the next generation of scholars, is a major reason for the small postgraduate training system. The World Bank (2005) estimates suggest that, in the DRC, only 17 percent (1,330 out of 7,899) of members of the academic and research staff have a professorial rank (which requires a doctoral degree). In addition, compensation for university instructors is less than adequate, and faculty members must work at more than one institution, or take extra positions in industry or government, in order to survive.

If the shortage of qualified faculty helps to explain the small size of postgraduate education, the converse is also true. The DRC produces very few doctoral degrees locally. Many faculty members with doctoral degrees pursued all or part of their postgraduate training abroad. Moreover, loss of doctorally trained faculty members to retirement, brain drain and even high mortality rates raises concerns about the risk of extinction of the professorial staff in some universities (Ngondo a Pitshandenge, 2005).

Postgraduate training, known as the "Third Cycle" (*le Troisième Cycle*), typically has two levels. The first leads to an advanced degree, *Diplôme d'Etudes Approfondies* or *Diplôme d'Etude Supérieures*, commonly known as DEA or DES (or its equivalent in medical fields). At this level, the program consists of courses and seminars, some of which (including psychology, pedagogy and foreign languages) are prescribed for all candidates regardless of their field of study, and completion of a thesis. For teaching and research staff at the university, promotion to the rank of *Chef de Travaux* (a rank immediately below that of a doctoral-degree holder), requires not only completion of the first postgraduate level but also the publication of a minimum of two articles. This rank is required of all teaching or research staff at the university who wish to pursue a doctorate.

Although admission to the DEA/DES level is open to all students with a *Licence* (equivalent to the bachelor's degree) from an accredited institution, students who enroll at this level have historically tended to be members of the academic or research personnel at the institutional level. Admissions criteria are less stringent for individuals already employed by the university, given that universities recruit the top students in their graduating classes at undergraduate level, as junior lecturers, than they are for individuals outside the university system.

The second level of postgraduate education leads to a doctoral degree. The program, which is research- rather than course-based, consists of the preparation of a doctoral dissertation under the supervision of a group of faculty members from the student's area of study and from other disciplines. According to Felix Ulombe Kaputu, who earned his doctorate from the University of Lubumbashi and taught there for many years before pursuing his scholarly career in the United States and Japan, the ideal doctoral candidate is "self-motivated, hard-working, innovative, communicative, challenging existing lines" and, to some extent, a "disciple of the master [i.e., faculty supervisor]" (Felix Ulombe Kaputu, personal communication, December 6, 2009).

Postgraduate training in the DRC is confronted by significant challenges. Financial support is largely a matter of individual responsibility, as the government does not typically provide research or training grants for postgraduate education. Lack of adequate institutional infrastructures, such as libraries and research labs, poses a serious challenge. For instance, in a survey of various higher-education stakeholders at the University of Lubumbashi, Dibwe dia Mwembu (2003) found that 92 percent believed that university libraries and labs were inadequate for scientific research. Access to technology, particularly to computers and to the Internet is very limited in a country where essentially 0 percent of the population owns a personal computer and 0.1 percent has an Internet subscription (World Bank, 2009). These issues negatively impact the quality of higher education in general and postgraduate education in particular.

Although challenges in the Congolese higher-education system may be daunting, this country—with its incredible natural resources as well as significant social, economic and environmental challenges—presents opportunities for international research collaborations. It is useful for potential international collaborators to be aware of certain issues. First, the shortage of individuals with postgraduate training in Congolese higher education and the scarcity of information about the higher-education system might make it difficult for international researchers to identify potential Congolese collaborators. Second, inadequate access to technologies, research equipment, and library resources imply that potential Congolese collaborators may enter collaboration at a disadvantage. Third, and on the other hand, the fact that postgraduate training in the DRC is increasingly international (due to cooperation with foreign institutions and governments) means that there is a pool of potential Congolese collaborators who are familiar with international research norms and practices. Fourth, in a country where academics face difficult living and work conditions, potential Congolese academics may enter collaborations with some expectations of possible benefits they will derive from the collaboration, such as financial resources, publication, research equipment, special training and personal achievement. Open dialogue around this issue, at the outset of the collaboration, might help to avoid future misunderstandings or disappointments.

Japan (Takehito Kamata)

Since 2004 all Japanese national and public universities have been independent of the national government coordination process, with self-governing systems for management, budget, personnel affairs, and so on. These universities established institution-level boards of directors and created their own management systems under their presidents' leadership. At the same time, Japanese private universities began efforts to reinforce the management structure and promote their unique educational programs and research.

Japanese universities have implemented changes in programs and curricula since 2004. For example, the universities are able to take the initiative in program development and promote unique research areas and activities. At the same time, obtaining research funds has become more competitive among the universities.

In the field of natural sciences, the koza is the smallest unit of the academic research system in universities. The koza is a group headed by a professor who has primary control and authority over an associate professor, assistants and graduate students (Coleman, 1999). The professor is in charge of the laboratory and leads the koza. Members of the koza system observe the seniority-based hierarchical structure, in which the professor's authority is strong. The graduate students in the koza system are expected to understand the hierarchical structure and maintain harmony among the members—key factors to achieving a successful graduate-student life in the koza.

In the koza system, students learn research skills, engage in research and complete a thesis or dissertation. Once the students join a koza, they usually do not switch to another koza during their doctorate program. They are expected to work closely with other members of the koza and engage in research activities under one professor's leadership. Maintaining harmony in the koza is the most essential skill fostered through research activities, and maintaining harmony with a professor is the primary discipline for Japanese graduate students. The students are not supposed to provide critical comments on research topics or engage in academic debates with senior scholars. Instead, students are expected to listen to the professor's advice and follow his guidance. Students in the doctoral programs do not have formal training in the ethics of research activities.

One of the unique aspects of the koza system can be observed in requests for funding. Young researchers and students are expected to put their advisor's name on the application form when they apply for competitive research funds (Sawa, Terasawa & Inoue, 2005). Sharing research-achievement credit with a professor is quite important in order to maintain harmony in the koza system, and members in the koza are dependent on the professor's authority. There is a relationship of trust between a student and a professor in Japan.

Students in the koza system also need to consider their postgraduate careers. After completing doctoral programs, graduates seek careers in private corporations, universities and research institutions. Professors are in charge of finding careers for their graduates. When students apply for jobs, the most critical factor is a professor's support.

Japanese students must pay their own tuition for their programs; however, there are special situations that may make it possible to obtain tuition exemption or tuition reduction. The Japan Student Services Organization offers scholarships to Japanese students; these scholarships also support Japanese students in doctoral programs. In addition, universities have their own scholarship opportunities for students in their doctorate courses.

Promoting and enhancing international research activities have become top priorities within the Japanese national universities. Yonezawa, Akiba and Hirouchi explain the national universities' research efforts this way: "National universities tend to focus on internationalization in research, keeping a more active presence and competitiveness in the global academic community" (Yonezawa, Akiba & Hirouchi, 2009, pp. 139–140).

The Japanese language is an ongoing issue for international research collaborations. Almost all programs in Japanese universities are offered in the Japanese language. Although writing and communication in English are common in the natural sciences, Japanese students have not typically gained these skills through undergraduate and graduate education. Coleman notes that the Japanese language is "Japan's most formidable barrier to international cooperation and completion in science" (Coleman, 1999, p. 183). This challenge prevents graduate students from joining and promoting discussion and other communication with students and scholars from other nations. In international collaborative research, Japanese scholars typically avoid sharing critical comments with other scholars and do not actively join discussions. They regard maintaining harmony in a group as the top priority throughout the research process.

Foreign scholars may not understand these customs engrained in the koza culture or the language issues. Thus, they misinterpret Japanese scholars' research attitudes and involvement as passive. In contrast, foreign scholars welcome and respect critical comments and active discussion from different perspectives on research subjects, methods, processes and conclusions. The organizational communication skills and cultural practices learned in the koza system and the lack of linguistic experience constitute significant barriers for Japanese scholars when communicating with foreign scholars in international research collaborations.

Poland (Marta A. Shaw)

Graduate education in Poland has a long and reputable tradition. The Jagiellonian University in Cracow, the second oldest institution of higher learning in Central Europe, granted its first doctoral degrees as far back as the fifteenth century. The Polish system of higher education is based on the German model and features a strong tradition of individual research.

Doctoral education in Poland is currently in a period of significant transition. Before 1989 there were relatively few doctoral programs, and the academic job market was easily able to absorb graduates, even to the point where it was quite typical for universities to employ young academics before they obtained their doctoral degrees (Kwiek, 2003). Since the political transformation of 1989, the popularity of doctoral programs has increased dramatically for reasons related to the volatile job market, a high graduate unemployment rate and the relative attractiveness of an academic career (Krasniewski, 2008). Also, the government introduced a new funding formula that provided strong incentives for higher-education institutions to offer doctoral programs, leading to a dramatic increase in the number of graduate students, from fewer than 2,700 in 1990 to over 30,000 in 2008 (Central Statistical Office, 2008). With a stable number of academic positions, young academics have faced enormous competition. Since only a fraction of them have been able to secure jobs in academia, many have had to seek employment elsewhere, often in other countries where the demand for holders of advanced degrees is greater. The majority of doctoral programs have yet to respond to these changing dynamics. So far, the process and content of graduate education continue to be based on the assumption that all students are being prepared for academic careers (Juchacz & Kwiek, 2007).

Unlike in many European countries, an academic career in Poland involves the attainment of two academic degrees: Doktor (or Doctor of Philosophy) and Doktor Habilitowany (or Doctor Habilitatus). There are two paths to obtaining a Doctor of Philosophy degree. A candidate can either enroll in a formal course of study or conduct independent research under the supervision of a senior faculty member. Polish law on higher education does not require students to complete a sequence of classes before beginning their research, and leaves open the possibility of obtaining a PhD without completing a formal study program (Law on Higher Education, 2005). Whether enrolled in a formal program or not, Polish doctoral students take very few classes and restrict their focus almost entirely to research. As a result, they are likely to assume considerable responsibility for their own experience in graduate school and conduct their research very independently. They are often forced to be strategically inventive in coping with constraints such as insufficient access to data, inadequate facilities and limited funding. Students travel abroad to use better libraries, rely on informal networks for information and support, and deal frugally with the resources they do have, learning how to make a little go a long way. In their efforts, they are usually left to their own devices and the help of an academic advisor.

The majority of funding for doctoral students in Poland comes from the state budget, and state institutions do not charge tuition for full-time students. Except in a few disciplines, most notably medicine, students do not generally get many opportunities to participate in collaborative research with professors or peers, and it is seldom the case that funding for graduate students is associated with any kind of research activity. The entire system values and encourages individual contributions, so professors are less likely than elsewhere to invite students' participation in grants or research projects. There are, however, numerous grants and scholarships funded by the European Union that are available exclusively to students, and participation in any such program greatly enhances a student's academic and employment prospects. International internships are also very popular among Polish graduate students.

The requirement of a second academic degree, the Doctor Habilitatus, is perhaps the most distinctive feature of the Polish system of graduate education. Prior to obtaining this degree, academics cannot supervise Master's or PhD students, review dissertations, vote or chair organizational units of departments (Act on Academic Degrees and Title, 2003). Habilitation opens up the possibility of becoming a senior faculty member and receiving the academic title of "Professor."

In order to receive the degree, a candidate must already have a PhD and substantial scientific or artistic accomplishments. They must also submit a habilitation dissertation that makes a significant contribution to the disciplinary field. The dissertation may consist of a series of publications on a single topic or, in some cases, a scientific or artistic project. The primary criterion, however, is that it must contribute significantly to the development of the candidate's scholarly discipline. The need to obtain a second advanced degree channels the scholarly activities of young academics in one direction and limits their pursuit of other interests until they receive the Doctor Habilitatus degree. Junior faculty members at higher-education institutions are expected to complete the habilitation process within 8–10 years of obtaining a PhD, and failure to do so may result in their dismissal. Because the awarding of the Doctor Habilitatus degree is based on peer review, the flexibility of junior faculty members in Poland varies greatly depending on the character of their immediate academic community.

Since Poland joined the Bologna Accord in 1999, the Doctor Habilitatus degree has been a centerpiece of controversy in discussions about the reform of Polish higher education (Majcher, 2008). Given the pressures of European harmonization, a few successive governments have considered eliminating the degree and thus shortening the course to an academic career in Poland. The argument is that the degree is a relic of the past that hinders the productivity and creativity of Polish scientists at a stage of their careers when their potential is the greatest, preserves excessive power in academic communities, and creates bottlenecks in the development of academic staff for the growing systems of higher education. Those who defend the Doctor Habilitatus, however, see it as a vital tradition in Polish higher education that safeguards the high standards required of senior academic staff.

The requirement for a second academic degree has significant implications for the involvement of junior academics in international research collaborations. The emphasis on focused and individual research places Polish scientists at somewhat of a disadvantage in developing collaborative projects. International projects may enhance scholarly prestige for some, but, for others, research activity that is not directly related to the subject of the Doctor Habilitatus dissertation may prove to be a hindrance in their academic career. Junior faculty must balance their own interests with the concerns and expectations of the communities that ultimately determine their academic fate. In international collaborations, these pressures may make researchers reluctant to pursue agendas considered to be controversial or to publish findings that may not find favor with immediate superiors.

The past legacy of Polish science and its relative inexperience in dealing with many ethical issues inherent in a free-market economy, particularly those surrounding partnerships between academy and industry, create distinctive challenges for international collaborations. The legacy of the previous political era is also perceived by some to shape key generational differences in how academics approach the opportunities and constraints inherent in the research system. In the previous political milieu, the researchers who were able to accomplish their goals were often those who found ways to play a difficult and sometimes hostile system. The ability to successfully subvert the bureaucratic structures of the Communist state was often considered a virtue, even if not by most, then certainly by many intellectuals. In the perception of some faculty members in Poland interviewed for this chapter, the tradition of playing the system continues to be a factor in Polish science, particularly in instances where policies affecting researchers are seen as unjust or counterproductive. The majority of difficulties in international research collaborations are thus likely to stem from diverse definitions of what constitutes ethical behavior, and different experiences with structures aimed at protecting research integrity. In practice, collaboration with scientists accustomed to the existence of a significant gray zone of contextually defined ethics requires clear and open communication of common rules and role boundaries. Successful cooperation will require a clear basis of understanding and communication from the earliest stages of collaborative efforts.

Brazil (Sonia Vasconcelos and Martha Sorenson)

The potential for knowledge production and technological transfer in Brazil is enormous. The country now has more than 80,000 PhDs, among which more than 35,000 are thesis supervisors. The accelerating rate at which PhD degrees are being awarded means that Brazilian researchers and scholars will grow in comparison with the international academic community (De Meis, Arruda & Guimarães, 2007). The Action Plan of the Brazilian Ministry for Science and Technology has the clear goal of making the Brazilian system of science, technology and innovation highly competitive.

Brazilian graduate programs are distributed among public and private universities and federal institutes (Steiner, 2007, p. 176), although doctoral training is carried out mainly in the federal and state universities. Among the distinctive features of graduate programs in Brazil is strong federal control. All graduate programs receive their credentials from a federal funding agency, Coordination for the Advancement of Higher Education Personnel (CAPES). Also, every graduate program is linked to an undergraduate research program run by the universities. Federal agencies provide beginning students with small fellowships and they serve as a continuous source of new graduate students.

A feature that serves to emphasize the high priority assigned to scientists' teaching obligations is that applications for the major competitive grants are often limited to faculty members who are accredited as thesis advisors in the higher-ranking graduate programs. For a graduate program to receive a maximum score from CAPES, publication in international journals, especially papers co-authored by graduate students, is of particular importance. To increase students' international visibility in their thesis projects, doctoral students are encouraged to submit at least one manuscript to an English-language, peer-reviewed international journal prior to their thesis defense (Vasconcelos, Sorenson & Leta, 2009b). International collaborations have a fundamental role in today's knowledge economy, particularly as a crucial driving force for students' mobility. The Erasmus Mundus Program, in which Brazil participates, is a mobility program with the clear aim of internationalizing European higher education, and international collaborations within and outside Europe comprise an important part of its scope. The Brazilian Ministry for Science and Technology has made an effort to promote collaborative projects, especially in engineering and emerging technologies. The U.S.–Brazil Higher Education Consortium Program (2006–2009) is another initiative that fosters students' mobility and exchange programs.

International partnerships have linguistic and ethical features that are not always acknowledged or identified. What is seen in Brazil is that young researchers lag behind E.U. colleagues, for example, in writing manuscripts and communicating face-to-face. In stark contrast with graduate programs in Brazil, graduate training in many E.U. universities stimulates the acquisition of English and other languages (Commission of the European Communities, 2007). In most graduate programs in Brazil, linguistic ability is taken for granted and its importance is underestimated by policy-makers (Meneghini & Packer, 2007; Vasconcelos, Sorenson, Leta, Sant'ana & Batista, 2008; Hermes-Lima, Polcheira, Trigueiro & Beleboni, 2008).

We should note, however, that many international collaborative works are expected to result in publications in English-language international journals. Currently, most Brazilian graduate programs do not have formal policies to support students' work for publication. Also, plagiarism has not received the attention it merits in Brazilian universities. In a recent meeting of the American Chemical Society (2009), George Bodner, from the Society's Ethical Committee, reported that confusion about what constitutes plagiarism among graduate students is widespread. In Brazil, focus-group interviews suggest that the concept of textual plagiarism, in particular, is blurry even among some senior scientists (Vasconcelos, Leta, Costa, Pinto & Sorenson, 2009a).

Confusion about the limits of textual borrowing and appropriate paraphrasing is not peculiar to Brazilian scientists, as this problem has been noted for researchers from other countries (Garbisu & Alcorta, 2003; *Nature*, 2007). What should be noted for Brazil is that this "confusion" has not been systematically addressed in graduate programs. This situation may have detrimental effects on international collaborative projects involving young Brazilian scientists.

Overall, these particular features can prevent Brazilian graduate students from taking full advantage of available bilateral exchange programs, with the result that the benefits of these international collaborations may be distributed unevenly between the two parties.

Another important contrast is in the approach to ethics and research integrity. Research ethics occupy only a minor place in most graduate education curricula. The Brazilian Bioethics Society (SBB) was founded in 1995, and has since tried to promote bioethics training in graduate biomedical programs. However, bioethics training in Brazil has many challenges to meet when it comes to graduate education. There are initiatives to raise awareness of the need to provide training in ethical concepts, but at this point it seems evident that Brazilian graduate students cooperating with colleagues from developed countries need to be better prepared to discuss how to share research protocols, data and ideas. For them to develop their own voice in ethical approaches, it is fundamental that Brazilian doctoral students have their own ethical standards clearly in mind. This is a relevant point, especially if we assume that in cross-cultural collaborations a balanced dialogue based on particular cultural and moral perceptions of particular issues, such as individual rights and justice should be established (Marshall, 2005; Chattopadhyay & De Vries, 2008). Otherwise, the ethics of collaboration itself in a multicultural context will not play any role in these collaborative works (Subedi & Rhee, 2008). International collaborations between researchers who have different views and expectations about research and publication ethics can easily lead to awkward misunderstandings. Cross-cultural problems in international collaborations have been discussed at length elsewhere (Global Science Forum, n.d.; *Nature*, 2008), and they should not be assumed to be irrelevant in the Brazilian scientific community.

As a final remark, Brazil has much to gain and much to offer based on the participation of graduate students in cross-cultural collaborations.

United States (Christine C. Lepkowski and Melissa S. Anderson)

The U.S. system of graduate education is extensive in scope. According to the Carnegie Foundation for the Advancement of Teaching (2009), 413 institutions offer doctoral programs in the United States. In 2008 these institutions awarded 48,802 research doctoral degrees, 32,827 of which were in science and engineering (Fiegener, 2009). As a scholar of the graduate-education system has written, "By cross-national standards, this country has the largest, most decentralized, and most highly differentiated set of arrangements for advanced education" (Gumport, 2005, p. 428).

The federal government has two primary roles in U.S. graduate education. As the major funders of academic science, various federal agencies support doctoral students indirectly through grants awarded to students' advisors. This system places significant responsibility for the financial support of doctoral students on their supervisors, who serve as principal investigators of competitively awarded funding. Federal support is also provided to some doctoral students through training grants awarded directly to the students or to their institutions. In their regulatory role, government agencies also impose requirements on doctoral programs, such as the recently enacted requirement that all doctoral students (and others) supported by funding from the National Science Foundation must be provided training in the responsible conduct of research.

As a system, graduate education in the United States has three distinctive features. The first is openness. Nationwide there are many doctoral programs, and they collectively admit large numbers of students. A commitment to educational opportunity that characterizes much of U.S. higher education extends to many graduate programs as well. Students can and do frequently apply to many graduate programs in an effort to find the best match for their own interests and goals.

Second, the system is driven by competition. Like their counterparts worldwide, doctoral students work for the break-throughs and publications that signal achievement in science. To this general form of competitive effort are added more specific types associated with the U.S. system. The general openness of graduate programs means that many more doctoral students are trained than can be employed in academic research. As most doctoral programs are still oriented largely to careers in academic research, there is significant competition for university positions. Doctoral students in the sciences recognize that, in order to be considered for faculty or research positions, they will likely need to complete several years of post-doctoral training with substantial output of publications. They also know that, in many cases, their futures will depend on their ability to secure funding through the same competitive federal grant system that their advisors participate in. They learn to respond nimbly to notices of new funding initiatives.

Third, the U.S. system is characterized by rather elaborate structural support. Most doctoral programs exist within the institutional framework of a graduate school, which oversees programmatic and curricular changes, assesses programs and awards the doctoral degree. The student–advisor dyad is therefore embedded in layers of institutional policy and oversight. This structure imposes, to some extent, standardization of doctoral degree programs across disciplinary fields.

Beyond these systemic features, U.S. doctoral education evidences a rather distinctive set of expectations. Students commonly engage in open debates, challenge existing assumptions, aim for innovative ideas and approaches and participate as partners in research projects. There are exceptions to this general mode of conduct—in hierarchically driven labs or highly controlled projects—but, for the most part, the U.S. system encourages individual achievement and an open, even assertive, stance in doctoral education.

The distinctive features of doctoral education in the United States have implications for international collaborations in research. The openness and competition characteristic of the system can foster modes of interaction that may be seen as inappropriate in some other national contexts. Students who are accustomed to freely taking the initiative to contact any scientist at any level of the hierarchy may cause offense in a system whose norms require persons of like rank to interact. In some cases, U.S. students' competitive urgency, driven by their awareness of the need for an edge in the grant system, may conflict with a more deliberate approach taken by scientists whose national systems provide stable support. Students who are well-acquainted with U.S.-specific standards and regulations on scientific integrity may not be adept in navigating the subtleties of applying and interpreting such standards in different cultural contexts.

Conclusion

International science serves as a basic reference point for many young researchers. They think in international terms, and, for many, doctoral training itself is international—that is, carried out at least in part in another country. They are attuned to international standards of research, publication, measures of quality, opportunities, research agendas and "hot" areas of research. Their travels and exposure to other research systems make them familiar with how research is done, how funding is provided, how integrity is (or is not) maintained, and how expectations are translated into standards and procedures in other countries. In short, young scientists are agents of international cooperative research.

Still, their core doctoral experiences imprint them with different assumptions about what matters most in their work, how people should behave, what counts most in pursuing scientific achievement, and what career mistakes they should avoid. Such assumptions can shape the ways in which they work with scientists in the international context, as students or later as colleagues.

Those who initiate collaborative projects should be attuned to the influence of ingrained assumptions derived from different graduate training and should openly address problems that they think might stem from such differences. It takes time and effort to pay deliberate attention to core assumptions about how work should be done and anticipate resulting challenges to cross-national projects. Not doing so, however, can lead to frustration, misunderstanding, stalled progress or derailed initiatives. The benefits are well worth the investment of time and attention.

Note

1. Authors Chiteng Kot through Vasconcelos contributed equally to this chapter and are listed in alphabetical order.

References

ACS (The American Chemical Society). (2009). *Confusion, not cheating, major factor in plagiarism among some students*. Retrieved from http://portal.acs.org/portal/acs/corg/content.
Brazilian Bioethics Society (SBB). (n.d.). Retrieved from www.sbbioetica.org.br.
Carnegie Foundation for the Advancement of Teaching. (2009). *Graduate instructional program classification: Distribution of institutions and enrollments by classification category*. Stanford, CA: Carnegie Foundation for the Advancement of Teaching. Retrieved from http://classifications.carnegiefoundation.org/summary/grad_prog.php.
Central Statistical Office (2008). *Higher education institutions and their finances in 2008*. Warsaw: Central Statistical Office.
Chattopadhyay, S., & De Vries, R. (2008). Bioethical concerns are global, bioethics is Western. *Journal of Asian International Bioethics, 18*(4), 106–109.
Coleman, S. (1999). *Japanese science: From the inside*. New York, NY: Routledge.
Commission of the European Communities. (2007). *Framework for the European survey on language competences*. Retrieved from http://ec.europa.eu/education/policies/2010/doc/com184_en.pdf.
Coordination for the Advancement of Higher Education Personnel (CAPES). Retrieved from www.capes.gov.br.

De Meis, L., Arruda, A. P., & Guimarães, J. A. (2007). The impact of science in Brazil. *IUBMB Life, 59,* 227–234.

De Witt, N. (1961). *Education and professional employment in the U.S.S.R.* Washington, DC: United States Government Printing Office.

Dibwe dia Mwembu, D. (2003). *Le rôle social de l'Université de Lubumbashi* [The University of Lubumbashi's social function]. Retrieved June 6, 2005, from www.ssrc.org/programs/africa/publications/Chapter1.pdf.

Erasmus Mundus Program. (n.d.). Retrieved from http://ec.europa.eu/education/external-relation-programmes/doc72_en.htm.

Fiegener, M. K. (2009, November). Numbers of U.S. doctorates awarded rise for sixth year, but growth slower. *InfoBrief,* NSF 10-308. Arlington, VA: National Science Foundation.

Garbisu, C., & Alcorta, I. (2003). Plagiarism or plain survival? *The Scientist, 17,* 10.

Global Science Forum. (n.d.) Retrieved December 12, 2009, from http://www.oecd.org/departme nt/0,335,en_2649_34319_1_1_1_1_1,00.htm/

Gumport, P. J. (2005). Graduate education and research: Interdependence and strain. In P. G. Altbach, R. O. Berdahl, & P. J. Gumport (Eds.), *American higher education in the twenty-first century: Social, political, and economic challenges.* Baltimore, MD: Johns Hopkins University Press.

Hermes-Lima, M., Polcheira, C., Trigueiro, M., & Beleboni, O. (2008). Perceptions of Latin American scientists about science and post-graduate education: Introduction. *CBP-Latin America Comparative Biochemistry and Physiology—Part A: Molecular & Integrative Physiology, 151*(3), 263–271.

Jin, B., & Rousseau, R. (2005). *China's quantitative expansion phase: Exponential growth but low impact.* Paper presented at the 10th International Conference of the International Society for Scientometrics and Information.

Juchacz, P. W., & Kwiek, M. (2007). Doctoral education in Poland. In S. Powell & H. Green (Eds.), *The doctorate worldwide* (pp. 77–87). Maidenhead: Open University Press.

Krasniewski, A. (2008). Transformation of doctoral training in Poland. *Higher Education in Europe, 33*(1), 125–138.

Kwiek, M. (2003). Academe in transition: Transformations in the Polish academic profession. *Higher Education, 45*(4), 455.

Li, P. (2008). Woguo boshisheng peiyang jishi youhua: Zhaosheng zhidu yu kecheng shezhi de shijiao [Enhancing Chinese doctoral training system: Admission and curriculum aspects]. *Zhongguo Gaojiao Yanjiu* [Chinese higher education research], *10,* 26–29.

Lindquist, C. B., & Rokitiansky, N. J. (1963). Graduate education in the U.S.S.R.: Contrasts with advanced study in the U.S. *The Journal of Higher Education, 34*(2), 73–84.

Majcher, A. (2008). The battle over professorship: Reform of human resource management and academic careers in a comparative perspective. *Higher Education Policy, 21*(3), 345–358.

Marshall, P. A. (2005). Human rights, cultural pluralism, and international health research. *Theoretical Medicine and Bioethics, 26*(6), 529–557.

Meneghini, R., & Packer, A. (2007). Is there science beyond English? Initiatives to increase the quality and visibility of non-English publications might help to break down language barriers in scientific communication. *EMBO Reports, 8,* 112–116.

Ministry of Education and Science of the Republic of Kazakhstan. (2008). *Государственный Общеобразовательный Стандарт Образования Республики Казахстан: Послевузовское Образование, Докторантура.* ГОСО РК 5.04.034-2008, Retrieved December 5, 2009, from www.edu.gov.kz/fileadmin/user_upload/2009./GOSO_dok_6_05_08.doc.

Ministry of Education China. (2002a). *Jiaoyu 50nian dashiji (1960nian–1969nian)* [Education 50-year memorabilia (1960–1969)]. Retrieved December 1, 2009, from www.moe.gov.cn/edoas/website18/85/info4985.htm.

Ministry of Education China. (2002b). *Jiaoyu 50nian dashiji (1980nian–1989nian)* [Education 50-year memorabilia (1980–1989)]. Retrieved December 1, 2009, from www.moe.gov.cn/edoas/website18/87/info4987.htm.

Ministry of Education China. (2002c). *Jiaoyu 50nian dashiji (1990nian–1999nian)* [Education 50-year memorabilia (1990–1999)]. Retrieved December 1, 2009, from www.moe.gov.cn/edoas/website18/89/info4989.htm.

Ministry of Education China. (2008). *China education yearbook 2008.* Beijing: Renmin jiaoyu chubanshe [People's Education Press].

Ministry of Education China. (2009). *Percentage of academics with overseas-study experiences taking prominent positions in the education and science sectors.* Retrieved December 3,

2009, from www.moe.edu.cn/edoas/website18/level3.jsp?tablename=1256021701783630&i nfoid=1256174071845262.

Ministry of Science and Technology. (2007–2010). *Action plan*. Retrieved from www.mct.gov.br/ upd_blob/0021/21432.pdf.

National Health Council (CNS). (n.d.). Available at www.conselho.saude.gov.br.

Nature (2007). Plagiarism? No, we're just borrowing better English. *Nature, 449*, 658.

Nature (2008). The path to productive partnerships. *Nature, 452*, 665.

Ngondo a Pitshandenge, S. (2005). L'Université congolaise à la croisée des chemins: Vers l'extinction du corps professoral de l'Université de Kinshasa [The Congolese university at the crossroad: Towards the extinction of the professorial staff at the University of Kinshasa]. *Journal of Higher Education in Africa, 3*(2), 101–110.

OECD Global Science Forum. (n.d.). Retrieved from www.oecd.org/department/0,3355,en_2649 _34319_1_1_1_1_1,00.html.

OECD, & EBRP/The World Bank. (2007). *Reviews of national policies for education: Higher education in Kazakhstan*. Paris: OECD Publishing.

SARUA (Southern African Regional Universities Association). (2009). *A guide to the public universities of Southern Africa*. Wits, South Africa: SARUA.

Sawa, A., Terasawa, T., & Inoue, S. (2005). *Kyousou ni katsu daigaku* [Toward the restructuring of the science and technology system in Japan]. Tokyo: Toyo Keizai Shimpousha. (In Japanese.)

Smolentseva, A. (2003). Challenges to the Russian academic profession. *Higher Education, 45*(4), 391–424.

Steiner, J. E. (2007). The Brazilian research universities. In P. G. Altbach & J. Balan (Eds.), *World-class worldwide: Transforming research universities in Asia and Latin America* (pp. 173–188). Baltimore, MD: Johns Hopkins University Press.

Subedi, B., & Rhee, J. (2008). Negotiating collaboration across differences. *Qualitative Inquiry, 14*/6.

Tettey, W. J. (2009). Postgraduate studies in Africa: The looming crisis. *International Higher Education, 54*. Retrieved from www.bc.edu/bc_org/avp/soe/cihe/newsletter/Number57/p13_ Tettey.htm.

U.S.–Brazil Higher Education Consortium Program (2006–2009). Retrieved from www.ed.gov/ programs/fipsebrazil.

Vasconcelos, S. M. R., Leta, J., Costa, L., Pinto, A., & Sorenson, M. M. (2009a). Discussing plagiarism in Latin American science: Brazilian researchers begin to address an ethical issue. *EMBO Reports, 10*, 677–682.

Vasconcelos, S. M. R., Sorenson, M. M., & Leta, J. (2009b). A new indicator for the assessment of science and technology research?. *Scientometrics, 80*(1), 217–230.

Vasconcelos, S. M. R, Sorenson, M. M., Leta, J., Sant'ana, M. C., & Batista, P. D. (2008). Researchers' writing competence: A bottleneck in the publication of Latin American Science? *EMBO Reports, 9*(8), 700–702.

Wang, L. (2005). Yingxiang boshisheng jiaoyu chuangxin de jidui maodun [Issues impacting doctoral education]. *Zhongguo Gaodeng Jiaoyun* [China Higher Education], *13*(14), 33–34.

Wang, W. (2008). Woguo woshisheng peiyang xianzhuang-jiyu sisuo gaodeng xuexiao de diaocha [Chinese doctoral training status: Based on investigation about four colleges and universities]. *Daxue. Yanjiu yu Pingjia* [Higher Education Research and Evaluation], *11*, 42–48.

Wilsdon, J., & Keeley, J. (2007). *China: The next science superpower?* London: Demos.

World Bank. (2005). *Education in the Democratic Republic of Congo: Priorities and options for regeneration*. Washington, DC: World Bank.

World Bank. (2009). *ICT at a glance*. Retrieved December 4, 2009, from http://web.worldbank. org/WBSITE/EXTERNAL/DATASTATISTICS/0,,contentMDK:20459133~menuPK:1192 714~pagePK:64133150~piPK:64133175~theSitePK:239419,00.html.

Yonezawa, A., Akiba, H., & Hirouchi, D. (2009). Japanese university leaders' perceptions of internationalization. *Journal of Studies in International Education, 13*(2), 125–142.

Zhao, Y. (2008). W daxue boshi peyang cunzai de wenti yu gaijin duice [Issues of doctoral training at W University and strategies for improvement]. *Dangdai Jiaoyu Kexue* [Modern Education Science], *15*, 12–16.

Zhou, P., & Leydesdorff, L. (2006). The emergence of China as a leading nation in science. *Research Policy, 35*(1), 83–104.

14

The Emergence of International Postdoctoral Training

John B. Godfrey

Globalization is re-shaping networks that organize and integrate science and engineering research, and the functions that research universities play within these networks. Complex research problems outstrip the capacity of even the best-funded institutions. Rising costs are driving adaptation as institutions seek participation in distributed arrangements and partnerships. Faculty research is located along transnational pathways and supported by collaborations and shared funding arrangements that must negotiate not only different legal and regulatory environments, but the often-bewildering diversity of institutional cultures in the universities and other organizations that participate in these networks. Globalization poses new risks and opportunities for every research university. The moment is transitional, and the outcome uncertain. Frameworks for global research are emergent, and protocols of collaboration and competition are unresolved. Overhead costs are high for universities, but opportunity costs for delaying entry may be far higher. Viewed through a different frame, however, the continued development of advanced global research rests on its workforce, particularly on the mobility and entrepreneurship of highly talented early-stage scientists and scholars. These mobile postdoctoral researchers move to leading centers around the world to find opportunities to work with senior investigators in state-of-the-art facilities in order to lay the groundwork for their careers (Adams & Wilsdon, 2006; UNESCO Institute for Statistics, 2009). It is the mobility of these postdoctoral researchers that helps build and sustain the productivity of the global research enterprise.

The first pulse of this global movement came nearly a century ago when it was recognized that talented and ambitious young U.S. researchers could benefit from exposure to the centers of science in Europe. Leading universities faced a shortage of leading research scientists who could help the U.S. catch up with Europe. Few institutions had such talent within their own ranks. The development of the research-based doctorate and the postdoctoral fellowship were innovations to meet the calls to improve national standing in science and advanced research. Postdoctoral training allowed promising young researchers to spend a year or two working in a well-equipped laboratory under the tutelage of a senior scientist, free from other commitments. From the outset, this advanced training was an international undertaking, as postdoctoral fellowships sent Americans abroad and brought talented young researchers to the United States. The circulation of gifted and ambitious postdoctoral researchers among universities and research centers in the United States and Europe foreshadowed the closer global linkages and collaborations that have arisen with such speed among universities in the twenty-first century.

The idea of the postdoctoral fellowship emerged during World War I, when the National Research Council (NRC) came to grips with the problem that the research capacity of the United States badly lagged behind that of Europe (Assmus, 1993). The NRC concluded that doctoral education was not closing this deficit. Tensions between the teaching and research missions of the university had become acute with the growth of graduate education in the pre-war period. Critics charged that the rapid expansion of doctoral education diluted talent, with many students engaged in merely repetitive technical work. Further, most universities were ill-equipped and faculty were insufficiently experienced themselves to mentor young researchers. Doctoral students and freshly appointed young faculty spent too much time teaching and too little in the laboratory (Hawkins, 1979). In 1910 the president of the Carnegie Foundation for the Advancement of Teaching noted that "in many institutions, the creation of a graduate school has practically put an end to research," and that while the interest in research had grown in American colleges, this growth "was in no such proportion as the graduate school has grown, and the growth of one has had too little to do with the growth of the other" (Curtis, 1969, p. 8).

In 1919 the NRC created the first postdoctoral research fellowships as a mechanism for identifying and supporting promising young scientists at the start of their research careers. The NRC also sought to stimulate a greater commitment to research within the leading universities that hosted these predoctoral fellows (Curtis, 1969; Rand, 1951). The first fellowships were awarded in physics and chemistry, followed by additional awards in the medical and biological sciences. The postdoctoral fellowship helped give birth to a second innovation: the formation of the research group. Postdoctorates took on the role of day-to-day management of laboratories of leading scientists, helped train doctoral students in the laboratory and research skills, and freed the senior scientist to pursue funding and to supervise the ideas that channeled the daily operations of the group (Etzkowitz, 1992).

The postdoctoral fellowship begot a third innovation, as many of the most talented of the first generation of postdoctoral fellows traveled to leading centers in England, Germany and elsewhere in Europe for research training.[1] The NRC provided a number of international fellowships in its first several years, but it was the Rockefeller Foundation's International Education Board (IEB), established in 1923, that became the primary funder for the development of international postdoctoral research and training.[2] In its brief history, the IEB built the first scaffold for the international mobility of scientific research (Curtis, 1969; Gray, 1941; Kohler, 1985). The IEB awarded grants to selected European research centers to help them recover from the turmoil of the post-war years, and established a system of postdoctoral fellowships to support the advanced training of talented young U.S. and European scientists at these centers. Between 1924 and 1933 the IEB funded 509 researchers from 35 countries to take postdoctoral appointments in the natural sciences in the United States and Europe.

These postdoctoral fellowships had an immediate impact on U.S. university-based research and doctoral education, and fostered a new degree of international collaboration. Their significance can be seen in the development of the career of David Dennison who, as a new PhD in physics at the University of Michigan in 1924, accepted an IEB award to pursue his research in Europe. A year earlier, Oskar Klein, a colleague of Niels Bohr, had visited Michigan to teach the first advanced courses in the new field of quantum physics. While in Ann Arbor, Klein helped advise Dennison on his research and arranged a visit by Bohr, who, impressed by the quality of Dennison's work, invited him to his new IEB-funded Institute for Physics at Copenhagen. Dennison spent the next three years developing his research and working with leading physicists in Copenhagen, Zurich and Cambridge. In 1927 he returned to Michigan to take up a faculty appointment. He was soon joined by Otto Laporte, George Uhlenbeck and Samuel Goldsmit, highly accomplished theorists he had met in Europe and who formed the University of Michigan's first research group in quantum mechanics. The consequences were far-reaching for U.S. science and physics research: their collaboration led to Michigan's Summer Symposium on Nuclear Physics, which convened leading theorists from around the world in the 1920s and 1930s to work out fundamental problems in quantum mechanics (Coben, 1972; Dennison, 1974; Meyer, Lindsay, Barker, Dennison & Zorn, 1988). The NRC recognized the decisive impact that these investments had made in such a short time, and in 1934 redirected funding to other fields (Rand, 1951).

Dennison's postdoctoral experience had a transformational impact both on his career and the development of theoretical physics in the United States. The IEB and NRC awards presaged the massive growth in postdoctoral training that followed World War II, when federal agencies became the principal funders of postdoctorates to help fuel the rapid expansion of the U.S. science and engineering workforce. In 1946 the National Institutes of Health (NIH) initiated its postdoctoral fellowship and training grant programs, and the National Science Foundation (NSF) followed several years later on a much smaller scale. By 1963 NIH funding supported nearly 7,000 postdoctoral positions, and the NSF funded nearly 250 early-career researchers in the natural and behavioral sciences and engineering (Curtis, 1969). Sources for postdoctoral funding diversified in the following years, and by 1994 federal research grants funded just over half of 36,158 postdoctoral appointments, and non-federal sources funded nearly one-third (NSF, 1994).

The postdoctoral fellow became an essential part of the workforce of the university research enterprise, and such an appointment was soon considered a requisite transitional stage for a research career. The NSF's 2006 *Survey of Doctorate Recipients* showed that 45 percent of persons who had earned U.S. PhDs in science, engineering and health fields within the previous five years followed their degree with one or more postdoctoral positions, an increase of one-third over the 35 percent of SEH degree recipients who had taken up postdoctorates two decades earlier (Hoffer, Grigorian & Hedberg, 2008).

Over the past three decades, growing numbers of non-U.S. citizens have come to the United States for doctoral education. Equally, postdoctoral opportunities in the United States have attracted talent from around the world. These knowledge migrants raised concerns about the impact of a "brain drain" to the United States on scientific and economic development elsewhere in the world (Bekhradnia & Sastry, 2005). The end of the Cold War opened new pathways for young talent to follow ambition across once-closed borders. The United States remains the greatest beneficiary. During the five-year period from 1960 to 1964, non-U.S. citizens with temporary visas received 10.2 percent of PhDs awarded by U.S. institutions in all fields; by 2002–2006, when the number of doctorates awarded had nearly quadrupled from 58,699 to 211,886, this share had increased to 27.8 percent (NSF, 2009; Thurgood, Golladay & Hill, 2006). The growth in the number of postdoctoral fellowships awarded to non-U.S. citizens saw a similar four-fold increase. In 1977 just over 6,000 non-U.S. citizens/non-permanent residents held post-doctoral appointments, comprising about 32 percent of these positions. In 2006, about 28,000 non-U.S. citizens/permanent residents held just over 57 percent of all postdoctoral positions (NSF, 2008).

For many researchers around the world, a postdoctorate in Europe or the United States has become a critical step for early-career development (Committee on Science, Engineering and Public Policy, 2000). The global pull of the U.S. doctorate feeds part of this workforce, as many international students who earn PhDs in the United States opt to stay for a postdoctoral appointment. An NSF survey of Chinese engineering and science students showed that over 30 percent intended to remain in the United States for postdoctoral research (Johnson, 2001). Yet, not surprisingly, 80 years after Dennison's sojourn in Bohr's laboratory, the motivation for a U.S. PhD to look for post-doctoral positions overseas has weakened. New PhDs who are U.S. citizens often are reluctant to move outside the U.S. postdoctoral research network and risk the chances of finding a good job.[3]

Other countries are catching up quickly to the United States, investing in postdoctoral research positions and encouraging the mobility of top young researchers. Member states of the European Union are investing in the expansion of the science infrastructure and increasing the size of their research and development workforces. While the postdoctorate was uncommon in the United Kingdom in the 1960s, nearly one-quarter of PhD recipients who completed their degrees between 2002 and 2007 took postdoctoral positions in higher education institutions (Haynes, Metcalfe & Videler, 2007). Cambridge has about 3,000 postdoctoral positions, roughly equal to the number of doctoral students and faculty, and 80 percent of these appointments are held by non-UK citizens (Salje, 2007). Britain's anxiety about a brain drain, when many of its most talented researchers went to the United States for postdoctorates and a fair proportion remained, has given way to the expectation that the most highly skilled researchers will spend a portion of their early careers overseas and then return; a higher percentage of persons who have held postdoctoral positions abroad have a greater number of highly cited publications and attribute career benefits to their experience (Bekhradnia & Sastry, 2005).

The postdoctoral position was also uncommon in France before the 1970s. Most PhDs found permanent government positions and most scientists were employed in universities or national research institutes and centers. In 1996, fewer than 20 percent of French doctoral recipients took postdoctoral positions, and two-thirds of these were outside France (Martin-Rovet, Terouanne, Thibaud & Neher, 1998). In the mid-1990s, in part because of the difficulty of finding research employment in France, at least 1,500 young French scientists held postdoctoral positions in the United States, but no more than 100 U.S. researchers worked in France (Martin-Rovet & Carlson, 1995). The creation of the European Research Area in 2000 has helped lower barriers to postdoctoral mobility within Europe, and countries have established prestigious programs to identify and attract the most talented researchers. The creation of a new postdoctoral designation in Germany, junior research group leader, has opened an alternative to the arduous postdoctoral *Habilitation* thesis that has been the traditional qualification for securing a professorship. This new option fosters the development of highly accomplished early-career researchers ready to move directly into faculty positions when they have established an independent research program. These positions represent only a small portion of Germany's postdoctoral positions, however (Hornbostel, 2007).[4] Across Europe, a number of flagship awards share a similar purpose with the IEB fellowships from over 80 years ago. The Humboldt Foundation supports German postdoctoral fellowships abroad and funds highly talented foreign researchers seeking an opportunity in a German research center. The Rubicon program of the Netherlands Organization of Scientific Research is a comparable program, and others are located elsewhere in the European Union.

At the regional level, the European Research Area has implemented high-profile postdoctoral awards. The Marie Curie Networks provide postdoctoral research opportunities and encourage cross-border mobility of young E.U.

scientists and engineers. These awards include grants to help researchers re-integrate with their home country (European Research Area Expert Group, 2008). A recent report, however, notes a number of challenges for postdoctoral researchers within the European Union, including the potential for the development of a two-tier research workforce with nomadic junior researchers circulating from one short-term contract to another while senior researchers hold permanent positions based on seniority rather than performance (Commission of the European Communities, 2008).

In Asia, most new PhDs are hired as laboratory assistants and technical personnel, and the postdoctoral position is a relatively recent innovation. In terms of propulsive growth, China has become the regional leader in doctoral training and postdoctoral research. While in 1989 only about 1,000 science and engineering doctorates were conferred in China, over 12,000 doctorates were awarded in 2003 (NSF, 2007). China's postdoctoral system, created in 1985, is funded and centrally administered at the national level, with most positions designated for national universities, laboratories and institutes. Industry-based postdoctoral positions were instituted in 1994 (Gang, 2007). Yet more than one-third of China's new PhDs take postdoctoral positions abroad, joining those who earn their doctorates out of the country. China's expanding gross domestic research and development expenditures may reduce the number of new PhDs seeking positions overseas. To build national science capacity and to keep talented young researchers engaged as universities and the domestic research and development sector grow to absorb this workforce, the government encourages researchers to seek early-career development opportunities abroad. In 2008 the China Scholarship Council launched a program of postdoctoral fellowships to help support nearly 2,500 researchers abroad (China Scholarship Council, 2009). India also has instituted postdoctoral research positions. New PhDs, particularly those with degrees from the national institutes of science and technology, are now expected to have a postdoctoral position, preferably abroad. Government departments and agencies have instituted flagship postdoctoral programs as part of the national strategy of research development (Ananth, 2007). Smaller, but equally dynamic, economies with intensive research investments, such as Korea and Singapore, encourage postdoctoral mobility and sponsor programs to attract talent from abroad. These strategies are designed to foster collaborative regional and global research networks while improving higher education and research infrastructures (UNESCO Institute for Statistics, 2009).[5]

At its origins, the postdoctoral position allowed the most talented young scientists opportunities to move to leading centers where they could learn the art of research "free from the financial problems that plague graduate students, and free from the distracting load of teaching and paper-grading that is generally the lot of the young academic scientist" (Rand, 1951, p. 77). From these beginnings as an incubator of scientific leadership, the postdoctoral position has become a key part of the research and development networks for a research network that moves among centers in Asia, Europe and North America. Short-term concerns about brain drain have given way to recognition of the long-term benefits to be had from participation in global research and development networks, and that the mobility of talented early-career scientists stimulates relationships that help build national research productivity. The significant growth in the volume of international research collaboration that has taken place since the 1990s correlates with growth in the number of international postdoctoral fellows, particularly in North America and Europe.[6] Globally, however, grave disequilibria put many countries at a disadvantage in the global research network, particularly in Africa and Latin America, where research universities do not exist or are poorly supported, and the postdoctoral researcher is rare.

International postdoctoral training faces other challenges. While a postdoctoral appointment remains a mandatory transitional step before a faculty appointment in many fields, it no longer is a pass-key to such a position. Unlike David Dennison and other young scientists whose careers the NRC and IEB advanced 80 years ago with prestigious fellowships, many postdoctoral scholars face job bottlenecks and can no longer expect to move on to faculty appointments and independent research careers. International postdoctoral researchers, particularly those from Asia, may face significant additional career risks: of being caught in a cycle of dependency on sponsors for visas and work permission; of being too distant to benefit from home-country networks for career advancement; and of being caught in a succession of short-term appointments, isolated by language and culture, with little likelihood of transition to research independence and job security (Armbruster, 2008). These problems may be particularly acute for women, who represent nearly 30 percent of the world's science and technology researchers (UNESCO Institute for Statistics, 2009). Such obstacles and disparities not only impede the career paths of the postdoctoral researchers who animate the globally distributed research enterprise, but also bear on the capabilities of this network to meet the world demand for innovation in science and technology.

Notes

1. This followed the earlier wave when, in the last decades of the nineteenth century, many young scholars went to Germany for the new doctorate, or spent a number of months observing the methods of Helmholtz and other leading practitioners of European science.
2. The NRC awarded 1,359 postdoctoral fellowships from 1919 through 1950 (Rand, 1951).
3. Since 2004 the NSF's flagship International Research Fellowship Program has made 242 awards, less than half those made by the IEB over a similar period.
4. The German Research Foundation (DFG) and other foundations fund about 120 fellowships.
5. Singapore's Lee Kuan Yew Postdoctoral Fellowship Program and the Korea Science and Engineering Foundation (KOSEF) Postdoctoral Fellowship Program.
6. An assessment of the scale and impact of international research collaborations can be found in Adams (2007).

References

Adams, J., & Wilsdon, J. (2006). *The new geography of science: UK Research and international collaboration.* Leeds, UK: Evidence Ltd. Retrieved from www.demos.co.uk/publications/thenewgeographyofscience.

Adams, J., Gurney, K., & Marshall, S. (2007). *Patterns of international collaboration for the UK and leading partners* (summary report). Report commissioned by the UK Office of Science and Innovation. Leeds, UK: Evidence Ltd.

Ananth, M. S. (2007). *Postdoctoral careers in India.* Retrieved from www.humboldt-foundation.de/web/31661.html.

Armbruster, C. (2008). The rise of the post-doc as principal investigator? How PhDs may advance their career and knowledge claims in the new Europe of knowledge. *Policy Futures in Education, 6*(4). Retrieved from http://papers.ssrn.com/sol3/papers.cfm?abstract_id=891041.

Assmus, A. (1993). The creation of postdoctoral fellowships and the siting of American scientific research. *Minerva, 31*(2), 151–183.

Bekhradnia, B., & Sastry, T. (2005). *Brain drain: Migration of academic staff to and from the UK.* Oxford, UK: Higher Education Policy Institute. Retrieved from www.hepi.ac.uk/466-1181/Brain-Drain–Migration-of-Academic-Staff-to-and-from-the-UK.html.

China Scholarship Council. (2009). *2008 annual report.* Beijing, China: China Scholarship Council. Retrieved from http://en.csc.edu.cn/Nianbao.

Coben, S. (1972). The scientific establishment and the transmission of quantum mechanics to the United States, 1919–32. *The American Historical Review, 76*(2), 459–461.

Commission of the European Communities. (2008). *Better careers and more mobility: A European partnership for researchers.* Communication from the Commission to the Council and the European Parliament. Retrieved from http://ec.europa.eu/research/era/specific-era-initiatives_en.html.

Committee on Science, Engineering and Public Policy (COSEPUP). (2000). *Enhancing the post-doctoral experience for scientists and engineers.* Washington, DC: National Academies Press.

Curtis, R. B. (1969). *The invisible university, post-doctoral education in the United States.* Washington, DC: National Academy of Sciences.

Dennison, D. M. (1974). Recollections of physics and physicists during the 1920s. *American Journal of Physics, 42*(12), 1051–1056.

Etzkowitz, H. (1992). Individual investigators and their research groups. *Minerva, 30*(1), 40–41.

European Research Area Expert Group. (2008). *Opening to the world: International cooperation in science and technology: Report of the ERA Expert Group.* Brussels: European Commission, Directorate-General for Research.

Gang, P. (2007). *Postdoctoral training in China.* Retrieved from www.humboldt-foundation.de/web/31665.html.

Gray, G. W. (1941). *Education on an international scale: A history of the International Education Board, 1923–1938.* New York: Harcourt, Brace and Co.

Hawkins, H. (1979). University identity: The teaching and research functions. In A. Olson & J. Voss (Eds.), *The organization of knowledge in modern America, 1860–1920.* Baltimore: Johns Hopkins University.

Haynes, K., Metcalfe, J., & Videler, T. (2007). *What do researchers do? First destinations of doctoral graduates by subject.* Cambridge, UK: Career Research and Advisory Centre (CRAC). Retrieved from www.vitae.ac.uk/researchers/1271-107681/Two-new-publications-provide-insights-into-the-employment-destinations-of-researchers.html.

Hoffer, T. B., Grigorian, K., & Hedberg, E. (2008, March). Postdoc participation of science, engineering, and health doctorate recipients. *InfoBrief.* National Science Foundation, Directorate for Social, Behavioral and Economic Sciences. Retrieved from www.nsf.gov/statistics/infbrief/nsf08307.

Hornbostel, S. (2007). *Postdoctoral careers in Germany: Findings from the evaluation of young research group leader programs.* Retrieved from www.humboldt-foundation.de/web/31653.html.

Johnson, J. M. (2001, January 12). Human resource contributions to U.S. science and engineering from China. *Issue Brief.* Arlington, VA: Division of Science Resources Studies, National Science Foundation. Retrieved from www.nsf.gov/statistics/issuebrf/nsf01311.

Kohler, R. E. (1985). Science and philanthropy: Wickliffe Rose and the International Education Board. *Minerva, 23*(1), 75–95.

Martin-Rovet, D., & Carlson, T. (1995). The international exchange of scholars: The training of young scientists through research abroad. American scientists in France. *Minerva, 33,* 189.

Martin-Rovet, D., Terouanne, D., Thibaud, J., & Neher, E. (1998). *Higher education in France and the international migration of scientists.* Proceedings of an NSF Workshop: *Graduate Education Reform in Europe, Asia and the Americas and the International Mobilization of Scientists and Engineers.*

Meyer, C., Lindsay, G., Barker, E., Dennison, D., & Zorn, J. (1988). *The department of physics: 1843–1975.* Ann Arbor, MI: Department of Physics.

NSF (National Science Foundation). (1994). *Graduate students and postdoctorates in science and engineering: Fall 1994, selected data,* Washington, DC: Division of Science Resources Statistics. Retrieved from www.nsf.gov/statistics/gradpostdoc/94select.

NSF (National Science Foundation). (2007). *Asia's rising science and technology strength: Comparative indicators for Asia, the European Union, and the United States.* Arlington, VA: Division of Science Resources Statistics. Retrieved from www.nsf.gov/statistics/nsf07319.

NSF (National Science Foundation). (2008). *Graduate students and postdoctorates in science and engineering: Fall 2006.* Arlington, VA: Division of Science Resources Statistics. Retrieved from www.nsf.gov/statistics/nsf08306.

NSF (National Science Foundation). (2009). *Science and engineering doctorate awards: 2006.* Arlington, VA: Division of Science Resources Statistics. Retrieved from www.nsf.gov/statistics/nsf09311.

Rand, M. J. (1951). The national research fellowships. *The Scientific Monthly, 73*(2), 71–80.

Salje, E. (2007). *Postdoctoral careers in Great Britain.* Retrieved from www.humboldt-foundation.de/web/31657.html.

Thurgood, L., Golladay, M. J., & Hill, S. T. (2006). *U.S. doctorates in the 20th century: Special report.* Arlington, VA: Division of Science Resources Statistics.

UNESCO Institute for Statistics. (2009). *A global perspective on research and development.* UIS Fact Sheet. Retrieved from www.uis.unesco.org/ev.php?ID=7055_201&ID2=DO_TOPIC.

15

Preparing Students to Navigate Cross-National Differences in the Research Environment

The Role of Research Integrity Education

Elizabeth Heitman and Juleigh Petty[1]

The globalization of science that has transformed collaboration in laboratory and clinical research has also reshaped research education. Today, unprecedented numbers of undergraduate, graduate, professional, and postdoctoral trainees in the physical and life sciences seek formal research education and experience outside their home countries. International educational exchange and research collaboration contribute to the academic development and economic well-being of industrialized and developing nations. Many countries now compete for international students and actively encourage their citizens to study abroad (National Science Board (NSB), 2008).

The multi-directional flow of science trainees and scientific knowledge around the world raises challenges for research educators, who must prepare future investigators to navigate this new environment. Among the most prominent challenges is the need to ensure the integrity of research results and promote high ethical standards among investigators, wherever and by whomever scientific research is conducted. English and mathematics are taught worldwide as the international languages of science (Montgomery, 2004; Rees, 2009), but there are no universally accepted standards of responsible research practice or research ethics, much less worldwide regulation or oversight bodies governing research collaboration across cultural or national borders. The questions of who and what to teach about research integrity gain even more importance as the growth of international research collaboration brings greater, more intensive contact among investigators in different national settings.

Over the last two decades, much work has been done in the United States to determine what academic preparation is needed for research integrity, particularly as governmental agencies have recommended and even required federally funded research training programs to provide instruction in the responsible conduct of research and research ethics. Yet this process has been uneven and sometimes contentious (Steneck & Bulger, 2007), and the nascent field of research integrity education is still working to define its goals, methods, content, and place in the curriculum of specific fields (Kalichman, 2007; Bulger & Heitman, 2007; DuBois, Schilling, Heitman, Steneck, & Kon, 2009). Outside the United States, formal efforts to promote research integrity are at an even earlier developmental stage: in many countries attention remains focused on the essential steps of defining misconduct and establishing mechanisms for handling allegations of misbehavior, and much less heed is paid to education (Mayer & Steneck, 2007; Stainthorpe, 2007; Lempinen, 2009). As a result, trainees and faculty researchers abroad may have limited awareness and conflicting understandings of the established and emerging standards of ethical practice in their work, even as the need for cross-national consensus on such standards grows.

While a global cadre of science-policy-makers now seeks common ground on standards of ethical research and structures to support responsible conduct, academic research institutions in the United States already face the practical demands of applying established U.S. standards to international collaborative research and research education. In this process, trainees, faculty investigators, and institutional administrators can easily become caught in webs of competing and conflicting customs, policy, and regulation from which there is no easy exit.

U.S. Policy on Research Integrity Education in a Cross-National Context

The U.S. Institute of Medicine first promoted formal instruction on good research practices and research ethics in 1989; its recommendations focused squarely on U.S.-educated students and postdoctoral fellows working in U.S. environments (Institute of Medicine, 1989). When the National Institutes of Health (NIH) based the first requirement for research integrity education in the National Research Service Award training programs—open only to U.S. citizens and permanent residents—it, too, focused on national research priorities and native trainee populations (NIH, 1990, 2003). Many institutions have continued to interpret the call for research integrity education as simply a training grant mandate (Steneck & Bulger, 2007), ignoring the needs of other audiences.

This common, narrow perspective does not reflect the multiple changes in policy that began soon after the initial requirement took effect. In 1994 NIH expanded its statement to encourage instruction for "all graduate students and postdoctorates ... regardless of the source of support" (NIH, 1994), and in 2000 the Public Health Service (PHS) issued a short-lived policy that required research integrity education for everyone engaged in PHS-supported research or training (PHS, 2000). Following the passing of the America COM-PETES Act (2007), the National Science Foundation's (NSF) 2009 policy called for training and oversight in the responsible and ethical conduct of research for all trainees supported by the NSF (NSF, 2009). The NIH's most recent *Update on the Requirement for Instruction in the Responsible Conduct of Research* (2009b) describes instruction in the responsible conduct of research as "an integral part of all research training programs," in which both trainees and faculty should participate.

Integrating research integrity instruction into the research education of all trainees requires attention to their backgrounds and goals, as well as to the current and likely future contexts of their research (Bulger & Heitman, 2007). Beyond the native-born, U.S.-trained graduate students and postdocs in U.S. institutions, three groups of trainees in cross-national contexts warrant specific consideration from research integrity educators to address the particular circumstances they face: (1) international trainees in U.S. institutions; (2) U.S. trainees in global health programs; and (3) non-U.S. trainees on U.S.-funded projects abroad.

International Trainees in U.S. Institutions

The Institute for International Education (IIE), a non-profit organization that coordinates U.S. education programs worldwide, defines international trainees as anyone "enrolled at an institution of higher education in the United States who is not a U.S. citizen, an immigrant (permanent resident) or a refugee" (IIE, 2009). There are currently over 60,000 international graduate students and postdoctoral fellows in the physical and life sciences in U.S. institutions, most of whom received their undergraduate science education in their home countries (IIE, 2009). Their numbers have grown steadily since the 1980s, despite restrictions on visas imposed after September 2001 (National Research Council, 2005; IEE, 2009). Figures from the NSB indicate that more than one-third of students enrolled in U.S. graduate science programs and over half of postdoctoral fellows are from other countries, with 36 percent of earned doctorates annually going to students with temporary visas (NSB, 2008). Upon their return home, international trainees often continue collaborative work with their U.S. mentors. Moreover, in recent years almost three-quarters of international science trainees have reported that they planned to stay to work in the United States (NSB, 2008), where they become contacts for collaboration, educational exchange, and mentoring for investigators and students in their home countries.

International trainees who have not had U.S. research integrity education are likely to be unaware of basic U.S. guidelines and regulations (Heitman, Olson, Anestidou, & Bulger, 2007), and citizenship status is a significant predictor of trainees' acceptance of U.S. norms of academic research (Anderson & Louis, 1994). Most policies related to research integrity have evolved in response to specific problems and in specific settings, and so international trainees unfamiliar with the origins of U.S. policies may misinterpret their meaning and scope. Trainees who have learned practice standards abroad

may be conflicted by differing U.S. norms (Alexander & Williams, 2004); similarly, trainees with limited experience or instruction may experience culture-
shock if they use their culturally based "common sense" to address issues that
arise in their U.S.-based research (Heitman, 1994). In a setting where
researchers from many nations work together, different culturally based interpretations of guidelines and disagreements over standard practice lead to
more frequent disputes and accusations of misconduct than among investigators trained just within the U.S. system (Meyer & Bernier, 2000).

International trainees in U.S. programs need focused research integrity
education, because their academic success depends on their understanding
the structure of the U.S. academic research system and the standards to which
they will be held accountable. They need instruction that helps them interpret,
understand, and ultimately adopt the standards of the U.S. environment in
order to collaborate effectively with U.S. researchers, whether faculty or other
trainees. Thus they need background on the place of biomedical science in
U.S. society and the way in which ethical issues are discussed in the United
States, particularly the variable roles of legal and religious authorities and the
norms of discourse in academics and society at large. International trainees
who return to their home countries after completing a U.S. degree or fellowship program may also need preparation to re-enter their original research
culture, which may have changed while they were away. Such preparation is
particularly important for researchers returning as new faculty, especially if
they plan to maintain collaborations in the United States.

U.S. Trainees in Global Health Research

Over the past decade, partially in response to unprecedented funding for
HIV/AIDS from the President's Emergency Plan for AIDS Relief, many U.S.
universities have established global health programs that aim to redress international health disparities through treatment and prevention-oriented
research. Global health programs typically "promote interdisciplinary education, research and service partnerships to address health issues that transcend
national boundaries" (Vermund, Sahasrabuddhe, Khedkar, Jia, Etherington,
& Vergara, 2008). Such programs often afford extraordinary opportunities for
trainees—particularly medical students, residents, and clinical fellows—to
undertake research and service-learning in resource-poor countries with high
rates of HIV/AIDS and conditions that are rare or unknown in the industrialized world.

Trainees in global health programs can gain powerful insight into the
socio-political challenges of disease prevention, priority setting, and allocation of scarce resources in the communities in which they work. They can also
make meaningful contributions to local medical institutions and their patient
populations. As detailed by Crump and Sugarman (2008), however, global
health programs may present trainees with potential conflicts between their

clinical service obligations and other in-country opportunities and responsibilities for patient care for which they have limited preparation or supervision.

U.S. trainees who undertake global health research may also find themselves working in environments with little research infrastructure and few formal ethical resources. U.S. trainees in global health programs thus have distinct needs for research integrity education to prepare them to work effectively in settings characterized by human suffering and regulatory ambiguity. Their greatest need for research integrity education concerns when and how the standards of research at their U.S. institutions apply in their international environment. This means that trainees must know that many U.S. standards—such as the need for Institutional Review Board (IRB) approval of their project and adherence to data management standards—are still binding abroad. Next, it means that they must learn whether the host country and institution follow additional research standards, guidelines, or protocols, and how to adhere to them. Ultimately, it also means that U.S. trainees must understand how the process of doing research is conceptualized in the local context, so they can follow standards and guidelines in practice.

Beyond their educational responsibilities to the trainees themselves, U.S. institutions and global health programs have an obligation to international partners and their patients to prepare trainees to follow relevant rules and guidelines and to anticipate ethical and practical issues that may arise. Likewise, the sending institution or program should make provisions for trainees to have someone to turn to if they have questions or crises. Their preparation should include an orientation to the structures of ethical and regulatory authority and the social hierarchy of their host institution, and the ways in which ethical issues are raised and resolved in the host society. Over time, trainees' critical reflection on their own experiences should become part of the curriculum. Their assessment of unmet needs and insights into resolving questions may also contribute to the research capacity-building process of the host institution or larger community.

Non-U.S. Trainees in U.S.-Funded Research Abroad

In addition to affording research opportunities to U.S. trainees, many U.S. universities' global health programs are dedicated to providing research education to trainees from their local partner institutions. In some cases training is part of NIH-funded efforts to strengthen the host country's academic and public health infrastructures and create sustainable capacity for research and disease prevention; NIH/Fogarty International Center's AIDS International Training and Research Program and Global Infectious Disease Research Training Program are two such endeavors focused on capacity building in low- and middle-income countries (NIH, 2009a). In other contexts, such as in projects funded by the HIV Prevention Trials Network (HTPN) (2008), U.S.

teams provide research training abroad in order to establish and maintain local study sites in countries with limited research infrastructure.

In both cases, local trainees need research integrity education as a fundamental introduction to NIH-sponsored research and the ethics and organizational structure of the processes that they will be expected to follow (Rennie, Sugarman, & HPTN Research Ethics Working Group, 2009). NIH requires that all funded investigators and all institutions that receive NIH funding—including foreign collaborators and components of grants awarded to U.S. institutions—comply with the terms laid out in the NIH Grants Policy Statement (NIH, 2003). This document lists over 40 separate policies intended to promote "high ethical, health, and safety standards in both the conduct of the research [that NIH] funds and the expenditure of public funds by its grantees" (NIH, 2003). A U.S. institution that receives grant funds for international collaborative research is accountable to NIH for its international partners' compliance with applicable NIH policy. Compliance begins with understanding the standards with which one is required to comply; therefore, education on the relevant standards of research ethics and responsible conduct is essential for international collaborators.

Research integrity education for international trainees in U.S.-funded studies abroad, like programs for international trainees in U.S. settings, needs to present U.S. standards in ways that permit trainees to compare and integrate them with the norms and practices that they already know. Such education is not common worldwide, particularly in developing countries, where global health research is concentrated (NIH, 2003; Mayer & Steneck, 2007), and so U.S. research educators may need to provide international trainees abroad with the necessary conceptual vocabulary to discuss research integrity and comparative standards. They, too, need insight into U.S. ways of talking about science, ethics, and regulation to make sense of the multiple levels of standards and guidelines that may be applied to their work. If the larger research program depends on investigators at international sites working independently, without the regular presence of U.S. collaborators, it is essential that the local investigators and trainees know and understand relevant policies and procedures well enough to avoid confusion and non-compliance.

Curricular Design for Cross-National Research Integrity Education: From Rules to Professional Engagement

Tailoring curricula to the needs of specific audiences is a growing priority among research integrity educators, with important implications for international collaboration (Bulger & Heitman, 2007; Steneck, Heitman, Dubois, & Kon, 2010). Despite an increasingly comprehensive description of what acceptable plans for research integrity education might include, the NIH and NSF have consistently declined to prescribe a specific curriculum or format for any population on the "international perspectives" that should be provided for training in cross-national research. Educators must set their own agendas.

At present, few U.S. programs or curricular resources on responsible conduct of research address international issues (Heitman & Bulger, 2005; DuBois & Decker, 2009). The most comprehensive is the Collaborative Institutional Training Initiative (CITI), which, in 2007, made its online modules on responsible conduct of research available in Spanish and selected modules available in other languages. The CITI's developers have also prepared country-specific modules with health and educational authorities in several nations; this activity is fundamental to the CITI-affiliated Pan American Bioethics Initiative, sponsored by the Fogarty International Center (CITI, 2009). Similarly, the *ORI Introduction to Responsible Conduct of Research* has also been translated into Spanish, Japanese, Chinese, and Korean by U.S. researchers for their international collaborators (Office of Research Integrity (ORI), 2007).

The availability of translated key resources makes an important contribution to communicating U.S. norms and standards of research integrity and responsible conduct of research internationally. Nonetheless, translated materials typically present U.S. standards to researchers abroad in the same format as they do to their U.S. audience, with little interpretive guidance for other cultural systems. Materials that successfully place U.S. regulations and practice standards in context for their U.S. audience may backfire in translation for readers unfamiliar with the basic U.S. culture, academic system, or regulatory approach. Even the metaphor "rules of the road," used in the *ORI Introduction* to engage its original U.S. audience, gets lost in translation for Japanese and Chinese readers, who typically do not drive (Steneck, personal communication).

For effective cross-national education, U.S. materials must be placed in a cultural context and new materials must be developed. In recent years the ORI has funded three projects on research integrity education for international postdoctoral fellows in U.S. programs. Based on their work with postdoctoral fellows at the Children's Hospital of Philadelphia, Alexander and Williams developed a guide to teaching select topics in the responsible conduct of research to international postdocs (2004), and a set of video cases and a guidebook on mentoring (Williams, 2005). The National Postdoctoral Association (NPA) has recently established an online toolkit for research integrity education aimed at postdocs, which addresses cultural diversity and communication with international postdocs in the U.S. research setting (NPA, 2009).

While these projects address specific aspects of research integrity education for a particular international population and context, many cross-national research education programs demand a more comprehensive curriculum. Current NIH policy on research integrity education, detailed in the 2009 *Update on the Requirement for Instruction in the Responsible Conduct of Research*, promotes an expanded set of subject matter and requires active faculty participation, face-to-face instruction with substantive contact time and discussion, and instruction appropriate to the trainee's career stage (NIH, 2009b). Beyond the more traditional scope of responsible conduct of research, it presents three vast areas of professional concern as additional topics for inclusion: the role and responsibility of scientists in society; ethical issues in biomedical research; and the environmental and societal impact of science. Most importantly perhaps, the new policy's definition of research integrity and responsible conduct of research moves away from "adherence to rules, regulations, guidelines and commonly accepted professional codes or norms" (NIH, 2008) and "compliance with related PHS and institutional policies" (PHS, 2000), to "awareness and application of established professional norms and ethical principles in the performance of all activities related to scientific research" (NIH, 2009b).

Although the specific research environment or composition of the trainee class will define the ethical, regulatory, and practical issues for discussion, basic cross-national considerations can be defined in each of the subject areas that the NIH identifies.

Conflict of Interest

Since 1989 federal and institutional policy in this area has mushroomed in scope and complexity. Different income standards and financial expectations may make it seem as if financial conflict of interest affects only a small fraction of researchers and that the disclosure system is simply burdensome paperwork. Conversely, U.S. disclosure practices may seem superficial in contexts where bribery, graft, and corruption are systemic. This issue may be further complicated by cultural differences in gift-giving practices: researchers abroad may find that their collaborators and others expect gifts and exchanges of hospitality that may violate U.S. restrictions.

Personal and professional conflicts of interest are often of pressing concern to trainees and investigators from countries with small academic or scientific communities and strong family networks; where there are limited opportunities for professional advancement, success often depends on getting along with a few influential individuals who set the research agenda or allocate resources. Learning to negotiate such interpersonal relationships without ethical or scientific compromise may be more important in cross-national research than the U.S. focus on relationships with industry.

Policies Regarding Human Subjects, Animal Subjects, and Laboratory Safety

Apart from NIH requirements on education in the responsible conduct of research, other federal agencies require many trainees to receive instruction on U.S. regulation regarding the protection of human participants in research, the humane care and use of animals in research, and laboratory safety. Attention to international differences in practice and ethical perspectives in these three areas can illustrate that regulation does not capture every issue and that consensus or harmonization of standards will be necessary for increasing globalization of science.

Research with human subjects is the most regulated area of research in the United States, and in many countries the term "research ethics" refers almost exclusively to the ethics of research with human participants. U.S.-funded trainees in cross-national research contexts should know that U.S. regulations, interpreted by their own institution's IRB, govern their work. Educational sessions on these other guidelines—including the World Medical Association's *Declaration of Helsinki* (2008), the Council for International Organizations of Medical Science's *International Guidelines for Biomedical Research Involving Human Subjects* (2002), and commentaries from the National Bioethics Advisory Committee (2001) and Nuffield Council on Bioethics (2003)—can highlight the practical ethical challenges that trainees face in cross-national research. The U.S. Office of Human Research Protections (2009) publishes an online compilation of international regulations on human participant research that can also be used to explore other countries' requirements.

Research with animal subjects is a highly regulated area in North America and Europe; elsewhere, standards for animal research vary greatly. U.S.-supported trainees in cross-national collaboration must know that U.S. regulations, and their institution's Animal Care and Use Committee, govern their work. Beginning with the definition of "animal" in U.S. policy, however, trainees may be confused by regulatory structures that seem to conflict with diverse popular views and uses of animals. A focus on the scientific goals of humane care can often bridge cultural differences in ethical perspectives, as witnessed by the international use of the *Guide to Animal Care and Use* (Institute for Laboratory Animal Resources, 1996). Ethical and methodological questions may also be explored in publications from countries with little to no regulatory oversight of animal studies.

Training in laboratory safety is under the rules of the federal Occupational Safety and Health Administration, and safety is widely viewed as an aspect of research integrity (Heitman & Bulger, 2005). International trainees may be unpersuaded by U.S. standards that conflict with their cultural habits of dress or perception of risk. Discussion about standards of safe footwear may illustrate cultural differences in the perception of feet as well as of risk; a desire to keep street dirt out of the lab or clinic may prompt some international researchers to remove their shoes before entering. Similarly, proper waste disposal and chemical and biological hazards are often viewed differently by trainees from systems where community practices outside the lab regularly expose them to a wide range of dangerous materials.

Mentor–Mentee Responsibilities and Relationships

Expectations for mentoring among faculty and trainees can vary tremendously across nations, institutions, and disciplines, making the subject of mentor–mentee relationships and responsibilities vital for international research integrity education (Williams, 2005). Differing definitions of appropriate social roles and hierarchies must be uncovered and addressed early, beginning with what the trainee and mentor should call each other. In collaboration abroad, local trainees' knowledge of settings and cultural practices can facilitate their mentor's work, and mentors and mentees may be each other's interpreters, literally and figuratively.

Peer Review

Peer review is the foundation of objective science. In cross-national collaborative research, however, it can be difficult to know what knowledge, credentials, and experience qualify someone to review another's work, whether for publication, funding, or employment decisions. Peer reviewers' familiarity with local research contexts, standards of practice, and available resources is essential for understanding the professional record of a candidate for hiring or promotion. The small size of many international research communities may make blind peer review difficult.

Data Acquisition, Management, Sharing, and Ownership

Data recording and retention is another of the NIH's original topics for research integrity education for which policies and professional standards have expanded dramatically. Cross-national research involves many practical data-related considerations with ethical consequences. Recording and retention of data are affected by the differing availability of technologies and cultural practices around documentation: where a U.S. site uses secure computers with confidentiality safeguards, a collaborating site elsewhere may have only paper records and a publicly accessible white board (Petty, 2008). Trainees in the United States are expected to keep their notebooks and other records in English to ensure team members' access; however, international collaborators should be alert to English terms that may not be used the same way in different national settings and to the risk that investigators' limited fluency in English may result in incomplete or inaccurate records. NIH policies that seek to resolve questions of storing and sharing data and biological samples through centralized repositories may also create ethical conflict internationally. International collaborators may resist committing biological samples taken from their local communities to a U.S. site that does not seem "central," especially if the criteria for using shared samples appear to disqualify their local colleagues and trainees.

Misconduct and Policies on Handling Misconduct

International trainees in U.S. programs typically understand that fabrication and falsification of data are antithetical to the goals of science, but—like U.S. trainees in U.S. contexts—often need guidance to understand when data manipulation becomes misrepresentation and misconduct. More problematic are academic dishonesty and plagiarism, which international students and senior trainees report to be common practices in their home countries (Steneck & Bulger, 2007). Research educators may be hard-pressed to contradict such assertions when so many nations have no published standards. However, they have a responsibility to instruct trainees in the meaning of plagiarism in the U.S. environment, as well as to help them understand the expectations for original work and citation in academic presentations and publications. Such trainees' early efforts at writing manuscripts should receive particular attention if English is not their first language, because their desire for clearer phrasing may tempt them to use another's words without attribution.

Responsible Authorship and Publication

Standards for publication and authorship remain contentious issues in science, despite the increasing specificity and prominence of such guidelines as the *Uniform Requirements for Manuscripts Submitted to Biomedical Journals* (International Committee of Medical Journal Editors, 2008). Criteria for authorship and the meaning of authorship order vary significantly among disciplines and internationally, and trainees are often uncertain when and why their contributions may qualify for recognition. Discredited practices like honorary and ghost authorship remain common worldwide. International research results published in an indexed, English-language journal may not be easily accessible in the country where the work was conducted; rewriting a single study in a second language is considered duplicate publication. University policies that reward publication in English-language journals may also indirectly promote plagiarism: non-native speakers of English—whether trainees or faculty—may borrow phrases, sentences, and even entire methods sections from published articles that address similar topics.

Collaboration

The key research integrity question related to collaboration is "Whose standards apply and why?" Teaching trainees how to prioritize standards can help them avoid overlooking some elements of responsible conduct because they were paying close attention to others (Petty, 2008). The Department of Commerce's export controls also present an aspect of collaboration that warrants diligence. Since the 1980s, federal law has prohibited the transfer of information on certain key technologies from the United States to other nations. These restrictions limit the research that can be conducted by non-U.S. citizens in the United States and the information that can be shared with international trainees. Finally, the issue of communication—particularly over physical distance and cultural barriers and using electronic media—is central to collaboration and successful navigation of cross-national environments (Alexander & Williams, 2004; NPA, 2009). Where differing customs about communication (such as expression of opinion, written documentation, social status and institutional hierarchy, and shame and face-saving) are likely to affect research practice or trainees' academic success, they should be addressed as early as possible and as often as necessary.

Conclusion and Recommendations

The evolution of cross-national research collaboration illustrates how standards of research integrity ultimately develop within the profession, established and sustained by researchers themselves, not simply imposed as policy by external regulatory authorities (Heitman, 2002). Teaching research integrity for cross-national research gives educators an opportunity to foster analytic and communication skills, moral imagination, and a sense of collegial responsibility among a wide range of trainees. Research educators who engage trainees in exploring the ethical dimensions of their collaborations help find the common ground upon which scientific inquiry can flourish.

We propose the following recommendations to meet the challenges to international research collaboration related to education in the responsible conduct of research. First, UNESCO's Global Ethics Observatory (GEObs) should expand its global databases on codes of ethics, bioethics-related legislation, and educational resources (www.unesco.org/shs/geobs) to include codes, legislation, and curricular resources related to research integrity and responsible conduct of research. As GEObs builds its repository of materials for UNESCO's proposed Bioethics Core Curriculum, it should include curricular materials for research integrity and the responsible conduct of research. Second, professional organizations in science should communicate regularly with their international counterparts to (1) establish consensus on best practices and ethical standards in their disciplines; and (2) promote development of curricular materials and instruction in the responsible conduct of research in disciplinary training programs. Third, research-funding agencies should support comparative studies in standards of research integrity as part of their funding of international biomedical research.

Note

1.   This work was supported in part by grant #0551837 from the National Science Foundation (Ethics and Values in Science) and grant # R25 TW007697 from the NIH Fogarty International Center (Bioethics).

References

Alexander, M., & Williams, W. R. (2004). *A guidebook for teaching selected responsible conduct of research topics to a culturally diverse trainee group*. Rockville, MD: Office of Research Integrity. Retrieved November 1, 2009, from http://ori.dhhs.gov/documents/Alexander. RCR%20Guidebook.BW.pdf.

America COMPETES Act of 2007 (2007). Public Law 110-69, National Science Foundation, SEC 7009. Responsible Conduct of Research, p. 117. Retrieved November 1, 2009, from http://edocket.access.gpo.gov/2009/E9-19930.htm.

Anderson, M. S., & Louis, K. S. (1994). The graduate student experience and subscription to the norms of science. *Research in Higher Education, 35,* 273–299.

Bulger, R. E., & Heitman, E. (2007). Expanding responsible conduct of research instruction across the university. *Academic Medicine, 82,* 876–878.

CITI (Collaborative Institutional Training Initiative). (2009). Retrieved November 1, 2009, from www.citiprogram.org.

Council for International Organizations of Medical Sciences. (2002). *International ethical guidelines for biomedical research involving human subjects.* Geneva: CIOMS.

Crump, J. A., & Sugarman, J. (2008). Ethical considerations for short-term experiences by trainees in global health. *Journal of the American Medical Association, 300*(12), 1456–1458.

DuBois, J. M., & Dueker, J. M. (2009). Teaching and assessing the responsible conduct of research: A Delphi consensus panel report. *Journal of Research Administration, 40*(1), 49–70.

DuBois, J. M., Schilling, D. A, Heitman, E., Steneck, N. H., & Kon, A. A. (2009). Instruction in the responsible conduct of research: An inventory of programs and materials within CTSAs. Submitted to *Clinical and Translational Research, 2009.*

Heitman, E. (1994). Cultural diversity and the clinical encounter. In G. P. McKenny & J. R. Sande (Eds.), *Theological analyses of the clinical encounter* (pp. 203–223). Norwell, MA: Kluwer Academic Publishers.

Heitman, E. (2002). The roots of honor and integrity in science. In R. E. Bulger, E. Heitman, & S. J. Reiser (Eds.), *The ethical dimensions of the biological and health sciences* (pp. 21–28). New York: Cambridge University Press.

Heitman, E., & Bulger, R. E. (2005). Assessing the educational literature in the responsible conduct of research for core content. *Accountability in Research, 12,* 207–224.

Heitman, E., Olson, C. H., Anestidou, L., & Bulger, R. E. (2007). New graduate students' baseline knowledge of the responsible conduct of research. *Academic Medicine, 82,* 838–845.

HTPN (HIV Prevention Trials Network). (2008). *HTPN manual of operations.* Retrieved December 6, 2009, from www.hptn.org/MOP%20NEW%20CD/MOP%20CD/HPTNMOP2008.htm.

IIE (Institute for International Education). (2009). *Open doors 2009.* Retrieved from http://opendoors.iienetwork.org/?p=150814.

Institute for Laboratory Animal Resources. (1996). *Guide to the care and use of laboratory animals.* Washington, DC: National Academies Press.

Institute of Medicine. (2002). *Integrity in scientific research: Creating an environment that promotes responsible conduct.* Washington, DC: National Academy Press.

International Committee of Medical Journal Editors. (2008). *Uniform requirements for manuscripts submitted to biomedical journals.* Retrieved November 1, 2009, from www.icmje.org.

Kalichman, M. W. (2007). Responding to challenges in educating for the responsible conduct of research. *Academic Medicine, 82,* 870–875.

Lempinen, E. W. (2009, May 21). Chinese, U.S. science scholars and educators plan joint projects in ethics education. *AAAS News.* Retrieved November 1, 2009, from www.aaas.org/news/releases/2009/0521us_china_ethics.shtml.

Mayer, T., & Steneck, N. (2007). *Final report to ESF and ORI: First World Conference On Research Integrity: Fostering Responsible Research* (Lisbon, Portugal September 16–19, 2007). Retrieved November 1, 2009, from www.esf.org/index.php?id=4479.

Meyer, W. M., & Bernier, G. M. (2000). Potential cultural factors in scientific misconduct allegations. In Nicholas H. Steneck and Mary D. Scheetz (Eds.), *Investigating research integrity: Proceedings of the First ORI Research Conference on Research Integrity* (pp. 163–174). Washington, DC: Office of Research Integrity.

Montgomery, S. (2004). Of towers, walls, and fields: Perspectives on language in science. *Science, 303,* 1333–1335.

National Bioethics Advisory Committee. (2001). *Ethical and policy issues in international research: Clinical trials in developing countries.* Bethesda, MD: NBAC. Retrieved November 1, 2009, from www.bioethics.gov/reports/past_commissions/nbac_international.pdf.

NIH (National Institutes of Health). (1994, June 17). Reminder and update: Requirement for instruction in the responsible conduct of research in national Research Service Award Institutional Training Grants. *NIH Guide, 23(23).* Retrieved November 1, 2009, from http://grants1.nih.gov/grants/guide/notice-files/not94-200.html.

NIH (National Institutes of Health). (2000, June 5). Required education in the protection of human research participants. *Guide for Grants and Contracts* (Revised August 25, 2000). Retrieved November 1, 2009, from http://grants2.nih.gov/grants/guide/notice-files/NOT-OD-00-039.html.

NIH (National Institutes of Health). (2003). *Part II: Grants policy statement: Terms and conditions of NIH grant awards.* Retrieved November 1, 2009, from http://grants.nih.gov/grants/policy/nihgps_2003/NIHGPS_Part4.htm#_Toc54600062.

NIH (National Institutes of Health). (2008). *Research on research integrity.* Retrieved November 1, 2009, from http://grants.nih.gov/grants/guide/rfa-files/RFA-RR-09-004.html.

NIH (National Institutes of Health). (2009a). *Non-NRSA fellowships (F) and training (T) grants funding opportunities.* Retrieved November 1, 2009, from http://grants1.nih.gov/training/F_files_non_nrsa.

NIH (National Institutes of Health). (2009b). *Update on the requirement for instruction in the responsible conduct of research.* Retrieved November 25, 2009, from http://grants.nih.gov/grants/guide/notice-files/NOT-OD-10-019.html.

National Postdoctoral Association. (2009). *RCR toolkit.* Retrieved November 1, 2009, from www.nationalpostdoc.org/publications/toolkits/rcr-toolkit.

National Research Council. (2005). *Policy implications of international graduate students and postdoctoral scholars in the United States.* Washington, DC: National Academies Press.

NSB (National Science Board). (2008). *Science and engineering indicators 2008.* Arlington, VA: National Science Foundation.

NSF (National Science Foundation). (2009, August 20). Responsible conduct of research. *Federal Register, 74*(160), 42126–42128. Retrieved November 1, 2009, from http://edocket.access.gpo.gov/2009/E9-19930.htm.

Nuffield Council on Bioethics. (2003). *The ethics of research related to healthcare in developing countries.* Retrieved November 1, 2009, from www.nuffieldbioethics.org/go/ourwork/developingcountries/publication_309.htm.

Office of Human Research Protections. (2009). *International compilation of human subject protections.* Retrieved December 3, 2009, from www.hhs.gov/ohrp/international/HSPCompilation.pdf.

ORI (Office of Research Integrity). (2007). ORI developing presence on an international level. *ORI Newsletter, 15*(4), 9.

Petty, J. (2008). *Science in the clinic: HIV research in the era of evidence-based medicine* (Unpublished dissertation, Northwestern University).

PHS (U.S. Public Health Service). (2000). *Policy on instruction in the responsible conduct of research (RCR) – suspended.* Retrieved November 1, 2009, from http://ori.dhhs.gov/policies/RCR_Policy.shtml.

Rees, M. (2009). Mathematics: The only true universal language. *New Scientist, 2695,* 36–39.

Rennie, S., Sugarman, J., & HPTN Research Ethics Working Group. (2009). *Ethics guidance for research.* Retrieved November 1, 2009, from www.hptn.org/researchethics/HPTN_Ethics_Guidance.htm.

Stainthorpe, A. K., for the European Commission Expert Group on Research Integrity. (2007). *Integrity in research: A rationale for community action. Final report.* Brussels: EC.

Steneck, N. H., & Bulger, R. E. (2007). The history, purpose, and future of instruction in the responsible conduct of research. *Academic Medicine, 82,* 829–834.

Steneck, N. H., Heitman, E., Dubois, J. M., & Kon, A. A. (2010). *Responsible conduct of research (RCR) instruction in clinical and translational research education.* CTSA white paper (in preparation).

Vermund, S. H., Sahasrabuddhe, V. V., Khedkar, S., Jia, Y., Etherington, C., & Vergara, A. (2008). Building global health through a center-without-walls: The Vanderbilt Institute for Global Health. *Academic Medicine, 82,* 154–164.

Williams, W. (2005). *Mentoring international postdocs: Working together to advance science and careers.* Philadelphia: Children's Hospital of Philadelphia. Retrieved November 1, 2009, from http://ori.dhhs.gov/education/products/chop_mentoring.

World Medical Association (2008). *Declaration of Helsinki.* Retrieved November 1, 2009, from www.wma.net/en/30publications/10policies/b3/index.html.

Part VI

Toward Successful International
Research Collaborations

16

Reactive and Proactive Approaches to Facilitating International Collaborations

Camille Nebeker

As a scientist I clearly recognize my tendency to put blinders on in order to get from point A to point B as expeditiously as possible—later realizing I messed everything up by taking the wrong pathway. Sometimes walking down the hall and taking the elevator is more beneficial than jumping out the window to get to the ground. My intentions sometimes have the wrong impact on the project. I deeply appreciate the research administration's expertise in saying, "Elevator here, need to push the button and spend time it takes, but result is much happier for everyone."

This chapter considers international collaborations from the perspective of research administration. It reviews the kinds of challenges that international teams of scientific collaborators face and the resulting complications that institutional administrators must manage. When scientists collaborate, especially cross-nationally, they require institutional and administrative support. It is often difficult, however, for research administrators to anticipate the full range of complications that can and do arise in cross-national research projects. The question is: What should institutions do to prepare for challenges that come up in a wide variety of situations? The following actual cases illustrate some of the administrative issues that arise in international research, as well as the kinds of adaptations needed to manage research that is carried out in cross-national settings.

Cases

Case 1: Fetal-Alcohol Spectrum Disorder

A neuropsychologist from the United States was investigating fetal-alcohol spectrum disorder. Study participants included children residing in a Russian orphanage who had symptoms of prenatal alcohol exposure. The children participated in a number of cognitive and motor tests to assess behavioral effects of exposure.

One of the challenges of the project was maintaining financial accountability, specifically, ensuring that the appropriate persons associated with the study within Russia received payments. Ultimately, the primary institution in the United States contracted a commercial broker in Russia to ensure that financial transactions were carried out and subcontractors received payments in a timely manner.

Another complication involved the research subjects, that is, Russian children who were orphaned or abandoned. The process of obtaining consent and assent could not follow the traditional process one would expect in a study taking place in the United States. Specifically, the children did not have a parent to provide consent to participate, and it was not clear how the orphanage administrators would determine whether or not a child could participate in research.

Since orphaned children are no longer institutionalized in the United States, the only comparable situation the U.S. Institutional Review Board (IRB) could identify was when a U.S. child is a ward of the court. In that setting, the child is supposed to have an identified advocate who can speak in the child's best interest. Was that true for the Russian orphans?

In this case, the community (outside) member of the relevant U.S. IRB happened to be an immigrant from Russia who was familiar with the operation of orphanages. He explained that the Russian orphans did not have the same status as a U.S. child who was deemed a ward of the court. In fact, by introducing the process of obtaining assent from an orphan, the researcher could actually put the child at risk, since the child would not be expected or even have the right to make a decision about whether or not to participate. That decision would be in the hands of administrators who were acting on behalf of the institution.

To manage this conflict, the IRB had to compare the ethical expectations and norms of obtaining assent in the United States with those in the institutional culture in Russia and evaluate the overarching objectives of the research. The IRB reviewed the tasks the child would perform as a subject and deemed them to have minimal risk of harm. It also determined that if assent could not technically be given, it could occur in practice through a respectful interaction between each child and the research staff member who would carefully explain what the child would be asked to do and allow the child to discontinue participation if he or she appeared uncomfortable or unable to participate.

Case 2: Dengue Fever

A geographer was part of a multi-institutional, international team of researchers studying the incidence and transmission of dengue fever in Peru and Thailand. The study involved monitoring and tracking village residents using global positioning systems in order to identify high-risk areas and then developing disease-prevention strategies.

From an administrative perspective, the process of confirming permission to proceed with the research in the countries involved was very complicated, as was obtaining IRB approval from all the institutions engaged in the research, both within the United States and abroad. According to U.S. regulations on the use of human subjects, when a number of institutions are engaged in the research, each institution must review the protocol for human subjects' protection. There are, however, formal mechanisms that allow one IRB to rely on another IRB's judgment. Utilizing an inter-institutional agreement was clearly beneficial in reducing burden, protecting subjects and maintaining appropriate oversight.

Case 3: Tectonic Evolution

A team of geologists who were studying tectonic evolution in cooperation with faculty and students from a university in Indonesia conducted geological surveys, field mapping and large-scale data integration in Java and applied sophisticated technology to broadcast data back to servers in the United States. The field research team, comprising nearly a dozen faculty and students, were transported by vehicle miles into the forest to conduct their work. While in the field, a co-investigator experienced life-threatening appendicitis, requiring immediate evacuation from the field site. A collaborating senior scientist from the local region alerted authorities and requested emergency assistance at the nearest airfield.

Without appropriate risk management contracts set up in advance of departure, this scenario could have had tragic results. In fact, a member of the research team stated:

> His appendix was so disintegrated that it didn't break but just functionally came apart and filled his body with the fluid. The doctor said he had never seen a case so bad or so close to death. Without the insurance, the airplane would not have taken the job, so he would simply have died.

In this case, a life was saved as a result of careful planning and administrative engagement.

Case 4: Drug Trafficking

A sociologist who was studying drug trafficking in Southeast Asia's Golden Triangle collected data through interviews with drug lords, government officials, drug traffickers and prisoners. The project was designed to document the process of trafficking, so that more-effective policies could be developed to prevent drug export. It proved difficult to determine whether or not research subjects could be adequately protected, given the nature of the study, and subjects' ability to volunteer to participate was severely compromised, according to accepted standards of autonomous consent. In particular, participants in custody or in other vulnerable circumstances would likely be subject to forms of coercion that would be difficult to identify or prevent. Furthermore, if subjects' participation in this study became known to those affiliated with organized crime, the risks to subjects might increase because they were providing information about how drug trafficking takes place.

From the perspective of an IRB, the cultural differences were challenging to understand, as was the methodology used to identify potential subjects. To gather data on drug trafficking, the researcher planned to employ ethnographic field methods. Identifying potential subjects and determining what would be discussed would depend on the circumstances at the time. Since organized crime is a clandestine operation, it was essential for the researcher to develop reliable connections and to be trusted within the community. From an IRB's perspective, the proposed protocol was vague; however, from the researchers' perspective, the proposed method of following promising leads and making sound decisions in the field was essential.

In addition, giving gifts was crucial to gaining access to potential subjects. Developing the necessary relationships required accepting local customs and culture. Gifts valued within the rural locations in Thailand, Laos and Burma include Western cigarettes and alcohol. These substances enhanced respect and social status that then opened doors and allowed conversations about trafficking to occur. The ethical challenge is that gifting also created a reciprocal obligation in that those accepting a gift felt it necessary to divulge information about drug trafficking. In the context of U.S. standards, the accepted norm is to use appropriate monetary incentive payments (e.g., not in an amount to compromise one's ability to volunteer) for subject recruitment or compensation; however, among those engaged in this research, incentive payments would have been considered an insult because there was not enough money available for substantial payments. Instead, offering potential subjects Western goods and payment for dinners was considered a more appropriate strategy, even though the researcher could not be reimbursed for these expenses.

Considerations for Project Oversight

Each international research project is unique and brings with it various administrative challenges. Institutional officials, research administrators and faculty all have critical roles in facilitating and managing cross-national research ventures and must work closely together to ensure success. When all the relevant stakeholders are engaged in the early stages of research planning, potential challenges can be anticipated and addressed before the research begins, resulting in a more productive and responsible research environment. By contrast, when the planning and conduct of research are uncoordinated, unanticipated problems are more likely to arise, necessitating a reactive form of project management. The results can include increased administrative burden, compromised research partnerships, delayed research and threats to research integrity.

To foster productive cross-national research, it is important to recognize the perspectives and roles of those involved and identify successful approaches to planning and management of international collaborations. Awareness of the complexities associated with international science may avert some potentially daunting challenges.

Among the individuals involved in planning a major scientific initiative are the faculty researchers, international collaborators, institutional officials, sponsored-research administration personnel, members of institutional compliance review boards and staff members of funding agencies. Ideally, the process of sharing information among these stakeholders begins early in the research planning. Ongoing communication is critical to ensure that the work conforms to the mission and interests of the institutions and funders, that problems are anticipated and corrective actions implemented, and that the work complies with institutional policies and assurances.

Before the project is funded, it must be reviewed with regard to technical merit, personnel obligations, budget, availability of space, financial interests, cost requirements, intellectual property issues and regulatory compliance. For international research, additional review includes feasibility of cross-national cooperation, export control, insurance, permits, visas, additional compliance requirements and financial reporting requirements.

Once an institution receives funding to support research, work may not commence until certain administrative tasks are addressed. Those involved in award administration must quickly become familiar with the project's history and the research plan, establish connections with all relevant parties and communicate with partnering institutions to develop appropriate contracts. In addition, they must ensure that requirements of sponsoring agencies and participating institutions will be met, compliance reviews completed, and insurance obtained. Research administrators are also involved in financial reporting, review of export control rules, identification of travel warnings and restrictions, and emergency planning. Administrative oversight of international research can be quite complex, as the following examples illustrate.

1. Foreign travel. Travel to a foreign collaborator's worksite may be subject to a higher level of review and additional requirements. If faculty members travel abroad, the institution's risk manager needs to determine whether or not the employee has adequate insurance coverage and has received the necessary vaccinations, based on the travel destination and the potential hazards of the activities involved. It may also be necessary to develop plans for the researchers' evacuation in case of emergency or illness. In some cases, a risk manager may postpone the start of a project, due to travel warnings.

2. Export controls. In the United States and elsewhere, an export license or other governmental approval may be required for researchers who carry laptops, software or other equipment to an international destination. There may be exceptions for "tools of trade," depending upon the travel destination and

type of equipment. Researchers need to be aware of these regulations when traveling internationally, so they do not run the risk of exporting sensitive information or technology and becoming involved in potentially serious international incidents.

3. Foreign visitors.[1] Payments to foreign collaborators are complicated by regulations that limit the types of payment that can be made to foreign nationals. The type of visa held by the foreign collaborator determines whether or not wages, honoraria, scholarships, awards or reimbursements can be paid to the individual. In the United States, federal regulations also require foreign visitors be taxed on income earned in the United States. Foreign collaborators may be required to establish U.S. taxpayer identification, complete a number of federal tax forms and provide copies of their visas and other documents to receive payments.

4. Compliance review. The institution must ensure compliance with regulations governing research subjects, monitor restrictions on publication, evaluate intellectual property rights, review the terms of students' involvement, assess and manage financial conflicts, and provide training in the responsible conduct of research and other areas of compliance. While these compliance matters pertain to all research, there are additional challenges in cross-national contexts, when cultural differences may influence expectations and accepted practice.

For the researcher, administrative requirements involved in preparing for and monitoring international activities can be unfamiliar, overwhelming and difficult to navigate. Given the number of rules, additional documentation, requirements and regulations that must be considered—in the home country and all host countries—and the expertise that is needed to carry out the administrative work, it is essential that the researchers work closely and communicate often with research administrative personnel to ensure the success of cross-national projects. Likewise, research administrators must rely on other subject matter experts within the institution and work with them to manage these types of awards successfully.

Reactive and Proactive Oversight

The following two accounts of actual research projects illustrate some of the issues that may arise, particularly the twists and turns that occur in research management. The first involves research on sex trafficking conducted by U.S. researchers in Tijuana, Baja California Norte, Mexico, as political transitions, anti-corruption efforts and organized-crime wars escalated the risks associated with the project. The second is an example of efforts to develop an international cooperative agreement for scientific collaboration between two laboratories. They illustrate the difference between reactive management, in the former case, and proactive oversight, in the latter.

Reactive Research Management: Sex Trafficking

This study of sex trafficking was designed to analyze the factors influencing movement of women into the Tijuana sex trade. The study's particular aim was to examine recruitment, transportation and management of the sex industry and the connection between human trafficking and the criminal "underworld," with the goals of describing challenges involved in combating sex trafficking and proposing strategies to inform law enforcement, public health and human-rights efforts. Data collection involved interviews with individuals involved in the sex-trafficking trade, including government and non-government officials and commercial sex-industry operators and workers (i.e., prostitutes and pimps). Tijuana was selected as a data collection site due to its established sex-entertainment industry.

The study was funded in the autumn of 2007 and approved by the IRB at the researchers' home institution in January 2008. To begin the research, a co-investigator and a graduate student, both fluent in Spanish and knowledgeable about governmental infrastructure and organized crime in Tijuana began to initiate contact with potential subject groups. The graduate student, a native of Baja California, Mexico, served as the project manager and used his expertise about the community to engage established social networks. Concurrent with this research being launched, violence associated with drug cartels and Mexico's war on drugs was escalating. Efforts to rid law enforcement of ties with cartels resulted in massive turnover in law enforcement and government infrastructure, leading to great instability across the region. News media reported daily on murders, kidnappings and ongoing political upheaval. Headlines revealed the widespread violence: "Mexico Under Siege: Mexico Acknowledges Drug Gang Infiltration of Police" (Wilkinson, 2008); "12 Bodies Dumped near Tijuana School" (Ali, 2008); and "Drug Deaths, Violence Plague Border in Tijuana" (Beaubien, 2008).

It is not known how closely tied the sex industry is with organized crime and drug cartels; however, the study's co-investigator and the graduate student assigned to project management believed that there was a direct threat to the subjects and staff involved in data collection. In fact, many of those to be interviewed included the law-enforcement personnel involved in the overturned government. Approximately seven months into the study, the co-investigator raised concerns with the principal investigator that the intense violence could put subjects, staff and students at risk. The principal investigator disagreed with the co-investigator's risk assessment and questioned his motivations. As the lead investigator, he wanted the research to continue as planned and did not view the escalating violence as a threat to the study or to the project employees or participants. It was this conflict between the two investigators that prompted the co-investigator to request the administration's intervention and recommend the study be suspended for several months until the violence diminished.

Administrative Oversight

To begin to address the conflict, it was important for the research administrators to clarify the problem and identify those who could assist in addressing the issues. One concern focused on the risks to human subjects and to project employees associated with escalating violence in the Tijuana area. Another concern focused on the disagreement between the principal investigator and the co-investigator. Interaction with the U.S. federal-government sponsor was necessary, since the study would be delayed while data were gathered to inform a decision about the future of the project. Finally, it was also important for administrators to assess the feasibility of carrying out this research, given the drug wars and the conflict between investigators.

The university director of research initiated and coordinated communications among individuals best able to identify and mediate risks toward conflict resolution. The deliberations included the university's vice-president for research and graduate dean, sponsored-research administrators, the director of human resources, the coordinator of the human-research protection program, the chair of the university's IRB, experts in homeland security, local police with relevant expertise and the federal sponsor's program officer.

Several meetings and conference calls were scheduled to address the issues. The IRB temporarily suspended approval of the study until the risks to subjects could be re-assessed with input from representatives of an equivalent ethics review board in Tijuana. The federal sponsor and the U.S. Office of Human Research Protections were notified of the suspension. To understand risks to project personnel and research subjects, local police and homeland security experts were consulted. It became evident that the unprecedented violence in Tijuana, associated with the struggles for power and control within organized crime, and the possible connections between organized crime and the sex industry could put project personnel and research subjects at substantial risk of harm. In fact, during the months in which the study was suspended, nearly 500 people were murdered in the city of Tijuana. The study remained inactive until January 2009. By then, the intensity of the violence had lessened and the principal investigator had appropriately modified the study to reduce participants' exposure to risk.

An initial meeting was held to assess the problems reported by the co-investigator and project manager and to determine whether the interpersonal conflicts could be mediated. The differences in the investigators' perspectives on the management of the project had severely compromised their ability to proceed with a functional and respectful relationship. The co-investigator and the project manager subsequently resigned.

With the principal investigator now solely responsible for the project and with the endorsement of the sponsor to continue, the next steps were to determine whether and how students and other employees would be involved in the study and whether the university would allow the work to proceed, given ongoing violence and a travel advisory for the area. An added concern associated with the resignation of the co-investigator and graduate student was potential challenges in carrying out the project, should it be reactivated. While the co-investigator and graduate student had experience conducting research in Mexico, the principal investigator did not. This lack of experience was problematic in terms of qualifications to carry out the tasks. Specifically, the investigator did not speak Spanish, there was not a Mexican collaborator, and it was not clear whether established contacts within the health clinics used to facilitate data collection from some subjects would remain involved.

The strategy eventually taken to reduce risks to students and personnel was to employ experienced fieldworkers who were residents of Tijuana for data collection. To compensate for the lack of direct experience conducting research within Tijuana, the investigator was advised to partner with a faculty researcher with an established record conducting community-based research within Tijuana and to consider inviting a collaborator from a university within Baja California. Additional provisions were implemented for added protection of research subjects focusing primarily on the interview locations for sex operators.

Implications

One of the basic problems with this research project was that it was cross-national without a collaborating investigator in the host country. Initially, research subjects were Mexican nationals and prostitutes whose nationality was not known. Those responsible for data collection were both Mexicans and U.S. citizens. While members of the research team had specific knowledge of the area, there was no designated academic counterpart to the investigators in Mexico. Engaging a research collaborator from Tijuana who was knowledgeable about the relationships between the sex trade and the "underworld" may have been helpful in understanding the political climate and determining how to proceed amid the challenges of criminal warfare. Given the number of cross-national studies occurring in Tijuana and the long-established relationships between faculty, it was also considered respectful to engage an appropriate counterpart, competent in the areas of research and familiar with the local customs, culture and climate.

In general, international projects benefit from formal and well-established relations between investigators in the countries involved. When there is no international partner, extra precautions should be taken to ensure that the research is conducted in a manner that is respectful of local customs and that involves knowledgeable people. This step is critical, given the potential repercussions that could impact further research in a specific population or country.

A second problem was that there was no requirement for a local human-subjects review board to review or oversee the research. A local board might have been more knowledgeable about the specific risks associated with the research subjects targeted and more sensitive to the potential for escalating crime and violence related to the elections. Even when the funding sponsor does not require a local review of the proposed research and protocols in the host country, institutions could still require an on-site ethics review board to evaluate the research for human subjects' protection.

The next case illustrates a very different approach to the management of an international research collaboration.

Proactive Research Management: Cell Biology

In 2008 two faculty investigators, one in the United States and one in Europe, initiated plans to collaborate on research involving the use of stem cells to repair damaged heart tissue. This type of cross-national collaboration creates opportunities for faculty and students to expand the scope of their research. To formalize the collaborative relationship before any joint research began, the researchers' institutions developed a cross-national agreement for the two participating laboratories. The investigators both work on cell regeneration and planned to work collaboratively by exchanging research faculty, staff and students; developing joint research projects; and pursuing activities of mutual academic interest.

Administrative Oversight

In this case, research administrators developed the formal agreement with contributions from the faculty collaborators, institutional officials responsible for overseeing regulatory compliance, representatives from technology transfer offices, administrators from international programs and officials responsible for research ethics. Collectively, this team defined the purpose of the agreement, identified the individuals covered (e.g., students, faculty, technicians) and identified key points to address. The resulting agreement established the principles and conditions by which the institutions agreed to cooperate in academic exchanges and research. The agreement included the following: a summary of the legal frameworks of the institutions; the common interests and objectives of the collaboration; the purposes and terms of the agreement; procedures for coordination and follow-up; and agreements on research integrity, including data management, confidentiality, intellectual property, biosafety, publication, authorship practices and student mentoring. Other issues were identified and addressed later, such as the responsibilities of the institution when hosting students (e.g., insurance, housing, health care, etc.) and the need for documentation to track international exchange of students. From the institutions' perspectives, the areas that received the most attention in the agreement focused on intellectual property rights, nondisclosure of confidential information and responsibilities for scholars while hosting.

Implications

Many such collaborations are never formalized by written agreement and are nonetheless successful, despite the lack of administrative documentation. In fact, the bureaucratic and legalistic nature of a formal Memorandum of Understanding might have negative effects on the interests of the collaborating individuals and cause their relationship to falter at a time when it should instead be developed and nurtured. Much can be gained, however, by documenting the terms of the research relationship and nature of the collaboration in written form, so that there is a common understanding between individuals and institutions. An agreement can also mitigate risk by clarifying expectations in advance.

The partnering institutions' desire to formalize the collaborative relationships through a written agreement eventually exposed weaknesses in the research infrastructure. Since this collaboration did not involve a grant or contract, there was no mechanism by which research administrators would have been alerted to the laboratories' plans to collaborate or exchange personnel. This collaboration did not involve any formal international-student exchange program, so the campus international programs office would not have been aware that students were traveling internationally to participate in research, nor would they have known of students visiting from abroad. Essentially, since this collaboration was funded through the investigators' discretionary research budgets, the activity could have been carried out without institutional knowledge or oversight. This structural weakness could have put both institutions and personnel involved at risk, if something had gone wrong in the course of the collaboration.

Cross-national research is generally rewarding and productive, often adding tremendous contributions to the scientific record. It can also present significant challenges that can impede success—both scientifically and administratively. It is now a responsibility to explore beyond one's own existing geographic boundaries in creating new knowledge in the world. Each of the cases mentioned in this chapter has contributed significantly to the development and dissemination of scientific knowledge that will impact the health and well-being of individuals throughout the world.

Certainly, there are challenges, conflicts, controversies and compromises, yet all are generally manageable with the appropriate administrative and institutional engagement. However, even with the best planning and oversight, unexpected events may compromise research. It is important that both scientists and administrators communicate often and anticipate challenges that may arise in the context of international research collaborations, with the understanding that each project is unique and all have a vested interest in facilitating successful cross-national research.

Note

1.   The author gratefully acknowledges the contributions of Renee Lechner to the discussion of foreign travel, export control and foreign visitors.

References

Ali, A. (2008, September 30). 12 bodies dumped near Tijuana school. *Newser.com*. Retrieved from www.newser.com/story/38762/12-bodies-dumped-near-tijuana-school.html.

Beaubien, J. (2008, December 1). Drug deaths, violence plague border in Tijuana. *NPR.org*. Retrieved from www.npr.org/templates/story/story.php?storyId=97457815.

Wilkinson, T. (2008, October 28). Mexico under siege: Mexico acknowledges drug gang infiltration of police. *LATimes.com*. Retrieved from www.latimes.com/news/nationworld/world/la-fg-mexbust28-2008oct28,0,3196498.story.

17

Balancing Research Collaborations with the Realities of Working with Industry

Lessons from the Biotechnology Realm

Stewart Lyman

This chapter covers best practices that one should follow in conducting international research collaborations, with a particular focus on collaborations in the biotechnology and pharmaceutical research areas. It provides an overview of the nature and benefits of research collaborations, and then considers problems that can arise and the best ways to deal with them. For the purposes of this chapter, a successful research collaboration is one that produces useful data in a timely manner. If the data are not useful or cannot be acquired in a reasonable period of time, then the collaboration is not likely to be considered successful in the biotech and pharmaceutical arenas.

A research collaboration is based on a relationship in which both sides contribute something of value, but the two sides may make unequal contributions. For example, one side may provide a rare and valuable reagent for performing an experiment, with the other side generating the experimental data using that key reagent. One side may collect clinical samples from patients with a particular disorder, which are then analyzed by the collaborator looking for new biomarkers of the disease. Ideally, both sides in the collaboration will have some intellectual input into the design of the experiments, taking advantage of the expertise on both sides. A collaboration would not exist if one group merely decided to pay a second group to perform some scientific experiments. Instead, this arrangement would be categorized as a fee-for-service agreement, not a collaboration.

Collaborations must also be distinguished from reagent supply. This can be defined as providing a reagent, clinical sample or other material for the primary reason of fulfilling a publishing requirement. Reagent supply has virtually become a requirement of all quality scientific journals. These journals require, as a condition of publishing your article, that you provide any unique reagents used in the experiments (those that could not otherwise be readily obtained in the marketplace) to outside investigators who may request them. This is an entirely reasonable rule, because scientific advancement is supported when other investigators are able to confirm your initial research findings.

Reagent provision differs from collaboration, however, in that there is often no intellectual input from those who provide the reagent and no expectation of credit in terms of authorship or ownership of intellectual property. It is important to note, however, that research collaborations are often built around these biological reagents. These different types of reagents or materials include certain radiochemicals, monoclonal antibodies, small molecules, or recombinant proteins. Collaborations based on these materials often reflect their rarity, their affordability, or both. The need to gain access to clinical samples from patients afflicted with a rare ailment can likewise give rise to international biomedical collaborations. Oftentimes these rare diseases affect a single family, which may be located anywhere in the world. An international scientific group's analysis of an Italian family with a lethal sleep disorder led to a greater understanding of prion diseases (Max, 2006).

Collaborations need not be limited to drug or chemical entities. They can also involve devices of various types. Similarly, collaborations might also involve sharing new software to facilitate control of a device or evaluation of data. Finally, even providing a biological insight to inform the design of a particular experiment might be the basis for a scientific collaboration.

Benefits of Collaboration

What benefits accrue to scientists working in the biotechnology industry when they collaborate with other investigators, especially those in the academic world? This section reviews some of the most general benefits of scientific collaboration between industry and academic partners.

First, collaborations can expand your research program into new areas outside of your core competencies. Scientists at biotechnology or pharmaceutical companies, even those with very large research programs, cannot possibly be experts in all areas of biology and medicine. The scientific literature is so vast that keeping up with it is near impossible. Thus, seeking the assistance of other investigators with a complementary knowledge base can be extremely helpful in working out the possible utility of a potential new drug. Consider, for example, the case of the soluble form of the TNF (tumor necrosis factor) receptor, pioneered by the biotechnology firm, Immunex. They tested this soluble receptor for its ability to treat sepsis, but the clinical trials were a failure and the drug was of no benefit. However, working with an outside collaborator, the company found evidence to suggest that the drug might be useful in the treatment of rheumatoid arthritis. In this case, the clinical trials were extremely successful, and the drug went on to become the best-selling biological drug, with worldwide sales of $7.4 billion in 2008.

Second, collaborations can sometimes enable you to get data inexpensively, without committing personnel or developing new models, techniques, or costly reagents. These are very difficult times for biotechnology and pharmaceutical companies, due to the current economic recession. Even in good economic times, resources for internal research are limited. Reaching out to collaborators who have relevant animal models for a disease process that you are studying enables you to get data at a much lower cost than if you set up the model yourself. This is especially true if you are moving toward an animal model system that would be difficult to set up, such as those involving zebrafish or primates. Years of work, not to mention considerable sums of money, can be saved by having an experienced investigator do the studies with you, rather than trying to reinvent the wheel and set up the model yourself.

Third, collaborations can support regulatory compliance. Regulatory agencies in virtually all countries that license drugs for sale require evidence that your drug works in some sort of model system before proceeding on to clinical trials. Relevant data obtained from external collaborators can help to bolster regulatory filings. It is a good idea to establish an agreement at the start of such a collaboration that the investigator will work with you to provide the data in a form that will be acceptable to the regulatory agency. Since these requirements differ from country to country, your collaborator may need to supply you with country-specific versions of the data and findings.

Fourth, collaborations can help you to earn the goodwill of the academic community. This goodwill can be earned in several ways. By providing new molecules to interested academic researchers, you establish a working relationship with them. Their insights in such areas as functional activities of the molecule in other cell types or tissues, metabolism of the molecule, or a biological pathway may be extremely valuable in helping you prioritize your work. These insights might lead you to send the molecule into clinical trials or to avoid doing so. As academic collaborators share results of their studies with you, the information will likely help shape your existing research and development programs.

Fifth, collaborations can enhance your ability to publish papers in top scientific journals. Scientific collaborations have been shown to result in higher citation rates for published articles (Figg, Dunn, Liewehr, Steinberg, Thurman, Barrett et al., 2006). Even if you make an initial discovery on your own, the help of a collaborator can get you the additional data you need to publish the results of your research in a top journal. I once worked on a project describing a new ligand–receptor pair, one that was potentially associated with a classic mouse mutational analysis that dated back decades. We set up a collaboration with several talented outside geneticists, who were able to prove the connection between our molecule and the known mouse mutations. This work was done very quickly (in a matter of weeks), because the investigators we worked with had all of the tools and reagents on hand to complete the study. The resulting publications in a top journal enhanced the reputations of all associated with the project.

Sixth, collaborations can facilitate clinical investigations in certain cases. In addition to running basic-research programs, many academic investigators conduct clinical studies at their university hospitals. If the results from preclinical studies done with these researchers look promising, they may have the wherewithal to transition the pre-clinical program into a clinical one. Finding one of these collaborators early means not having to look for a second investigator later.

Seventh, collaborations with investigators in other countries can facilitate access to patient samples with a different genetic make-up. For example, population genetics are such that patients in different parts of the world can react quite differently to a drug under development. Being able to get samples from people with diverse genetic backgrounds can facilitate an understanding of how a drug may work in distinct populations. This information can then be used either to redesign the drug or to come up with a second one targeted at a specific population. Having access to diverse genetic samples can be a very valuable asset in the drug-development world.

Academy–Industry Collaboration in the International Context

In the United States, the Bayh–Dole Act, passed by the U.S. Congress in 1980, has had the unintended consequence of facilitating collaborations between U.S. biotechnology and pharmaceutical researchers and those in other countries. It regulates how universities interact with biotechnology and pharmaceutical companies by specifying the rights and obligations of all parties involved. It also defines the operating rules for current technology-transfer policy, but there are differing viewpoints on how the Bayh–Dole Act affects the terms set forth in Material Transfer Agreements.

In my experience, from the point of view of biotechnology or pharmaceutical companies, these different interpretations of the Bayh–Dole Act have negatively impacted interactions with university technology-transfer offices. Twenty years ago, academy–industry collaborations could begin very rapidly, because many universities would approve Material Transfer Agreements within a matter of days. These days it's a completely different story. Many university technology-transfer administrators believe that it is their job to generate additional revenues for their institutions through licensing fees. They are the ones responsible for approving Material Transfer Agreements that are sent to them by biotechnology and pharmaceutical companies. The majority of universities want to negotiate the terms of these agreements, as well as licensing accords, in endless detail. The technology-transfer officers live under the specter of unknowingly giving away the rights to some drug that might earn their university millions of dollars. The net result is that negotiations move at a glacial pace, sometimes dragging on for one to two years. Collaborations are slowed down and sometimes abandoned. Cutting-edge science simply cannot wait on these types of delay.

I recommend that biotech and pharmaceutical companies, instead of spending years negotiating, find a collaborator who can get the project done without delay. The place I recommend looking for such collaborators is overseas, in places like Western Europe or Japan. Non-U.S. universities and research organizations that are not funded by the U.S. government are not affected by the Bayh–Dole Act. As a result, non-U.S. institutions end up being easier to work with than academic laboratories in the United States that are supported by federal research funds, as most are. Negotiations with research institutions and universities outside the United States can often be completed quite rapidly. Sending reagents or clinical samples to other countries in support of research collaborations is definitely more complicated than sending these same materials domestically within the United States. This disadvantage is outweighed, however, by the advantages of being able to establish the primary collaboration on a much more expeditious basis.

General Considerations before Entering into a Research Collaboration

There are a number of points that scientists should consider before entering into a research collaboration (Lyman, 2008a; Vicens & Bourne, 2007). The considerations in this section are relevant to both domestic and international collaborations.

The Goal of the Collaboration

Most research collaborations in the biological sciences are developed to gain a better understanding of underlying scientific principles or to answer a specific question. The likelihood that the collaboration will help you reach this goal will inform your decision as to whether or not you want to engage a particular group.

Investment Required

Some collaborations require large amounts of material to do the experiments, and others take up a significant amount of laboratory personnel's time. Some collaborations can be accomplished on a non-paying basis, but others can only be set up with funding. The resources available to each of the competing groups will determine whether or not the collaboration makes sense for both parties.

Potential Payoff

Some collaborations are established to confirm findings initially discovered by a particular research group. Other collaborations can take you into new areas of science that are beyond the scope of your own scientific expertise. These types of studies could reveal new clinical indications for a drug or a new use for an industrial enzyme. If the potential payoff of a collaborative venture is large, then this would be a strong reason for setting it up.

Collaborator's Expertise

It is very helpful to know, at the outset of a collaboration, the level of expertise of the people with whom you are considering working. They may be new investigators in the field or leaders with decades of experience in the area. There is nothing wrong with working with young investigators, though they may lack the funding or manpower resources that a more experienced investigator may have.

Collaborator's Work Style

Simply put, some people are easy to work with, whereas others are not. If someone has a reputation as being difficult to work with, do not assume that your experience with them is likely to be any different. Check around to see if you can find others who have worked with the person in question, and find out if they are easy to work with and highly ethical. Pay attention to any warning signs you come across. Oftentimes, you have a choice of different lab groups that you can approach to get help in answering a scientific question. Getting background information on investigators in other countries may be especially challenging. Note that there is no requirement that you collaborate with someone who asks you to (Lyman, 2007).

Existing Collaborations

Sometimes it pays to have multiple collaborations in the same area of investigation. For example, one might want to test a new anti-tumor agent in a number of different cancer models before deciding on a particular clinical-trial plan. However, working with multiple individuals in the same area can lead to problematic ethical issues related to data sharing, publication priorities, and so on. Be very careful in undertaking overlapping collaborations, which require excellent communication skills to pull off successfully.

Ease of Working with Collaborator's Technology-Transfer Office

Sometimes it is not just about how easy the investigators are to work with, but also how easy it is to work with their institution, specifically, the technology-transfer office. Some are easy to work with, others have very tight paperwork requirements, and still others can literally take years to sign off on any agreements that need to be in place before starting the collaboration. With all types of research agreements, substantial investment of time and money may occur while the details are being sorted out. My experience has shown me that a lengthy time period for negotiating the terms of a collaboration often prevents the collaboration from taking place at all. As discussed above, much of this negotiating time can be sidestepped by setting up collaborations with scientists outside of the United States.

Considerations before Entering into an International Research Collaboration

"A clever person solves a problem; a wise person avoids it," according to a quotation attributed to Albert Einstein. Anticipating potential problems is the first step in avoiding them (Lyman, 2008b). This advice is particularly applicable to international research collaborations. Distance only serves to magnify financial, cultural, and language issues that might impinge on a collaboration. However, international collaborations have been shown to be positively related to a scientist's future research output (He, Geng, & Campbell-Hunt, 2008). Here I identify areas that are potential stumbling blocks to successful international research collaborations.

Scientific Data Quality and Integrity

In the course of a collaboration, decisions often need to be made about the interpretation of data. Scientists in different countries may receive different types and levels of training on these issues, and cultural norms on how experiments are done may vary from country to country. In addition, educational requirements and norms vary within a country as well. These differences can lead to serious conflicts in research collaborations. What happens if one group asks for the inclusion of a control group that a collaborator does not believe to be necessary, or cannot afford to include for financial reasons? Suppose one group challenges the believability of the data because the data look too good? Are the data supported by raw notebook information that is available to all parties? I have seen cases in which the people who ran the experiments felt that the data that they generated were of high quality, but the collaborators strongly disagreed with this interpretation.

It is helpful to have a mechanism or procedure in place to resolve these types of conflict on both ends. In my experience, however, many organizations do not have an established way of handling these situations when they arise. The most egregious example of a problem that can arise is suspicion or accusation of scientific fraud. It is difficult to police fraud in your own country; it is even more difficult to detect it when the work has been done in other countries. Fraud usually comes to light when other investigators try to replicate findings that are both new and important. Fraud involving non-cutting-edge research will generally not be detected. Sometimes, what may appear to be fraud is simply work that is of very poor quality or poorly presented. The best practice here is to agree at the outset that either party to the collaboration can request the raw data to see how the conclusions have been reached. In the rare case that problems do arise and the collaborators cannot agree on a solution, they should resolve to look to a mutually agreed-upon third party to help resolve the conflict.

Colleagues of mine were caught up in a well-known case of scientific fraud in oncology research in Germany in the late 1990s. An investigation by the German Research Foundation (Deutsche Forschungsgemeinschaft) determined that a large number of published papers by scientists at the University of Lubeck contained manipulated data (Hagmann, 2000). My associates were unable to verify the data produced by their German collaborators and subsequently retracted their papers that were done in collaboration with this group.

Publication and Presentation Issues

At the outset of any collaboration, some understanding should be reached on who is to be included as an author on any manuscripts that arise from the collaboration. This includes deciding who will take the positions of first author and last (senior) author, and which party or parties in the collaboration will make the decisions on authorship. Expectations in this regard may vary due to the research culture in place in different countries. For example, it may be customary in some countries to include as authors the research technicians who performed the studies. In other countries, they may not be included as authors, since they often have not made any intellectual contribution to the work, even though they performed the experiments. It is helpful to talk these kinds of issues through at the very outset of the collaboration, before any bad feelings arise.

A similar understanding needs to be reached among all participants on public presentations of data that arise from the collaboration. Who will be the ones to present the data at national or international meetings? How can meeting assignments be divided up in a fair manner? What if one group has fewer financial resources and cannot afford to travel to meetings to present the data?

Finally, collaborators should be made aware at the very outset of any potential restrictions (such as disclosure concerns related to patents) on presenting the data in a variety of settings (departmental, university, national, and international meetings). If you are concerned about not getting proper credit for the contributions of your group to the overall effort, then you should discuss how your collaborators, as part of their presentation, would apportion credit to you and your colleagues. Again, it can be helpful to identify a third party in advance who can help resolve these types of conflict.

Competing Collaboration Requests

It is very common to receive competing collaboration requests for "hot" reagents, such as the only known monoclonal antibody to a cell surface receptor, or a recombinant protein that is difficult to express. These requests may come from researchers all over the world. One should be sure to avoid a country-specific bias when getting requests from different countries.

Geographic factors may come into play in how you handle these various requests. For example, it may be quite expensive to ship this key reagent to the other side of the world, especially if it needs to be kept on dry ice or if it is a potential biohazard. If recipients are asked to bear the expense of having the reagent sent to them, then investigators who are less well-funded are at a significant disadvantage in obtaining the material for their studies.

In addition to geographic factors, there are a number of ethical issues to be considered in dealing with potentially competing collaborations (Lyman,

2008c). Different groups may ask for your "hot" reagent to do what appear to be very similar, if not identical, experiments. Ethical concerns here are paramount, because one risks antagonizing a number of collaborators if these types of requests are not handled appropriately. Researchers must strive to treat all groups fairly and clearly inform them as to how you handle such requests. One should never send a particular reagent to two or more groups who are doing the same or similar experiments without explicitly telling all parties involved at the outset that the reagent is being provided on a non-exclusive basis to the scientific community. This norm may not exist in all countries, so it is especially important to make this point clear. Furthermore, it should be explicitly stated that reagents that are sent to collaborators are not to be shared with their colleagues without the express permission of the people who sent it. Researchers who operate in an area where obtaining certain reagents is difficult or impossible may assume that they can freely distribute the materials that you have provided them. Again, this is tied to the issue of local cultural norms.

Transport of Materials

Another factor that comes into play here is trying to get these specialized reagents across international borders. I had an experience a number of years ago when trying to send reagents to another country, only to find that they had disappeared without a trace, on two separate occasions, while in transit. I have also sent reagents on ice to other countries, only to learn that, for some reason, the reagents sat on a loading dock at the receiving institution for days before being delivered to the scientist on the address label. As a result, the reagents had denatured and were no longer usable, delaying the experiments until a replacement shipment could be sent. These experiences have led me to adopt the habit of emailing collaborators in other countries all of the information needed to track a package, whenever I send them a reagent. This has cut down on the incidence of packages going astray.

Legal, Regulatory, and Ethical Issues

Issues related to the legal, regulatory, and ethical management of collaborations should be covered in discussion with international collaborators at the outset of a collaboration. For example, investigators should come to an agreement on how any intellectual property that arises from the collaboration will be dealt with. They need to consider patent filings and ownership of inventions. Combination studies, in which reagents provided by two different groups are combined in one experiment, are problematic for a number of reasons. If separate companies supply the reagents, the issue is then who has a claim to ownership of intellectual property that may arise from such an undertaking. These types of studies are not uncommon and can be quite problematic.

There are a number of countries that do not accept international norms regarding intellectual property issues. Because they do not adhere to international guidelines, many organizations, including mine, made the decision not to file for patent protection in these countries and not to share any of our valuable reagents with investigators located within their borders. This obviously has put academic investigators in these nations at a disadvantage, compared to scientists in countries where intellectual property rights are respected.

Ethical issues also need to be addressed at the outset and throughout a collaborative study. It is important, for example, to be clear that any reagents sent for animal studies should be used only in animals and never administered to humans. One would be horrified to learn that a drug that was in the early stages of development to treat a particular disease had actually been given to a patient.

Informed consent, a concept now well-established in some countries, is not nearly as well-developed in other countries. It covers not only the administration of drugs, but also the acquisition of human tissue samples. They must be procured in an ethical manner that would meet the guidelines of regulatory agencies, professional societies, and the journals to which articles might ultimately be submitted. A number of years ago, one of my colleagues wanted to acquire patient samples from Poland, since he had a personal relationship with investigators there. A number of us were concerned, however, that we might run into ethical problems down the line since we could not confirm that the samples had been acquired with the appropriate informed consent. As a result, we decided not to acquire these clinical samples from Poland, and we looked for a source in the United States. Again, local customs vary in this regard, so this should be discussed in advance if it is a potential point of contention.

Financial Issues

One must be sensitive to financial realities when working with collaborators in other countries. Collaborators may not have money to spend on journal reprints, page charges for publishing articles, drafting figures, shipping reagents, or even mailing manuscripts. It may be appropriate to pay a collaborator to perform some experiments or just supply them with key reagents. Payments may or may not be allowable. Some groups are not allowed to take money in exchange for laboratory work as a result of institutional guidelines. The U.S. National Institutes of Health, for example, have strict regulations on how their researchers interact with drug companies, be they international or domestic. I had a collaborator in Germany who was doing some bioassays for me on a novel growth factor I had discovered. I wanted to defray the expenses incurred by his group in doing these studies, but his research institution's financial guidelines would not allow for direct payments. The solution was to pay instead the travel expenses of my collaborators, so they could attend a scientific conference in the United States to present our shared data.

One should be aware of the potentially high cost of sending large numbers of reagents internationally under controlled conditions (for example, packed in dry ice). An investigator in another country may not be able to afford to send you some unique materials that have been developed in their lab, unless you can pay for the shipping costs. In such situations, it is obviously in your interest to do so.

Another issue that arises as part of a discussion of financial considerations is whether collaborators working in different countries can afford to attend scientific conferences to present findings that were jointly derived. Investigators who are located far from where major conferences are held or who have limited travel budgets are at a significant disadvantage and may not get sufficient credit for a discovery if they are not able to travel to talk about it. An ideal solution would be for the wealthier partner to help fund transportation and meeting expenses for the other partner, although granting agencies may specifically prevent this type of expenditure. Finally, it is important to budget for visits between collaborators to discuss the work that has been done together.

Cultural and Language Issues

Cultural issues can complicate a collaboration between lab groups located in different parts of the world. For example, in some cultures, a female scientist would not be likely to challenge a male collaborator, particularly if he were from another country. Also, women's contributions to a collaboration may not be reflected in authorship or other credit due to cultural norms about women's role in conducting scientific research.

Issues related to hierarchy can sometimes lead to problems in collaborations between investigators in different countries. For example, the title "Professor" carries very different connotations in Europe, Japan, and the United States. In the United States, a professor is a university researcher at any level (assistant, associate, or full). By contrast, in Japan and Europe the title is reserved for those who function as head of a department or institute. It is useful to keep this distinction in mind if one is entering into a collaboration with a person bearing that title.

Communication and language issues can also complicate collaborations. English is the primary language for the publication of papers in the biological sciences. Suppose an investigator in the United States is working with a collaborator in Japan to complete some scientific studies, with the bulk of the work being done in Japan. When the work is completed, the general expectation would be that the Japanese lab would write up the data for publication. Sometimes, however, as has happened in my experience, an English-speaking partner needs to take over the writing task, so that the publication will be ready for submission to an English-language journal. This kind of situation has implications for authorship credit that need to be discussed openly. It can be difficult for scientists to assess each other's written language skills, and so this issue may not arise until toward the end of a collaboration.

In addition to having actual difficulties with language in working with collaborators, one also has to deal with more generalized communication norms. For example, in Japan, it is considered impolite to use negative words precisely, like saying "No." You are more likely to hear phrases such as "I personally like it" or "We'll meet internally and discuss it." One must become attuned to this. Finally, language issues can arise in a collaboration, and key points can become lost in translation due to idioms and colloquial expressions.

Counterfeiting and Piracy Concerns

As a working scientist I always tried my best to assist researchers from other countries when they sought my help. However, senior officials in my company often blocked collaborations because they were concerned about potential piracy and counterfeiting of drugs. Researchers have some legitimate concerns about sending complementary DNA (cDNA) to other countries where they may be used to produce counterfeit drugs (in the case of marketed products) or proteins that are not approved by regulatory agencies. Examples of such counterfeit biologics that have been reported include erythropoietin, granulocyte-colony stimulating factor (G-CSF), and human growth hormone. Much of the worldwide use of recombinant human growth hormone (as much as $2 billion worth) is actually based on its illicit rather than approved uses, including a drug that was illegally manufactured or sold (*The Growth Hormone Craze*, 2008). While piracy involving cDNA clones is not the concern it once was, this topic still concerns scientists working for industrial organizations. One must strive to balance the fear that reagents will be used in an illegitimate manner against the desire to help scientists in other countries gain access to materials that they would not otherwise be able to obtain.

Dealing with Problems in International Research Collaborations

There are no research organizations charged with helping to sort out general issues that may arise between collaborators working in different countries. If a study is being conducted under the auspices of a sponsoring group, such as the World Health Organization, then that group may help to smooth out any conflicts that arise from the collaboration. This is probably the exception and not the rule. In general, it will be up to the researchers themselves to sort out any disagreements or problems that arise. On occasion, institutional help can be obtained from university technology-transfer offices or other administrative offices. When issues like scientific fraud are suspected, science journals, as well as granting agencies, should be brought into the discussion.

Collaborative Challenges and Recommendations

The top challenges that are faced in international research collaborations are:

1. Communication. The problem is not just language but expectations as to what the collaboration can provide for each of the groups involved in it.
2. Credit. Each group will want to get credit for their hard work and ideas. This may involve publications in scientific journals or the popular press, or presentations at conferences.
3. Culture. Cultural norms differ from country to country. This can create difficulties in communication, data interpretation, and expectations of what each party in the collaboration is expected to do.
4. Financial issues. Collaborators may not all have access to adequate financial resources. This can lead to problems in affording resources required to perform experiments, as well as arranging presentations at international meetings.

To address these issues and ensure a successful research collaboration, it is important to work out details with regard to each party's expectations, explicitly and in writing, at the outset of the collaboration. This should include discussions of publications, presentations, intellectual property, communication frequency, and any ethical concerns. Stay in close contact, via regularly scheduled videoconferencing, telephone calls, or emails. This is especially important if any problems arise; if they do, discuss them in a timely manner. Be aware of changing conditions (such as personnel changes or loss of grant support) that can affect the outcome of the collaboration. These should be communicated as soon as possible to your collaborators. Remember that collaborations with investigators in other countries may be easier to set up than domestic partnerships, due to fewer legal and paperwork issues. In summary, my experience has shown me that the benefits of international collaboration can make the challenges well worth overcoming.

References

Figg, W., Dunn, L., Liewehr, D. J., Steinberg, S. M., Thurman, P. W., Barrett, J. C., et al. (2006). Scientific collaboration results in higher citation rates of published articles. *Pharmacotherapy, 26,* 759–767.

Hagmann, M. (2000). Panel finds scores of suspect papers in German fraud probe. *Science, 288,* 2106–2107.

He, Z.-L., Geng, X.-S., & Campbell-Hunt, C. (2009). Research collaboration and research output: A longitudinal study of 65 biomedical scientists in a New Zealand University. *Research Policy, 38,* 306–317.

Lyman, S. D. (2007). Must you collaborate with another scientist? *Drug Discovery News, 3*(12), 12.

Lyman, S. D. (2008a, March). Six questions to ask before setting up a scientific collaboration. *PharmaVoice,* March 2008, 68.

Lyman, S. D. (2008b). Preventing discord in research collaborations. *Genetic Engineering & Biotechnology News, 28*(13), 56–57.

Lyman, S. D. (2008c). When collaborations compete. *The Scientist, 22*(5), 28.

Max, D. T. (2006). *The family that couldn't sleep: A medical mystery.* New York, NY: Random House.

The growth hormone craze: Hearing before the Oversight Committee of the U.S. House of Representatives, 110th Cong. (2008). Testimony of T. Perls. Retrieved from http://oversight. house.gov/images/stories/documents/20080212150143.pdf.

Vicens, Q., & Bourne, P. E. (2007). Ten simple rules for a successful collaboration. *PLoS Computational Biology, 3*(3), e44.

18

Realizing Gains and Staying Out of Trouble

Melissa S. Anderson and Nicholas H. Steneck

We turned to the task of drawing this book together in mid-December, when an early winter storm rolled into Minnesota and Michigan, bringing the first snow of the season. As colleagues located in the northern part of the United States, we share the know-how of shoveling snow and bundling up on cold winter days. As research integrity scholars, we share an understanding of research problems in our common area and, of course, some fundamental research skills. We use computers with different operating systems, but have been able to work around this problem. In other words, we share many things, particularly our research interests, but also have some important differences. One of us likes the snow; the other is less sure about the joys of winter.

Researchers who work in international collaborations are drawn together by their common interests in research problems. The problems create for them a shared world in which they can seemingly work together without further complications. They share the same scientific assumptions and worldview. They use the same tools or provide tools that complement the work their collaborators are doing. They share a common technical vocabulary, even if they speak different languages. They often publish in the same journals and are members of the same professional societies. They all know how to shovel snow.

The obvious flaw in this picture is, of course, that our colleagues do not all know how to shovel snow. And while shoveling snow may not be relevant to successful international collaboration in research, there may be other things we share or do not share that are. In drawing together many views of international collaboration and the experiences of international collaborators, this is perhaps the most valuable lesson to learn. International collaboration may at first appear to be just a natural extension of the work of an individual or local group, but in practice it is much more. It is an activity that, of necessity, must move beyond the research itself and take into account differences in national regulations and their effectiveness, legal systems, personal and cultural styles, research environments, and, of course, all of the logistical problems that can arise when your colleague is not just down the hall or in another building. However, before turning to these differences there is one important point that bears brief discussion, the value of international collaboration.

Much to be Gained

Considerable attention has already been given to the importance and benefits of international collaboration in research. Countries develop strategies to promote collaboration and worry when competitor nations seem to be doing better than they are at it. Some areas of research, such as high-energy physics, pandemics or global economies, cannot exist without international collaboration. There is much to be gained from working with colleagues in other parts of the world. This aspect of this book should not be controversial. There are, however, two lessons about the benefits to keep in mind.

First, although our authors ran into and recognized all sorts of "ways to get in trouble," the complications they noted did not dampen their enthusiasm for international collaboration. This suggests that broad collaboration is a strong, natural part of research today and not something imposed by national bodies and economic goals. The reasons for collaboration, of course, vary. Sometimes it is based on the need for unique information. There are no rainforests in Minnesota or Michigan. Developing countries often do not have access to advanced clinical research equipment. Sometimes collaboration is based simply on the need to find a colleague who is interested in the same problem as you are or to increase the size of a team working on a problem. The saying, "more minds are better than one," is true for most areas of problem solving. Whatever the reasons, researchers enjoy and benefit from collaborations.

Second, some of the troubles mentioned throughout this book suggest that international collaboration should not by itself be seen as a benefit or be used as a measure of success, as sometimes happens. Joining with partners in other countries to increase the chances of getting published in an international journal might be encouraged in some countries, but this reason alone is not enough to sustain an international collaboration. Collaborations that are driven primarily by economic motivations can also lead to conflicts and tensions. Businesses compete; researchers are supposed to cooperate. To get the maximum benefit from international collaborations, they should be based primarily on intellectual justifications. When they are, the potential for benefit is high. When they are not, the door to "trouble" can sometimes be opened.

Many Ways to Get in Trouble

Despite our like-mindedness as editors of this volume and our common, rather smug confidence that we each know how to deal with a few feet (one or two meters) of snow, it's never a good idea to assume that all our ideas and strategies are aligned. Abiding by one city's post-snowfall parking restrictions while in the other's city would likely just lead to having to retrieve a car that the city towed away because it was in the wrong place at the wrong time.

Likewise, researchers who assume that everything they know about doing research in one context will transfer directly and without modification to any other context are asking for trouble. The chapters in this volume suggest that there are several important kinds of trouble that international collaborators should take steps to avoid.

Rules and Regulations

Most of the chapters in this volume address directly or indirectly the wide range of rules to which international research is subject. Bohnhorst et al. and Capron review the legal and governance issues that plague international cooperation. Inattention to law is one of the quickest and surest ways to get into trouble. Lyman points to the importance of having a practical understanding of regulations and procedures, whereas De Vries et al. emphasize the power of less-tangible, normative assumptions that require careful attention in the international context. Handley makes the critical point that taking advantage of the expertise of the diplomatic corps is a good way to avoid an international incident. This may seem like an obvious warning, but if you do not know the basic rules for responsible research in all the countries in which you are working, you are asking for trouble.

Finances and Logistics

Most researchers have a hard enough time dealing with the funding agencies and institutional financial systems in their own national contexts. Figuring out a collaborator's funding system and coordinating between the two can be more than a harried researcher can handle. Mayer and Chapman et al. explain how national systems have developed in ways that can make smooth coordination elusive. Adding the complexities of transferring materials and personnel between research sites and coordinating data collection on different continents can overburden even staff members with particular expertise in these areas. Nebeker and Pais/Xavier/Belani show just how difficult these problems can become. This is one area where it is more than likely that the rules of different countries will conflict and lead to seemingly irresolvable problems.

Research Environments and Culture

Knowing how to navigate one research environment does not immediately qualify one to navigate all others, even within a particular discipline. Social structures, scientific practices, custom, culture, institutional context and historical development all affect the way things are done in a particular research setting. The emerging developments in China that Sun describes are changing the way research is done there. Stegemann et al. suggest ways in which publication practices are subject to regional differences. The accounts by doctoral students in Anderson et al. illustrate how many factors influence laboratory norms in different parts of the world. Cultural influences are also significant, as shown in the first-person accounts by Adib Abdel-Messih and

Leckie. Just because laboratories and research settings around the world look basically the same does not mean that what goes on from day to day is the same.

Doing the Right Thing

Staying out of trouble is partly a matter of knowing how to behave. The chapters by Steneck, Boesz/Fischer and Stainthorpe review an array of recent initiatives aimed at making cross-national standards of behavior more transparent and accessible. The challenges of communicating these standards effectively to young scientists are considerable, as chapters by Heitman/Petty, Godfrey and Anderson et al. suggest. "Doing the right thing" might at first seem obvious, but can be more complicated than one anticipates.

Momentum toward Internationalization of Structures that Support Collaboration

Based on the various stories and experiences reported in this book, it is heartening to see the many ways in which the systems in place to support international collaborations are improving. The Internet has, of course, by itself created a more international world. Computers and the Internet greatly facilitate real-time international "travel" and communication. It is sometimes easier to talk electronically with a colleague halfway around the world than in person with a colleague down the hall. Live videoconferencing now adds the personal touch, provided it is possible to find a time when all of the participants would reasonably be awake. International collaborators can now store and access data any place in the world, and even control remotely run, complex experiments. Younger researchers have grown up in this world; experienced researchers are adapting to it.

International research collaboration is also slowly being facilitated by more cross-national collaboration in the areas of research administration, regulation, and the promotion of ethics and integrity. Rules for authorship are becoming more universal. Countries are working on ways to share materials and intellectual property, especially when there is a need to balance sharing with international security. Educators are developing ways to make it easier for students to study and do research in other countries. Researchers themselves are talking more about their own standards and values, which could, one day, lead to the adoption of a common code of conduct for research. All of these developments will, we hope, eventually yield a more complete worldview for international collaborations.

This somewhat sunny picture of the future of international collaboration unfortunately has one significant storm cloud hanging over it—international imbalances. Stegemann et al. are concerned that developing countries have not been equal partners in working out the worldview for international collaborations, and De Vries et al. and Capron suggest that developed countries may have too strong a voice. To succeed over the long-term, international collaborations must be balanced and take into account the needs and values of all of the partners, particularly at national levels.

National Research Systems: Somewhere between Global Research and Individual Researchers

As we noted at the outset, there is a sense in which research is universal and the same everywhere. A laboratory in Tokyo looks much like a laboratory in Konstanz or in Mumbai. Norms of presentation and publication, linked to the scientific method, support the apparent commonality of research by removing person- and place-specific references. There is usually nothing in a scientific article to suggest the influence of context on the work done. It would seem, then, that to work together internationally, all you have to do is put money and people together and you have a collaboration. But it isn't that simple. There are differences and variations at a number of different levels: national, disciplinary, institutional, departmental, laboratory and even individual. What proportion of this variation is due to differences at the national level? Unfortunately, current research and understandings do not provide a definitive answer to this question.

We have uncovered clues, however, that national-level variation—which has not previously received much attention—accounts for some of the variation in how research is done. Respect of hierarchy in interpersonal interactions is a function of norms transmitted during graduate training, which vary cross-nationally; this factor affects how quickly information can be exchanged and decisions made on a collaborative project. Targets of funding (individuals versus institutions) vary by national funding systems; this feature influences the degree of control that principal investigators have over a project's financial trajectory. Attitudes toward authority are linked to national or regional custom; the extent to which persons at higher levels can be challenged has implications for researchers' ability to call attention to questionable behavior as a means of ensuring research integrity. Differences in national research systems appear to have effects on collaborative work. How much, we don't know, particularly when viewed in light of all of the other factors that can influence international research collaborations.

Conclusion

For readers who have never had the joy (?) of shoveling snow, or who may never even have seen it, the experience is much like running an experiment. You need to begin by understanding the task you are about to take on: How deep is the snow? Is it wet or dry? Is there a wind? Can I get someone else to do the work for me? All snow is not the same, a fact humans discovered and could describe in great deal centuries ago. The same, we suggest, holds true for international research collaborations.

Collaborations are not all the same. They become more complex when they cross borders and become international. Working with colleagues in other countries offers many benefits. The way to avoid troubles is to understand the complexities and plan in advance how you will deal with them. As the chapters in this book make clear, this includes everything from personal differences in working habits, professional goals and basic values, to different levels of support and the availability of crucial equipment or resources, to the variations in the way research is administered, regulated and assessed in different parts of the world. Becoming aware of the challenges of working in the global arena and planning carefully in advance are, we believe, the best ways to avoid problems and ensure that both the researchers involved and the public that supports them gain maximum benefit from international collaborations in research.

Appendices

The issues addressed in this volume are of real consequence for researchers who collaborate internationally. For them, legal, financial, organizational and other challenges are compounded by the details of cross-national arrangements and the nuances of cultural exchange. The authors represented in the following appendices are distinguished scientists, each with years of collaborative experience in the international arena. Ibrahim Adib Abdel-Messih, Prem Pais, Kumar Belani and James Leckie were honored guests and presenters at the conference that initiated this examination of international cooperation. We are grateful to them for permitting us to publish their accounts of their experiences and their perspectives on what helps and hinders international research.

Egypt

Ibrahim Adib Abdel-Messih. Interview by Melissa S. Anderson

Would you please give some examples of what you see as challenges that come up when scientists work cross-nationally?

Actually, I will tell you more about situations than stories. First, there are very strong family ties in the Middle East in general and in Egypt specifically. When we want to conduct a trial, we should approach the community and the family as a whole, not different individuals. We have to first approach the village leader, the religious leader, the one we call the Mosque Sheikh or Imam. Then we approach the head of the family, for each individual family. And then in the last step—if we've gotten approval from all of the others—we approach the individual for the informed consent.

Would this be for any research or just for clinical trials?

I think for any research. If, for example, you want to conduct an environmental study and collect dust from the ground or some water from the river, they will question what you are doing. And you really have to announce beforehand, to the stakeholders in the area exactly what you're doing. So I think it's kind of a general approach to this closed community, especially in rural areas, more so than in the big cities. This rule applies to Egypt and many other Middle Eastern countries.

How would a researcher from another area know whom to contact. You need to start with the leaders of the local mosque. What would be the appropriate protocol for finding out the right chain of commands for getting approval for a study?

That's why I think the international researcher should really involve local researchers, local stakeholders, in the research protocol. A researcher cannot really just go to the village and think that he knows everything, thinking, "I can do everything alone. I have the knowledge. I have the experience. I have the scientific background, so I will go and conduct this research." Actually, especially in community-based research and in rural areas, this is nearly impossible because you need this special approach that reflects the culture of these communities.

So it would be a big mistake to go in any other way.
And it has happened, actually, it did happen. And it was a major factor that made many researchers fail to conduct their studies, because they think they know everything, and they don't need to consult anybody. And then they are faced with this situation.

In those cases, did the studies simply fall apart, or were there more significant consequences besides just dropping the study?
Well, yeah, there have sometimes been aggressive reactions, when people really didn't go about the project carefully. All the rumors start to come out: What are the real intentions of this research? What is this "foreigner" doing in our village? So it really can be dangerous and has consequences that really have to be controlled.

What other kinds of situations affect international scientific collaboration?
Another situation that affects international scientific collaboration is that religion plays a major role in this community. This community is very religious and religion influences daily living. For example, during Ramadan, you cannot really conduct a clinical trial that involves ingestion of any material or a blood draw, due to the fasting season. It's a complete fast until sunset. And there is a special way of life during this month, different than in the other 11 months in the year. You really have to plan to be away during this religious feast and the holy month of Ramadan, which is the month of fasting. And another thing is the tradition of travel during the feast. So your planning really has to consider this feast, the religious habits, religious ceremonies, fasting, celebrations and so on.

Now when you say there are difficulties with travel, do you mean the people there are traveling or that the people doing the research would have trouble traveling?
No, the people there are traveling, so subjects will not be available. And another point related to religion is the conservativeness of the community. These people in rural areas specifically and in Upper Egypt (in the south) are very conservative. For example, no male can talk with a woman without, for example, a female social worker or a female research team member attending them. And you cannot easily go into people's homes, unless you are accompanied by a person who is very familiar to them. It helps a bit being a physician. They respect a physician, and they can allow him to talk to females. But still it's very much preferable to be accompanied by a female member of the study team or by a local, trusted person in your home visits. You have to be very cautious when talking or laughing with females, you know, because people are very conservative.

Here's another situation related to the conservative perspective. I was a member of the Institutional Review Board, and there was discussion of a research protocol submitted. It was a proposal for a workshop that involved a questionnaire about sexual behavior in teenagers. And they wanted to ask questions of teenagers from different areas in Egypt, to study sexual behaviors and the possible risk of acquiring the HIV virus. We at the Institutional Review Board discussed it thoroughly, and we finally didn't approve this protocol, because we thought it was very high-risk. Even though there were no biological specimens or any other intervention, other than a set of questions, we thought that, in this conservative community, speaking about this subject to this age group could really put subjects, especially the girls, at very high risk with their families. This approach would not be acceptable in these communities. And all of that of course applies more to rural areas and small towns than to big cities like Cairo or Alexandria.

Are there other situations that can lead to problems?
One time we were doing a study, a cohort study, where we followed-up some kids and their families for some time. And we decided to do a parallel study—an observational study—where social workers would go to homes to observe and record different health hygienic behaviors. The point was to get some information about possible mode of transmission of *Helicobacter pylori* bacteria. This is a relatively newly discovered bacteria, and the epidemiology and the mode of transmission of this bacteria is not yet known or identified. We thought that an observational study of hygienic behavior in the high-risk group would help us to, you know, get some clues about the epidemiology. We sent social workers to stay about four hours at houses where infection was high, according to breath tests which at that time were the gold standard of detecting *Helicobacter pylori*. And after a week or so, we heard that sending a social worker or a health worker from the team to stay at a home for such a long time was starting rumors about the health status of this specific house. There were rumors that there was a serious or dangerous infection inside, and that's why the health team was staying so long inside, to fix the problem. This created real trouble for the people, so we had to stop the observational study, because of the trouble we caused for these families. They were selected according to the breath-test results, but it turned out to be a rumor about a serious infection—actually the literal translation was "epidemic"—in the house. This shows how misinterpretation can cause a lot of trouble.

What happened then?
Well, the original study was going on with no problems, because we had been there a long time in the village, and we had built mutual trust. We followed the rules that really should be followed, like involving local physicians and local health workers. So the original study about the *Helicobacter pylori* infection was going well, but this observation study really had to stop.

254 • I. Adib Abdel-Messih

Have you seen any cases of researchers from elsewhere in the world making mistakes that you would hope other international researchers would avoid?
Yes, actually, that's a very common situation. Many knowledgeable researchers are very good scientists, they are good at their work, they have all the background, but they are not culturally educated about these countries. So, as I mentioned before, they may not be aware of the conservative nature of the community. They talk freely to everybody, to women, to young girls, and they try to tackle all the study procedures themselves, and not use the local people enough. So this can cause them a lot of trouble, and we've seen that. And we've also seen others who followed the rules and respected these rules and were sensitive enough to realize that it's not only knowledge or science that makes these studies succeed. You have to be really culturally competent and sensitive to conduct such studies in these communities.

I remember during a certain vaccine trial, one researcher wasn't actually doing it all wrong, but he didn't follow our advice. He brought in the media—some video filming, some video recording—without getting the permission of the community. He thought "This will be very simple. This won't harm anybody. We're just recording what we are doing for the media, and this is very important." It actually led to very low compliance for the trial procedure just after this event. Subjects just didn't show up for the vaccination. At that time, it really caused a lot of trouble at the site. It was a violation, because it was filming mothers and their children, i.e., women. Men don't mind at all. On the contrary, they want to be in photos and they want to get "famous." But this was about women again and the conservative approach.

Where was the researcher from?
From the United States, but many foreign researchers really followed the rules, and they knew what to do, because they had other overseas experiences. They had done some background reading and educational orientation about the nature of these communities, and they did it the right way. They were very popular. After some time, they were considered like one of the family and part of the community, and not treated at all as a foreigner—with the extreme of even inviting them home to have lunch or dinner. And it was really different when they approached it from the right way, compared to when they thought they could do everything alone.

For example, in another vaccine trial, the same researcher from the United States just kind of stepped back and put us on the front lines—that is, the front lines of the study, dealing with people. He just answered questions, and he was there to support us and be very honest with the people. These people can be uneducated, illiterate, but very smart. They have a sense of who respects them, who respects their culture, who respects their community, and who thinks that he is the one who understands everything and doesn't need advice. So people have a good sense of that. It goes well if the researcher is really honest and respectful to these communities, if he bears in mind all these factors, for his own good and for the transparency of the trials, and if he is very honest about mentioning all the different aspects of the trials, and so on.

Going back to the *Helicobacter pylori* bacteria study, when we were getting started, there was that breath test which was new at the time. It was actually new all over the world. The scientist who invented the test taught us how to do the test. It involved ingestion of some powder mixed with liquid. Basically, you ingest it, and a half-hour later you give your exhalation breath specimen that will be analyzed to detect these bacteria. We had very good relations in that community, but everybody was kind of wondering, "What's in this powder? This is written in English. We don't understand what's on the label. They are trying new drugs in our community. We haven't seen this before." And so on. An Egyptian researcher volunteered to be the first one to take the test, and this helped them to see that "here's the physician who knows better" (in their opinion), the wise man, and he is taking this test, so it should be safe. Although they trust us as physicians, you still have to go sometimes the second mile.

The scientists actually didn't realize that this would help, but they followed him doing the same test after that. And then the official from the Ministry of Health was next, so people really got satisfied. This was done because the researcher sensed from the faces of people what they were thinking. So he just volunteered before anybody raised any concerns.

It reminds me of a physician in the United States who gives children spinal taps. And he underwent the procedure himself, so that he would understand what the children were going through.
Oh, a lot of suffering. It's a very tough procedure.

Well, I'm just going to keep asking until you run out of stories.
Here's another point: the relation between politics and research. Usually in the Middle Eastern communities, there's the effect of media and political issues, especially in the last, say, 10–15 years, with the wars in Iraq and Afghanistan. They have created lot of ... well, I would say frankly, the United States is not presented in the very best light. And this is due to the policies. And we were struggling hard when doing collaborations with U.S. researchers specifically, to explain to people that politics is different from research. Politics is different from science. You may not like the policy of XYZ, and I may not like it either, but I like the science out of the university because this is progress in human science. To explain this concept was really hard for us, while dealing with the effects of the media, bombing in Iraq, bombing in Afghanistan and the long-standing conflict in Israel—this politics thing. And, of course, the media in Egypt and the Arab world in the Middle East sometimes exaggerates the scene for the people.

So does ours sometimes.
Yeah, yeah, every country. So it's from one point of view. It exaggerates one side, and hides another side and so on. These politics are really closely related to research. I've seen it during the second war on Iraq. I remember in the year 2000 or sometime like that, the day that a major bombing happened, we lost something like 30 subjects from our vaccine trial, out of 90 enrolled. Actually politics affect research a lot, and this factor has to be taken into consideration when planning a study—maybe preparing people for the nationality of the researchers, and making sure they understand the concept of science, and how the people are different than the politicians. Although this is very hard usually, but it has to be at least tried, worked out.

You have focused largely on the subjects. Have you seen any situations in which a collaboration caused problems for the researcher, either Egyptian or U.S. or anyone else? Where in a sense it backfired or was so problematic or serious that it had repercussions for the careers of the researchers?
Of course, usually when researchers come to a foreign country, it's a sacrifice, and they expect that their career will be boosted by this research. They are really anxious to get most of the results in a short time, to get this boost. This sometimes actually conflicts with the initiative of the local researchers, because they think that they are conducting all the work and without them the work wouldn't have been conducted. Everybody has a point of view from a different angle. The researchers from other countries think, "I brought the research. I brought the funding." And the other's point of view is, "I conducted the research. Without me you could not have access to this community." This relates to the credit for presentations at conferences, publications and promotions if they work in the same organization. Everybody, of course, has high hopes for the effect of the research on his career, but there is always room for conflict, especially in the non-monetary areas like publication, like conference presentations. There are no solid rules in those areas. There are always gray areas and personal preferences that influence who is included in authorship and presentations, and so on. So this has to be clarified from the start, before starting the research. This will help a lot to minimize the conflicts or the potential for conflict.

There was a publication in Nature *about a year ago about having a "prenuptial agreement" for collaborators to get these things worked out* (Ledford, 2008).
I think it's a great idea, because we've seen many times, as long as this is not very well-defined from the start, conflicts happen, because everybody thinks he is the one who influenced the research, he is the one who put in the most effort and so on.

As long as we've moved on to researchers here, what about interactions in the lab or interactions in the course of actually doing the science?

There are always conflicts between the lab team and the field team. The lab people think that they are interpreting the results, that they are doing the hard work, they are risking infections with the specimens. The field people think that they are the research from A to Z, and nobody else is participating, other than doing his usual routine work. It's always like that. Lab people think that they are underestimated, unrecognized. So always, I think this is a general issue, it's not just with Egypt or with international research.

Moving on, based on your own experience, what do you think are the primary challenges in international research?

I can put them in terms of the different ways people look at research in different countries. For example, in Egypt, doctors are really a distinguished group, a very authoritative group, and even in rural Egypt, they call doctors "Hakim," an Arabic term that means "wise man." So he is not only knowledgeable in medicine, he is a wise man.

And so tell me more about what that means.

This means that there is a paternalistic approach in this research. It's from the Pharaonic times, when the priests were also the physicians. So there is a mixture between religion and medicine. These people have to be obeyed and followed because they are wise men, they are knowledgeable men, they are the men of God. So even now, this view of physicians is still present, and people cannot really accept it when the physician asks them to choose for themselves. We always hear, "If you don't know which is better, how could I know? You tell me what's better. I trust you." So this paternalistic approach is always there.

The concept of research, the word "research" itself, does not have a good translation in Arabic or in many African languages. Research, if you translate it literally, means an experiment, and this implies a bad thing, that you are experimenting on a person. Also, the concepts of placebo and randomization cannot be readily understood in these communities. You cannot really convince people with these concepts. At the end, they just say "Okay, you do what you see right. We trust you doctor. We don't understand what you're saying." Even if they say, "Okay, I'll sign the informed consent," on the inside, they don't really understand what a placebo means, what randomization means, and so on.

And there is an Egyptian group that studied the understanding of the informed consent process (Khalil, Silverman, Raafat, El-Kamary & El-Setouhy, 2007). The other reference which I found very useful on this issue was "Issues in the Design and Implementation of Vaccine Trials in Less Developed Countries" (Deen & Clemens, 2007).

Okay. Now what rules, policies, or regulations complicate the problem you've mentioned, if any?
The research community in Egypt is not yet fully mature, and it still has to be reformed, and well-defined. And basically, there are only a few rules, and the rules that apply are the rules of the community where the research is conducted. For example, the informed consent form. In these communities, the written informed consent is very difficult to obtain. Egyptians, like many others, as you know, are accustomed to signing only on documents related to a birth certificate or a death certificate or when selling their land. They're not interested in signing any other documents, although they will tell you, "Okay go ahead, I agree with what you say, but I will not sign any documents." So I think flexibility on this matter of written or verbal consents should be considered in these communities. Maybe sometimes audio-taping could replace written consent. In working in these communities, I've found that documenting the consent is the hardest part, not obtaining the informed consent. And this actually applies to many other countries. Again, the language used to describe the research procedures has no good translation or translation of the meaning—the word "experiment" and the word "research."

One thing also that we should really highlight in this chapter, if you think it will be useful, is the question, "What happens after the research is over?"

I had that in mind, so I'm glad you brought it up.
I always ask myself and colleagues this question, because we start by building up capabilities in the community where we are conducting research. Sometimes we set up a field clinic, we offer to make a physician available in the mornings and make this health service available for 24 hours. We offer free medication to the study subject, and sometimes this is expanded to their families and automatically expanded to their small community. So at the end, the trial actually affects the whole community for a long time, like for one or two years, and they are accustomed to this service. Instead of going far to the main health facility in their village or town and waiting for a long time and buying their medication, they have the physician available, conveniently located at their place. They enjoy welcoming smiles and they have good treatment, because the study team and physicians are aware that these are the trial subjects. They have to take good care of the study subjects. They have to pamper them to keep their voluntary participation active throughout the study. And then, after the study is over, everything is lost, all of the benefits, and they always wonder who is responsible for that. Is the researcher responsible? Is the researcher's organization responsible? Or are the local health authorities responsible for maintaining this level of care, if they approved the research in the first place? Or is the research ethics committee responsible for setting up some rules about this? So this really has to be thought about before the research, not just left to chance or circumstances.

Given the way the research is set up—episodic and not longitudinal—what would be a good solution here?
I think, yeah, it's a very tough situation, but the nearest solution that I can see is from the local health authorities. If they approve the trial to be conducted with this level of health care at their area, they have to make sure that this level of health care is maintained after the study is over. And they may even ask for extra budget amounts for that for some time, because, at the end, they are responsible for the health and welfare of their own people. The researcher is interested in the health and welfare of the people for some time during the trial, but not all the time, because that is not his responsibility.

What blind spots do you think scientists who have not collaborated previously might have?
I think, you know, the term that summarizes all of this is "culture competence" or sensitivity. They should get focused training about these issues that we discussed, and these issues should include history, religion and country-specific culture. And this will help them a lot to understand. And also they should actually have a lot of meetings and a lot of interaction with local researchers before conducting the trial, to get their views, to get their opinion. And I think, the main blind spots we discussed are what happens after the research is over, how we organize research, how we define different rules, how we make the most of our resources from science and from field-site resources and from local people. Also, how to involve local people in an efficient, culturally sensitive way. All of these issues have to be thought about before starting research studies.

What about effects on students or early-career scientists?
I think for a young researcher or a student, if they have, like, education for overseas country, that will help a lot—say, four or six months. Take, for example, U.S. Navy doctors in infectious diseases. They come to Egypt and Kenya to examine patients with infectious diseases that can be very rare in the United States or in the West. So to finish their fellowship, they have to have two months of this training. I had responsibilities in that program in Egypt. We visited all the infectious diseases hospitals, the skin clinics, where, for example, they can get the experience with diseases like leprosy, which they cannot see anywhere else in the developed world, and some other infectious diseases which are now rare in the world.

Well, to conclude, what kinds of advice can you give to scientists who have not yet begun an international collaboration?
Well, first, do a lot of homework. For example, before one travels on holiday, he browses travel websites on the Internet. What are the must dos? What are the best things he might like in this country? What are the best budget-saving ways for his holiday? So in the same way, he has to do some homework about

the country where the research is conducted. He has to get some understanding and sensitivity about all these cultural aspects of this specific country, about the religion, the culture, the history of this country. And during the conduct of the trial, he has to be honest, sincere, open to people. He has to follow the local norms and customs, try to get advice from local peers and colleagues. He has to share information and spread his knowledge so that people know how valuable scientific international research can be. And also, I think this is not just the researchers themselves. I think it's important to strengthen the research ethics committee, the local committee—strengthen and enforce their role and try to help them be economically and physically independent of any other influence. This helps a lot in conducting ethical research.

Well, is there anything else you'd like to add, Ibrahim?
One last point is about maintaining voluntary participation throughout the research. In these countries, if a subject signed the consent and enrolled himself in the research, that doesn't mean that he will participate in the research. So continuous participation and maintaining his voluntary participation has to be considered.

Also, throughout the research, information has to be shared through updates, meetings, regular meetings with locals, so people feel that these researchers are really transparent and careful to share information, share the situation with them.

Thank you.

References

Deen, J. L., & Clemens, J. D. (2006). Issues in the design and implementation of vaccine trials in less developed countries. *Nature Reviews Drug Discovery, 5*, 932–940.

Khalil, S. S., Silverman, H. J., Raafat, M., El-Kamary, S., & El-Setouhy, M. (2007). Attitudes, understanding, and concerns regarding medical research amongst Egyptians: A qualitative pilot study. *BMC Medical Ethics, 8*(9), doi: 10.1186/1472-6939-8-9.

Ledford, H. (2008). Collaborations: With all good intentions. *Nature, 452*(7188), 682–684.

India

Prem Pais, Denis Xavier, and Kumar G. Belani

This appendix discusses the evolution of clinical trials and clinical research in India. It focuses on regulatory issues and challenges specific to the country and to the development of multi-center studies in the country. In addition, it describes some recent experiences of research investigators in conducting research in India. Two of the authors (Pais and Xavier) present the perspective of Indian researchers. The other (Belani) adds his experience on collaborative research in India.

The Early Days

St. John's Medical College, a medical school in Bangalore, India, was started in 1963. In the last decade, it has ventured increasingly into clinical research, a field that, surprisingly, is still not very much a part of the activities of most medical schools in India. In 2004 St. John's Research Institute was established with its own dean, making St. John's the only medical school in India with an independent research institute. The research institute has a number of divisions covering both bench and clinical research. Despite its name, the clinical-trials division carries out a significant number of epidemiologic studies, mainly in the field of cardiovascular disease, in addition to clinical trials. It has focused on large, multi-center studies, and over the last 10 years the division has developed a network of collaborating centers all over the country.

In 1999 St. John's became the national coordinating center for the trial of reviparin and glucose insulin potassium infusion in acute myocardial infarction by the CREATE (Clinical trial of Reviparin and mEtabolic modulation in Acute myocardial infarction Treatment Evaluation) Estudio Cardiologicas Latin America (ECLA) Study Group (Yusuf, Mehta, Xie, Ahmed, Xavier, Pais et al., 2005; Mehta, Yusuf, Diaz, Zhu, Pais, Xavier et al., 2005). It gave us first-hand experience of the challenges and joys of multi-center clinical trials in India. We conducted this low-budget trial as a green-field study (that is, we carried out all activities in the study from obtaining regulatory approvals, drug import, storage and distribution), learning the regulatory requirements and getting them ourselves (as we could not afford a contract research organization). We set up a coordinating office, a central randomization system, developed non-carbon-required, case-report forms (NCRCRFs) and set up a network of participating centers. CREATE was the first clinical trial that most of these centers had been involved in, and we traveled extensively throughout the country training site personnel. Since many of these centers at that time did not have their own institutional review boards, we guided them in setting one up or obtaining clearance from the one independent ethics committee in existence at that time in India. CREATE included subjects from China and later from the ECLA group from South America. The international coordinator was at McMaster University in Canada. The project exposed us to international meetings and partners as well.

Since the CREATE trial we have conducted collaborative studies—clinical trials and epidemiologic studies—with industry and academic organizations, both national and international, and have worked in collaboration with the Indian Council of Medical Research. Our collaborating centers have now grown to 176. While we ourselves still obtain regulatory approval for our academically sponsored studies through the Indian Council of Medical Research and the Ministry of Health, we have fortunately been able to work through contract research organizations for other regulatory approvals.

The Evolution of Clinical Studies in India

Until the early 1990s, small uncontrolled clinical trials involving 8–10 centers and 200–300 subjects were all that were conducted in India. These were done mainly to satisfy regulatory requirements for minimal safety data on medications marketed abroad, before they were marketed in India. Such trials were largely unmonitored and of very spotty quality.

In the early 1990s, some multi-national pharmaceutical companies set up independent research divisions and started to include India in the multi-country trials being conducted by their parent company. Contract research organizations soon followed. They began to bid to include India in international trials. The main attractions of India were lower costs, a potentially large number of subjects and clinically skilled, English-speaking physicians. These organizations trained investigators and study staff at a few selected sites.

The Indian Council of Medical Research had been active in clinical trials regarding tuberculosis. Epidemiologic studies in the country were being done mainly by the Indian Council of Medical Research and some independent academic researchers. Such studies were mainly cross-sectional surveys of the prevalence of disease and risk factors, with some cohorts and registries in cancer. Regulatory requirements were minimal and, in research studies other than trials, non-existent. Institutional ethical review boards were few and far between.

A research team at the University of Minnesota in the United States attempted to collaborate with a research institution in India (not St. John's). The study was a multi-center, multi-national trial of a new, non-invasive device. There was no difficulty in obtaining ethical and institutional review board approvals in the home institution, or at institutions in France, Austria and Japan, but there was considerable difficulty in obtaining approval in India. It took considerable time to help them set up an institutional review board, and the board insisted that the volunteer patients get financial reimbursement for participating in the study. Eventually, the Indian site had to be dropped, because the research protocol did not call for financial payments to volunteers in this evaluation of the non-invasive device. Since then, the Indian Council of Medical Research has set up guidelines for institutions for setting up ethical and institutional review board committees (Indian Council of Medical Research, n.d.). It has also issued a mandate that clinical investigations may be conducted only after obtaining institutional review board approval.

Current Clinical Research in India

Over the last decade things have changed. Clinical trials are booming. By some estimates, India would be earning a billion U.S. dollars in the next few years from such trials ("Clinical Trials," 2006). Despite this, there is significant room for growth because India contributes only 1.5 percent of global patient enrollment and 2 percent of clinical trial volume ("India Preferred Destination," 2009). In most of these trials, however, there is little academic input. Investigators serve mainly to recruit subjects and follow study protocols. Regulations have also developed, and doing trials and (especially) academic studies in India through international collaboration is not as simple as in the early days of CREATE.

Getting Ethical Approval for Research Studies

The Indian Council of Medical Research has published ethical guidelines for clinical research in India, and for setting up institutional ethical review boards (Indian Council of Medical Research, n.d.). It has encouraged sites, especially academic ones, to set up their own institutional ethical review boards. The guidelines are broadly in line with those of the U.S. National Institutes of Health. It is now mandatory for all human research in India to obtain ethical approval from a properly constituted institutional ethical review board prior to the start of the research.

If a site has its own institutional ethical review board, it is generally required that ethical approval be issued by this board. (We know of cases, however, in which investigators have requested clearance from other boards because of "political problems.") When a site does not have its own review board, clearance may be obtained from a valid review board that is either independent or associated with another institution. The latter is not usually an option, because most institutional boards are reluctant to give clearance for another institution.

Since the CREATE days, things have improved, and most sites now have their own institutional ethical review boards. Even when sites in India have their own boards, it is wise for international collaborators to assist busy principal investigators by providing a template for application to hasten things along. With the boom in industry-sponsored trials, some sites, especially private corporate hospitals, charge substantial fees for ethics reviews, over $1,000 at times. Although in many cases they are willing to charge lower fees for low-budget or unsponsored academic trials, this is by no means always the case. Another problem is that often the members of review boards are unfamiliar with clinical trials and raise objections to issues such as the use of placebos. Such issues can usually be sorted out with diplomacy and persistence, but they lead to delays.

Regulatory Approvals for Industry-Sponsored and Academic Studies

The Drugs Controller General of India grants permission for clinical trials involving drugs or devices in India. In the case of industry-sponsored studies, only this approval is required. Documents to be submitted are the latest version of the protocol, the informed consent form with any translated versions to be used, letters of acceptance and biographical data from investigators, and at least one institutional ethical review board approval. Multi-national trials that have received approval and have commenced in other countries are eligible for expedited review.

Academic collaborations between Indian and non-Indian universities require additional clearance from the Health Ministry Screening Committee to ensure that Indian subjects and investigators are not being taken advantage of. The Indian Council of Medical Research acts as the secretariat for this clearance. In addition to the documents noted above, the Health Ministry Screening Committee requires the review board approval of each investigating site before considering the study. In the case of multi-center studies with a large number of centers, this requirement leads to delays. The whole process of submission, peer review and approval takes 3–6 months, or longer if clarifications are asked for. It is therefore important to apply for Health Ministry Screening Committee clearance as early as possible. For academic clinical trials involving drugs or appliances, approval by the Drugs Controller General of India is required before submission to the Indian Council of Medical Research.

Any international organization doing collaborative research with an institution in India must have such projects approved by the Indian Council of Medical Research, particularly if the projects involve funding from overseas and if they involve transfer of biological materials such as blood or serum. An international health division coordinates and facilitates approval of joint projects with international agencies and institutions, and the related procedures and application formats differ, based on the countries and agencies involved. The Indian Council of Medical Research has a specific, detailed review mechanism for projects. Studies other than clinical trials, conducted entirely by Indian centers, do not require any approval other than that of the ethical review board. It is now also a requirement that all clinical trials be registered with and approved by the Drugs Controller General of India.

Importing investigational drugs into India requires an import license; sending blood samples out of the country requires an export license. Both of these can be obtained once the study protocol is approved by the Drugs Controller General of India or the Health Ministry Screening Committee. Shipping cells out of the country for gene studies requires separate approval that is generally difficult to obtain. In one case we know of, in which the University of Minnesota was involved, obtaining permission for transport of biological materials has been difficult. The study involved an institution in southern India and was approved by the institutional review boards at both institutions. It involved collection of stool samples for sophisticated processing available in the United States. It has been several years, and the institution in India has been unable to transport the stool samples to the United States.

Challenges for the Clinical Investigator

Doing research in India is not easy for a clinician. Dedicated research time is not an option in most institutions, including "academic" ones. The clinical workload is heavy, and in medical schools the second priority is instruction of students and residents. It is therefore strongly advisable for each investigator to have a co-investigator who can share the work. First-time principal investigators need advice and help to set up a research team with research assistants.

Site Requirements

Apart from human resources, a trial site needs appropriate space for storage of medication (such as a dedicated refrigerator) and good communication facilities, including phones capable of supporting international toll-free calls, as well as an Internet connection with sufficient speed and bandwidth for online data entry and fax lines. In addition, in many studies centrifuges and freezers for storage of biological samples may be required. Until five years ago, such equipment could not be taken for granted in India. If a site is a promising one, providing it with what is required will not only help the study in question but also serve as an investment for future studies. Now most sites have Internet access and adequate telephone facilities, although many may still need help to set up storage for biological materials.

Laboratory Investigations

Clinical studies raise the question of where to do laboratory tests: at the site or in a central laboratory. It is best to permit safety and screening laboratory tests locally, provided the site lab has basic quality-control procedures. This will facilitate quick reports and study-related decisions, and also permit reports to be shared with study subjects—something that most subjects would like and that would result in more cooperative subjects. It is worth drawing attention to the fact that, in many hospitals in India, laboratory tests are paid for by the subject. Therefore, doing a second test in the local lab for which the study subject pays when the same test has already be done in a central study lab may not be feasible.

Investigational Products

Having obtained an import license, investigators can import drugs only through those ports and airports that have representatives of the Drugs Controller General of India. These sites include Delhi, Mumbai and Chennai, but not Bangalore, as we discovered to our cost in CREATE.

India has extremes of temperature. Much of the central and northern part of the country may have ambient temperatures exceeding 40°C (104°F) in the summer. These temperatures make transport and storage of medication a problem, with requirements for refrigerated trucks or well-insulated containers and air-conditioned drug-storage facilities at sites. At times, investigators may not appreciate the importance of maintaining temperature logs, since this does not form part of normal clinical practice, but it is critical in this climate. Trial teams do usually not have research pharmacists in the group. Drug management is carried out by the principal investigator and the research coordinator. Maintaining a drug accountability log is extremely important.

Randomization Procedures

Random assignment of patients to treatment and control groups is at the heart of a randomized clinical trial. When we (Pais and Xavier) started CREATE (Yusuf et al., 2005; Mehta et al., 2005), we used a system in which envelopes with randomization assignments were to be opened on site, once eligibility criteria were fulfilled. In a few cases, we found the system misused and changed to a central randomized system by which envelopes were kept in the coordinating office in Bangalore and sites called the office for drug allotment. We had to set up an office that was manned 24 hours a day, with a toll-free telephone line. We have since been able to set up a computer-based system.

Challenges with Study Subjects and Long-term Follow-up

Long-term follow-up is a special challenge in India. The country has no system of central registration (such as Social Security numbers in the United States) through which subjects or their health records can be traced. Neither is the national death registration system yet developed enough to permit tracking of deaths of study subjects.

Migration of subjects is a problem, as is the frequency with which mobile telephone numbers are changed. It is therefore crucial to record as many addresses and phone numbers as possible, not only of the subject but also of friends and family who may help in tracing the subject. These contact lists should be updated each time the subject is contacted. In the end, tracing the last few subjects often calls for home visits by social workers or study staff. With attention to detail, however, good follow-up is possible. In CREATE, which required a one-month follow-up, we were able to contact 7,775 of the 7,780 subjects randomized in India, at times using social workers.

Working with subjects in clinical research in India poses some special challenges. Obtaining informed consent requires more time in explaining the issues carefully to subjects. Subjects often respond by leaving the decision to participate up to the physician ("If you think I should, I will") or, at the other extreme, view participating in a trial as being made a "guinea pig." Often subjects want to consult with family and friends before giving their consent to participate.

Among poorer subjects, one has to be careful that consent is not given to obtain free treatment or monetary benefit, while at the same time compensating subjects adequately for travel, meals and—importantly—wages lost, especially in the case of daily-wage earners. For some subjects, trials may be their only source of medical care. Issues of continuation of care, including medication at the end of the trial, are dilemmas that must be addressed.

Additional Challenges

Two other challenges that may not be peculiar to India are issues of media coverage and investigator payment. Media in India tend to sensationalize any incidents that may arise from clinical research, especially clinical trials, and often publish accusatory articles and air television stories without first getting a fair idea of the issues or expert opinion in the area. As clinical trials are becoming more common, media interest has declined somewhat.

The second issue, however, is not improving. Industry-sponsored trials are ready to pay ever-increasing investigator fees. Now some investigators are reluctant to be part of lower-budget, academic studies. This is an area of real concern and needs to be addressed by the medical scientific community in India. The message we try to convey to our partner investigators is that the studies they are involved in should constitute good science and should answer questions of local importance and relevance. By participating in collaborative studies, the clinical investigators can expect to improve their skills and knowledge, as well as the health of the population. They become part of a broader scientific community and make new friends. They may also make a little money, but the money must not be the primary motive.

Strategies for Running a Successful Multi-Center Study

If you plan to set up a clinical study in India, what would be some good strategies to follow? Based on the St. John's experience, we give the following general advice. Wherever possible, work with investigators with a record of good research work. Include some new investigators who seem enthusiastic and committed. Always give investigators a sense of shared ownership in the study by getting their input on the protocol and having meetings in which they are encouraged to play an active role. Be sure that publications fairly list everyone who has a right to be included as a co-author.

Be a little skeptical about the numbers investigators say they can recruit. They tend to give numbers from their clinic without much thought to inclusion and exclusion criteria, the number who will not consent, those who come from afar and may not be available for follow-up and, most of all, the time required of the principal investigator to recruit subjects.

Once the study is running, maintain frequent and friendly communication with investigators and their teams. Much diplomacy is called for, as investigators can be prickly. Apart from telephone calls it is important to have face-to-face meetings, so plan meetings, at least annually, at which business is combined with socializing. Many problems have been sorted out at the dining table, or over cocktails. Organizing opportunistic meetings to coincide with conferences does not seem to work, in our experience, as investigators are busy with other conference-related meetings, both scientific and personal.

We now provide advice in some specific areas, based on the St. John's collaborative experience.

Choosing Investigators and Sites

In the case of multi-center studies, the usual way to choose collaborating investigators is to use lists maintained by contract research organizations or by the pharmaceutical industry. Contract research organizations tend to go to the same sites again and again. Pharmaceutical industry lists are often generated by the marketing department of the company, which is more concerned about sales generated by the potential investigator than his or her scientific ability.

Instead, it is useful to start with people whom one knows personally and can work with comfortably. In a country as large as India, we have found it useful to have a regional steering committee, with committee members from different parts of the country to act as regional coordinators who can advise about potential collaborators from among their acquaintances, provide input into developing the research protocol and stay in contact with investigators from their own regions. It is worthwhile to include a few first-time investigators for each new trial, thereby developing a growing pool of collaborators. Practical experience has shown that large hospitals and busy clinicians do not always make good investigators, even in teaching hospitals. In the end, the motivation of the investigator is key. We have had excellent recruitment and data quality from smaller private hospitals.

The proper selection of a collaborating principal investigator is most important when collaborating with India. Some time ago, the University of Minnesota tried to embark on a multi-center clinical trial with several sites in India. The study was brought to the Indian Council of Medical Research for review and approval. There was a lot of difficulty in getting this study launched. The Indian Council of Medical Research required a single principal investigator from India. The three sites in India could not come to an agreement as to which researcher should serve as the principal investigator. Since one of the investigators was in Delhi, the Indian Council of Medical Research listed him as the principal investigator. We found out that when doing such studies with the involvement by the Indian Council of Medical Research, the principal investigator must submit to the Council 30 copies of the research proposal, five copies of Council forms, five copies of the duly signed material transfer agreement (in case the transfer of biological material is involved) and all clearances from the institutional review board. Unfortunately, in this case, the designated principal investigator was unable to fill out the required forms, assume a leadership role or attend joint meetings with the Council, despite having shown considerable interest in planning meetings both in Delhi and in the United States. We also learned that, since the project was registered in that researcher's name, the University of Minnesota could not designate a new principal investigator unless the original principal provided a release to the Council. In the absence of this release, the university could not continue the study with India under the same protocol, and India was eventually dropped as a site for the multi-center study. Before embarking on a study with India, the collaborating parties should review the requirements of the Indian Council of Medical Research and ensure that participating investigators understand and are able and willing to comply with these rules.

Keeping on Top of the Study

Even once a research team is in place, it remains important for the principal investigator to keep on top of the study and supervise the team closely. This does not always happen. Sometimes a call to the principal investigator reveals that he or she is unaware of the goings-on at the research site.

At all times, stay on top of the study. Do not let tasks pile up. Alert sites about overdue patient visits. This is particularly important, given the risk of subjects being lost to follow-up. Monitoring visits should be seen as opportunities to work with sites to improve study quality and solve problems, rather than policing. Monitors should be carefully trained in communication. Investigators get upset when researchers whom they see as "non-clinicians" tell them what to do. It is also important to check source documents during visits. Sometimes large public hospitals do not have adequate record systems, and investigators may have to develop their own study-specific source documents.

Contract Research Organizations

A large number of contract research organizations, both large and small, have started working in India. They can take away many of the hassles associated with trials, but they are expensive. Using their services in a low-budget academic study may not be feasible. In addition, even when one does employ such a group, it is better for the investigators themselves to know the regulations and rules involved than to leave them to the contract organizations. In the case of academic studies, where approval by the Indian Health Ministry Screening Committee is required, contract research organizations are unable to be of help, as application must be by the principal investigator. We note that, overall, contract research organizations are not very popular with investigators. They tend to train, rather than inform, investigators and research staff, and they focus more on monitoring and audits than on science

Advantages and Challenges of Clinical Studies in India

In summary, we see both advantages and challenges in pursuing collaborative clinical studies in India. Language is an advantage, in so far as Indian scientists speak English, the most common language used in scientific collaborations. Their clinical skills recommend them as collaborative investigators, and they have access to a large patient base. The Indian health-care system is improving in organizational terms, and it provides a lower-cost environment for some studies. We have also benefited from good information-technology systems and logistics.

Among the challenges are the difficulties of working with investigators who are over-burdened with clinical work and patient loads and the instabilities of research teams in India. Working through the Health Ministry Screening Committee's system of approvals to get clearance for projects can be daunting. Though the patient populations in India are a significant draw for international collaborations, they also involve challenges of long-term follow-up and compliance. The inadequacy of hospital records is also problematic.

References

Clinical trials: Concern over liberal permission. (2006, January 3). *The Hindu.* Retrieved from www.hinduonnet.com/2006/01/03/stories/2006010316521200.htm.
Indian Council of Medical Research. (n.d.). *Guidelines.* Retrieved from www.icmr.nic.in/guidelines.htm.
India preferred destination for clinical trials: Study. (2009, August 10). *The Hindu.* Retrieved from www.hinduonnet.com/thehindu/holnus/099200908100321.htm.
Mehta, S. R., Yusuf, S., Diaz, R., Zhu, J., Pais, P., & Xavier, D., et al. (2005). Effect of glucose insulin potassium infusion on mortality in patients with acute ST: segment myocardial infarction. *Journal of the American Medical Association, 293*(4), 437–446.
Yusuf, S., Mehta, S. R., Xie, C., Ahmed, R. J., Xavier, D., Pais, P., et al. (2005). Effects of reviparin, a low molecular weight heparin on mortality reinfarction and strokes in patients with acute myocardial infarction presenting with ST: segment elevation. *Journal of the American Medical Association, 293*(4), 427–436.

Singapore and China

James O. Leckie. Interview by Melissa S. Anderson

You have indicated that you have experience in both Singapore and China. The rate of growth of the research enterprise is different in those two countries, and what they have to build on is also quite different. So the question is, how do those differences show up when you are collaborating with people from those countries? What is different about collaborating with China and Singapore, compared to collaborating with somebody down the hall from you there at Stanford?

First of all, let me give you some context. I've been working with a group in Singapore since the late 1990s. We had a very large, three-year, multi-million-dollar research project, initially called the Clean Water Program. It was focused on research issues important to Singapore about reclaiming and recycling 100 percent of their wastewater. It was out of that research collaboration that we developed an ongoing, educational graduate program in environmental engineering which is still going on today. Through the research activity we quickly learned of both structural and cultural differences in the conduct of research.

There were no language problems. English is the operational language in Singapore, due to its colonial history. It's a multi-ethnic community dominated by overseas Chinese (85 percent), with 10 percent Malay and 5 percent Indian.

It is effectively a single-party country and is very much a top-down society. People accede to the designated leaders. Individuals at the rank-and-file level seldom take initiative. They essentially wait to be told what to do, even in the academic institutions. Consequently, it's been very difficult for them to attract and hold top-notch Western faculty because you can't operate in a Western mode.

I'll give you some examples we encountered once when we were developing a proposal for a joint project. We had a field site and were doing some exploratory work, trying to identify where we would put a field site for part of the research. My crew is pretty independent. The way I generally operate is that I identify and attract good people, give them lots of responsibility, and basically hold them accountable, but I don't micromanage. I expect them to come to me when they have real questions and real issues to deal with. So they often are essentially free agents to a very large degree, when they have a highly targeted issue to deal with.

In this case, my research associate was charged with working with a group in Singapore to identify a field site, develop a justification for the field site and then put together a budget to develop and operate the field site. And just as he would here, he searched out people at all levels, including the professor who was overseeing the Singapore end of the operation, but without asking for permission, because it's just simply not an issue when we deal with that kind of thing here in the States. He also went to the machine shop and asked people if they could fabricate a few small items and talked to a number of the students and so forth. When the professor in Singapore heard that my research associate had been dealing with his people without his permission, he went ballistic, and I got communications that didn't make any sense to me. And so I compounded the problem by saying, "Well he's operating on my instructions, and we need to get this done. We don't have a lot of time." And then I got a note saying that I hadn't asked permission. We worked it out pretty quickly, but there were a number of ruffled feathers on their end.

You learn the social culture, sometimes, by making one mistake after the other. I'm typically very direct in dealing with people, so on my next trip to Singapore, I asked for a meeting very early on with this fellow. And I went in and I just told him, "I can't be coming to Singapore every week. I need to have an operational format that is efficient. And we don't have a large budget for preparing this thing, so we all need to work together. This business of asking for permission is just getting in the way of getting the work done." And I was immediately told that I'm operating in Singapore, not at Stanford, and I have to follow the Singapore rules, and Singapore rules don't allow staff from some other institution to just go and work with the staff at the university. So I basically was told I had no choice, and I said that we didn't budget on that basis of doing everything three times. So I actually damaged the relationship for the duration. We're cordial now, but in the end I never worked with that particular fellow even though I had to deal with him to get the field site organized.

So what we've begun to develop is a sense of how the institution operates. It really is a top-down structure, which is essentially perpendicular to the way we do things at Stanford. At the research level, we're very horizontal. And in order to attract really good people, including good students and good staff, you really have to give them lots of leeway, with the condition of course that they are operating as part of a group.

I've found that the Singapore culture is very indirect. Often the person you are dealing with in negotiating on details can't make the decision. So I often go there and spend two or three days working on a particular issue, and we arrive at our conclusions, and I say that now we have to implement them, and the one I'm talking to can't do that. Now he has to basically go back up the chain of command, so it takes two or three meetings to get something done.

And you have to be very, very mindful, when there is a glitch or a problem or somebody makes a mistake, that you don't confront it directly, because, to my surprise, losing face is even more important in Singapore than it was in China, in the academic institution anyway. So it's just simply not very efficient, and you have to accept that as part of the deal. You have to allocate more time and more resources to get things done.

The top-down structure permeates the decision process in ways that would be unacceptable in the West. For instance, principal investigators on projects, even if they are awarded funds from an outside agency to do research, can't make the kinds of decisions that my U.S. colleagues and I would make with respect to how we staff our projects. Often the department chair or somebody farther up the chain of command will decide who gets hired, who the postdoc is, who the research staff are on that project, sometimes even when they don't have the needed expertise whatsoever. Even though you brought in the money and you're running a program, and as the principal investigator you are ultimately legally responsible for completing the project, you don't often have complete control over staffing. That is a huge issue from the point of view of how you run a research operation. So it's a continuing challenge.

I'll give you another example. I once was designing a research activity with this fellow, and he brought to me very early on several drafts of his part of the proposal. And on it, he had the name of a division head who was associated with the overall program but had nothing to do with his research activity. The division head had no expertise relevant to the proposal and was not going to contribute anything. I told my collaborator, "Look, that guy's not doing anything. Take his name off." And he said, "Well, I can't." Then I said, "Well then, take my name off." And so we had a real confrontation, and in the end my collaborator took the name off, and it resulted in an attempt to fire him. In the end, I felt responsible since I had actually generated the issue by insisting that we follow the rules that I'm accustomed to. And after that, the division head tried to put his name on manuscripts, and I insisted that he was not going to be a co-author.

So these issues are real. Often they don't surface because no one challenges them. And the junior faculty pay a very high price to the more-senior faculty who have worked their way up into positions of power. The people who grew up in that culture often don't like it, but they accept it as simply the way the world's constructed. But when you're dealing with a colleague who comes from a Western culture, where the mode of operation is dramatically different, it often causes a lot of problems. And there are some Western researchers in Singapore who just simply give up. They say, well, it's too difficult to operate in that environment.

What has made it worth the effort for you? What were the benefits of that collaboration?

My current research collaborator is very clever, very innovative. We're working on the same topic. Scientifically, he's very strong. He just happens to have developed his career in Singapore.

In that earlier situation, if there had been any kind of irreversible decision that I couldn't deal with, I would have just simply pulled out. I think my success rested primarily on the fact that I'm very senior, I come from a very prestigious institution, I have a very strong international reputation, and the university valued that.

Another point. There has been a big push by the government in Singapore to develop a knowledge-based economy, and they've been investing a lot of money, working very hard in that direction. So they're looking down the line at developing intellectual property, which will then spin off into economic activity. So they would like their students to be innovative and creative, which would lead to new ideas and new products and services, and so on. So they look at Silicon Valley in California as being kind of a model for that. But their educational system is structured in such a way that you're taught not to challenge, not to question, not to be different from your classmates. And so by the time they go to university, they've learned that you don't take risks, because the penalty for failure is sometimes quite severe, in the sense that you would be forced out of school or ostracized. By the time they get to university, they feel very comfortable sitting back, waiting to be given information, but they're not taught to think critically, not taught to think independently. At the university, they behave in exactly the same fashion, and the politicians seem puzzled as to why, in spite of all their programs to try to foster innovation and creativity, it just simply didn't happen. They can't attract really good students from the West, at the graduate level anyway, because they won't stay in the system that operates in that fashion. Their own students with a streak of innovation or creativity want to go overseas to university, and often they don't come back. It's a big dilemma for them.

There's a lot of frustration. When I first went there, I didn't quite understand why they're continually looking for outside leadership. They don't try to develop internal leadership, and I didn't quite understand why. But I think that this is an ongoing issue. Always going outside to find leadership means that you never really develop internal leadership. And often they go for senior people, who are at the end of their careers, to start things, and when one retires, they go back outside of Singapore again. If you continue to bring in outside people, you never really modify the parameters that constrain the development of the kind of culture and environment that you need to foster— what they hope for—which is a more open, creative environment for their students and for their faculty. So the structure is rigid, and the staff don't take risks, because they know what the penalty is if you do anything other than what is exactly prescribed, even though sometimes you can solve problems in innovative ways. They basically go to the handbook and look up the procedure, and they follow it to the letter.

In a lot of ways, although I'm critical of some aspects on the academic end, Singapore's been enormously successful. And it is successful, I think, partly because the government has adopted the Mandarin philosophy of governance, in the sense that they have looked for the very best and the very brightest to pull into government, and they compensate them quite well. They identify young people, send them off, pay for their education, and obligate them to come back and work for the government for a number of years. So they have an enormously talented civil service, and they've been very astute about preventing corruption at the operational level, so Singapore really is a society that works.

Now China.

China's quite a different situation. First of all, it's changing at an enormous rate, both economically and culturally, in the broad, social-culture sense. The one-child policy is having an enormous effect on China. Families that have only one child invest their whole effort to make sure that child gets educational opportunities, whether that child is a boy or a girl. And so a lot of the universities in China have very large female enrollment. You have young women majoring in law and medicine and engineering and science and doing very well. I run an executive leadership program in conjunction with the Development Research Center of the State Council for the business community in China, and you find that increasingly women are the chief executive officers, sometimes sole owners of fairly sizeable businesses. They're having a big impact, but women take a different view of the world than men, and I think that that's going to change China in ways that will actually be pretty profound.

The central government has decided that education is the key to their continued future growth, and so universities in China have been receiving incredible financial support. Their infrastructure is world-class, and virtually every campus I've been on is being rebuilt, if it hasn't been already, and in some cases they are building whole new campuses out of whole cloth. They're attempting to provide seats for many more young people. Right now, their enrollment's very large, but, given their population, it's actually a small fraction of the young people that eventually they'll have to accommodate at university level.

So interacting with the academic community in China these days is kind of a breath-taking experience. They are not short on resources. To put this in context, at Stanford University, there are six faculty members in our environmental engineering program. At Tsinghua, they have 70 faculty in just environmental engineering, and they had just gotten permission to hire 30 more. Now that, for me, is mind-boggling.

Then my colleagues said that it sounds like a huge number, but, in fact, all of the universities in China are being required by the government to provide what we would call consulting services to industry, villages and municipalities, to help solve their water- and air-pollution problems. And so a very large portion of the money that comes in is essentially funding a consultancy of sorts. Many of their students get student projects doing that, but the projects are very practical, very applied.

Even though China is pretty much still a top-down society, in many respects they are actually quite democratic at the operational level. At the faculty meetings I've sat in on, the junior faculty speak up, they're listened to, they often are involved in group contingents sent overseas.

They don't seem to lack resources in any real way. Their equipment and their physical facilities are increasingly world-class. The problem in China is that they're not given the freedom to work on fundamental or basic research, at least in my field of environmental engineering. So they're not creating cutting-edge solutions or intellectual property. They're in a mode of solving problems that in the Western world an engineering consultancy or operational engineering business field would take care of. In other areas of engineering they are not constrained by such practical problems and, for example, in computer science, bioengineering or electrical engineering, they are fast becoming competitive at a world-class level.

I think their leadership—both political and academic leadership—want world-class universities, and so you have to have the infrastructure and equipment. Actually a lot of the best research is done at the Institutes of the Chinese Academy of Sciences. They are a whole series of labs, not a single place. They're distributed all over. There they do much more fundamental work and award PhD degrees.

What else have you seen through your collaborative projects in China?
There's a surplus of human resources. They are able to throw lots of manpower at projects. Their students are funded, so the faculty don't have to go out and get money for students the way we do in the United States. So their students have access to resources once they are admitted, and the faculty don't have to generate those. Because they are expanding, they have access to a very large pool of talented manpower for their projects, both students and researchers. And that's very much in contrast to what we have here. So when we talk about a concept with them, and if they get excited about the concept, they can basically take the next step the morning after, because they have a large pool of students who are looking for projects and also a very large array of faculty whom they can pull into these projects. So they can move much more quickly than we can. They don't try to run away with the projects; they still try to collaborate and keep you involved. But we have to write a proposal, and it takes six months, if we're lucky and get funded, and so we're often running behind on these things.

Their resources are going to continue to multiply over time, because they have this enormous pool of young people that they're attempting to move through the educational system. They hope to educate a much larger fraction of their population over time, so their university system will continue to expand dramatically.

One issue that comes up in collaborative work, especially with students, is the matter of plagiarism. They don't feel that they're doing anything wrong when they copy material verbatim and incorporate it into written reports that they then submit as their own. In discussions with the students and even with some of the faculty, they seem puzzled by why that would be controversial. The notion is that, if the authors didn't want you to use their material, they wouldn't publish it, but since it's published and accessible, it should be free for everyone to use in any way.

I have no evidence of other kinds of problems with research integrity. But there is no oversight that I'm aware of, where people really worry about the intellectual integrity of their activities and worry about the validity of attribution. From that point of view, I think it is probably something that should be worried about, especially at the rate at which they're expanding their academic institutions.

What do you think are the primary challenges of doing international research?
The world is pretty small, and so I think it's important for students to have an international experience. We get a lot of that by virtue of international students coming to the United States. Our students are often in class and in the laboratory with international students, but if you go to a place like China, it's pretty homogeneous. And so even though they may have all the resources, they don't get the cross-cultural experience. Several Chinese universities have decided to convert their graduate programs to English, because they want to attract foreign students. One reason may be that they want to become more of an international university, but I think also they want their own students to interact with international students. Again, I think it's important.

For a lot of the interesting problems on natural systems, you almost are compelled to do collaborative work because you can't work in some other country, typically, without having a local partner. There's an overhead you pay, in the sense that it takes time to adjust to the culture, you invest an awful lot of time in travel and communication, and so on. And there are a lot of people who have tried it and then decided they didn't want to pay the overhead. They just don't want that extra cost of sitting on a plane for 18 hours to go to Singapore, or whatever. And so they just say it's not worth their time. For others, if you do fieldwork, you're almost compelled to work internationally.

What do you think scientists need to know before they embark on international research collaborations?
Well, for one thing, you do pay a time and energy cost above and beyond the research itself. There's travel time, and if you're working in a third-world nation, you can even have health risks. I mean, any number of things can pop

up, and if you haven't thought it through, that can have consequences. And you have to be aware of potential problems, and you have to make the judgment as to whether that cost is worth the outcome and the experience.

There can be language barriers. And if you're working with a group that doesn't have access to resources, sometimes you have to provide resources beyond your own needs in order to make it work. We have a group working in Tanzania now on sanitation. They literally had to build a laboratory to do analysis—set it up at the local university and plan to leave it behind for the students and faculty. You have to sell that to the funding agency. If you're accepting money from the National Institutes of Health, you have to explain that you need all these purchases, because you have to build a laboratory at your field site and then leave it behind.

So there are a number of things that people, especially young people, don't anticipate. It sounds exotic to work in some of these places, but the costs can be real and sometimes there actually can be actual health consequences. I had amoebic dysentery for about 20 years that I couldn't get rid of. I acquired it in Central America when I was a young faculty member. I was a little bit naïve at that time. I think now I would recommend that people really do a pretty thorough read-up on current health standards in some of these places.

Thank you.

Contributors

Ibrahim Adib Abdel-Messih is a Clinical Research Scientist at the Influenza Vaccines Clinical Development program, Novartis Vaccines & Diagnostics, Siena, Italy. He is working on vaccine clinical trials to develop pandemic and interpandemic influenza vaccines. His past work in research started when he joined the Enteric Diseases Research Program (EDRP), U.S Naval Medical Research Unit (NAMRU-3) in Cairo. His research was focused on pediatric diarrheal diseases and providing necessary information to make evidence-based decisions regarding the use of enteric vaccines. His work has been published in many peer-reviewed journals. He is also an active member of the NAMRU-3 Institutional Review Board.

Sergio Alvarado-Menacho, CD, is Professor in Prosthetic Dentistry of the Oral Rehabilitation Department in the Dental Clinic at the School of Dentistry in San Marcos University in Lima, Peru. He is Consultant Editor of *Revista Odontológica San Marquina* (*San Marcos Dentistry Journal*), member of the Asosiación Peruana de Editores Científicos—APECi—(Peruvian Scientific Editors Association), and also serves as Professor in the School of Dentistry in the Garcilaso de la Vega University and San Martín de Porras University in Lima, Peru.

Donald M. Amundson, JD, is an Associate General Counsel in the University of Minnesota's Office of the General Counsel, which he joined in 1996. His legal practice focuses on international activities and agreements, external sales and general business matters. Mr. Amundson received his law degree cum laude from the University of Minnesota after earning his baccalaureate degree summa cum laude from St. Olaf College, where he was also a member of the Phi Beta Kappa Honor Society. His prior legal experience includes private practice at the Dorsey & Whitney law firm as well as in-house work for several corporations. Mr. Amundson has been practicing law since 1980.

Melissa S. Anderson, PhD, is Professor of Higher Education and an affiliate faculty member in bioethics at the University of Minnesota, where she also chairs the university's Senate Research Committee. Her work over the past 25 years has been in the areas of research integrity, research ethics and academy–industry relations. Dr. Anderson's research, funded by the U.S. National Institutes of Health (NIH) and the National Science Foundation, has focused on the research environment in relation to scientific work and graduate and postdoctoral training. She is currently principal investigator of an NIH-funded study of international research collaborations.

Kumar G. Belani, MBBS, MS, is Professor of Anesthesiology in the Medical School at the University of Minnesota. He holds joint appointments in the Departments of Medicine and Pediatrics. He is also adjunct Professor in the Department of Environmental Health Sciences in the School of Public Health, University of Minnesota. In addition to his research interests and expertise in Pediatric Anesthesiology, Malignant Hyperthermia and Anesthesia for Solid Organ Transplantation, Dr. Belani has been active in the Office of International Medical Education and Research to promote global health education and research for the last decade. More recently he has been actively involved with the Academic Health Center at the University of Minnesota and the University of Minnesota Physicians to promote education, research and clinical programs in India.

Christine C. Boesz, Dr. PH, is retired Inspector General of the National Science Foundation, and serves as an international consultant in accountability, specializing in research and financial integrity. She represented the United States at the Global Science Forum as it developed guidelines for research integrity and the handling of research misconduct in international collaborations. She serves on the Advisory Board of the U.S. Government Accountability Office that sets financial auditing standards for federal, state and local governments. She has published articles dealing with managed health-care organizational and compliance issues.

Mark A. Bohnhorst, JD, has been a practicing attorney for 34 years. Since 1992, Mr. Bohnhorst has served as an Associate General Counsel for the University of Minnesota, with concentrations in research compliance and negotiation of research contracts, including agreements for international research. Since 2001, Mr. Bohnhorst has been an invited speaker on issues of export controls and preserving openness in research at meetings of the National Association of College and University Attorneys, the AAU Senior Research Officers and the National Council of University Research Administrators.

Alexander M. Capron is a globally recognized expert in health policy and medical ethics. He teaches torts, as well as law, science and medicine. He also teaches at the University of Southern California (USC) School of Medicine and is co-director of the Pacific Center for Health Policy and Ethics, a campus-wide inter-disciplinary research and education center. He returned to USC Law in fall 2006, after four years on leave as Director of Ethics, Trade, Human Rights and Health Law at the World Health Organization in Geneva. Professor Capron's publications include *Law, Science and Medicine*, 2nd ed. (with others, 1996), *Treatise on Health Care Law* (with others, 1991) and *Genetics, Ethics and Human Values* (edited with Z. Bankowski, 1991). Professor Capron received a BA from Swarthmore College and an LLB from Yale University, where he was an editor of the *Yale Law Journal*. He was appointed by President Bill Clinton to the National Bioethics Advisory Commission, where he served for five years. He is a trustee of the Century Foundation, president of the International Association of Bioethics and a member of the Institute of Medicine.

David W. Chapman is the Birkmaier Professor of Educational Leadership in the Department of Organizational Leadership, Policy, and Development at the University of Minnesota. His specialization is in international development assistance. He has worked on development assistance activities in over 45 countries and has authored or edited 10 books and over 125 book chapters and journal articles, many of them on issues related to the development of education systems in international settings. His research has examined, among other things, corruption in education, the impact of national policy on school practice and the role of higher education in national development.

Felly Chiteng Kot is a PhD candidate in Higher Education Policy and Administration at the University of Minnesota. His research focuses on international higher education partnerships in sub-Saharan Africa. He serves as a Graduate Research Assistant on Professor Melissa S. Anderson's NIH-funded study of international research collaborations. Felly Chiteng Kot is from the Democratic Republic of Congo.

Raymond G. De Vries, PhD, is Professor in the Bioethics Program, the Department of Obstetrics and Gynecology and the Department of Medical Education at the Medical School, University of Michigan. He is the author of *A Pleasing Birth: Midwifery and Maternity Care in the Netherlands* (2005) and co-editor of *The View from Here: Bioethics and the Social Sciences* (2007). He is currently working on a critical social history of bioethics, and is studying: the regulation of science; international research ethics; the difficulties of informed consent; bioethics and the problem of suffering; and the social, ethical and policy issues associated with non-medically indicated surgical birth.

Reyna M. Durón, MD, is an active neurologist and research scientist from the National Autonomous University of Honduras. Her involvement in academic medicine and scientific research includes participation in the design and development of research protocols in several fields of neurological research, including epidemiology, medical anthropology, neurogenetics, quality of life and neurocisticercosis. She has been involved in multi-disciplinary and international collaborations, especially regarding epilepsy disorders. She is currently the Director of the *Honduran Medical Journal.*

Peggy L. Fischer, PhD, is the Associate Inspector General for Investigations in the National Science Foundation's Office of the Inspector General. She has been with the Foundation in the Office of the Inspector General in varying capacities since 1992. Currently she is responsible for managing the Office's investigations into all allegations of wrongdoing and research misconduct, as well as its outreach efforts. Her previous experience includes serving as a Senior Program Officer for the National Research Council's Board on Biology and as the Director of Research and Development for a biotechnology company. She held two postdoctoral positions after receiving her doctorate in cell biology.

Olena Glushko, PhD student in Higher Education, is a Graduate Research Assistant in the Postsecondary Education Research Institute, Department of Organizational Leadership, Policy, and Development, University of Minnesota. Her research interests are in the areas of institutional public-image and ranking, research and development, and institutional advancement.

John B. Godfrey, PhD, has been at the University of Michigan since 1993. He has been Associate Director of the International Institute and is now Assistant Dean for International Education at the Rackham Graduate School, where his responsibilities include issues of international graduate education and research and the development of international collaborations and policies. He also administers the school's support for graduate research training programs and inter-disciplinary initiatives. He sits on a number of university committees for international engagement. He has made presentations on international graduate education in Europe and Asia, and has worked with the Council of Graduate Schools on a range of international issues.

F. Gray Handley, MSPH, is Associate Director for International Research Affairs at the National Institute of Allergy and Infectious Diseases (NIAID), of the U.S. National Institutes of Health (NIH). In this role, he oversees and coordinates NIAID's international infectious disease and immunology research activities and serves as a senior advisor to the NIAID Director, Dr. Anthony Fauci. Previously he served for five years as the U.S. Health Attaché, PEPFAR Coordinator and U.S. Department of Health and Human Services (DHHS) Regional Representative in Southern Africa, stationed in Pretoria, South Africa. During his career he has served in many global public health and biomedical research positions, including: Associate Director for Prevention Research and International Programs at the National Institute of Child Health and Human Development (NIH); Science Attaché and DHHS Representative in South Asia, U.S. Embassy New Delhi; Associate Director for International Relations at the Fogarty International Center, NIH; International Organizations Health and Narcotics Officer for the U.S. Department of State; and International Health Advisor in the DHHS Office of the Secretary, the Office of Health (USAID), the National Institute of Environmental Health Research (NIH), the World Health Organization, the White House Office of Management and Budget and the Office of the Assistant Secretary for Health, Department of Defense.

Elizabeth Heitman is Associate Professor in the Center for Biomedical Ethics and Society at Vanderbilt University, with appointments in the Departments of Medicine, Anesthesiology and Religious Studies. Her primary research addresses the evaluation of education in the responsible conduct of research, and the cultural awareness and professional socialization of students and researchers. Dr. Heitman is the Director of a four-year research ethics education program for Costa Rican biomedical researchers and research ethics review committees, in conjunction with the Hospital Nacional de Niños in San José, Costa Rica, and sponsored by the NIH's Fogarty International Center. She is also principal investigator for an NSF-sponsored study of international science graduate students' experience of U.S. standards of practice in ethical research. Dr. Heitman is the author of numerous essays on ethics education, the role of institutional ethics committees in clinical medicine and health policy, and cultural aspects of health and health care. She is the co-author of *The Ethical Dimensions of the Biological and Health Sciences* (with Drs. Ruth Ellen Bulger and Stanley Joel Reiser).

Yiyun Jie is a doctoral candidate in the Comparative and International Development Education Program at the University of Minnesota. Her research interests focus on internationalization of higher education, cross-border higher education programs and university international partnerships. She is working on a dissertation on international partnership in cross-border higher-education programs. Currently she serves as a research assistant to the Assessment Committee in the Department of Postsecondary Teaching and Learning at the University of Minnesota. Her work has focused on first-year college program evaluation and assessing student learning and development outcomes.

Takehito Kamata is currently a doctoral student in the Department of Organizational Leadership, Policy, and Development, at the University of Minnesota. He is a board member of the Truman and Reta Wood Community Leadership Scholarship at Minnesota State University, Mankato.

Aliya Kuzhabekova is a doctoral student in Higher Education Policy and Administration at the University of Minnesota. She has received a "Bolas-hak" scholarship from the President of Kazakhstan to pursue her education in the United States. Prior to her studies in the United States, she was employed in various administrative positions at universities in her country. She has a number of publications in language policy in Kazakhstan, which she completed during her Master's training in linguistics. She also co-authored articles on regulation of emerging technologies in the United States when working for the Center for Science, Technology and Public Policy at the University of Minnesota. Her current research interests include higher-education economics and finance in international contexts, and the role of higher education in building science, technology and innovation capacity in developing countries.

James O. Leckie has been on the Stanford Environmental Engineering faculty since 1970 and is an environmental chemist interested in the application of chemical principles to the study of pollutants' behavior in natural aquatic systems and in engineered processes. His research contributions have been extensive in the areas of adsorption chemistry, human-exposure analysis and membrane science. In 2005 he became a member of the National Academy of Engineering, and received the American Society of Civil Engineering Rudolf Hering Medal in 1981. Presently, he is co-Director of the Singapore–Stanford Partnership program in Environmental Engineering & Science, and Director of the Center for Sustainable Development & Global Competitiveness at Stanford University. He is also Appointed Chair Professor in the Department of Environmental Science and Engineering at Tsinghua University. Professor Leckie holds a BS degree in Civil Engineering from San José State University (1964), and MS (1965) and PhD (1970) degrees in Environmental Sciences from Harvard University.

Christine C. Lepkowski is a PhD student in Higher Education at the Department of Organizational Leadership, Policy, and Development at the University of Minnesota. She is a graduate research assistant in the Postsecondary Education Institute studying research misconduct and international research collaborations. Her research interests include gender and women in higher education.

Stewart Lyman, PhD, is Manager of Lyman BioPharma Consulting LLC, through which he provides advice and scientific and managerial expertise to the biotechnology and pharmaceutical industry. Dr. Lyman has 25 years' experience in research and biotechnology. Dr. Lyman identified numerous important growth factor genes during his 14-year tenure at Immunex Corporation, including flt3 ligand, Steel factor, Ephrin B1 and TSLP. He also served as the Director of Extramural Research, where his group managed about 2,500 research collaborations with over 1,000 academic investigators worldwide during a four-year period. He holds 21 U.S. patents and has authored or co-authored 129 scientific publications.

Tony Mayer is a geologist who has pursued a career in research administration and management, initially with the UK Natural Environment Research Council. He is the Europe Representative of the Nanyang Technological University (NTU), Singapore. Formerly Director of COST (European Cooperation in Science and Technology) in Brussels and Senior Science Policy Advisor to the European Science Foundation, Strasbourg, he joined NTU in 2007. He was also the Scientific Secretary of the European Research Advisory Board. In 2007 he co-organized and co-chaired the First World Conference on Research Integrity, held in Lisbon.

Meredith McQuaid, JD, is Associate Vice President and Dean of the Office of International Programs at the University of Minnesota. In this capacity, she promotes the global dimensions of teaching, research and engagement across all colleges and campuses of the university. She works with university leaders, faculty, students and staff to create global opportunities; expand international and inter-disciplinary components of teaching, research and public engagement activities; recruit and support international students, faculty and staff; and facilitate development of critical inter-disciplinary and international partnerships important to the university's strategic plan.

Juan Miyahira, MD, is Professor in the Department of Medicine, School of Medicine of the Universidad Peruana Cayetano Heredia (Cayetano Heredia Peruvian University), Editor-in-Chief of the *Revista Médica Herediana* (*Heredian Medical Journal*), and President of the Asosiación Peruana de Editores Científicos—APECi—(Peruvian Scientific Editors Association). He works in the Nephrology Division at the Hospital Nacional Cayetano Heredia (Cayetano Heredia National Hospital) in Lima, Peru.

Camille Nebeker, MS, is Director of the Division of Research Affairs at San Diego State University, where she oversees the university's research infrastructure, including regulatory compliance programs, research ethics initiatives and research promotion. In addition to responsibilities in research administration, she has received funding from the National Institutes of Health, the Office of Research Integrity and the National Science Foundation to develop ethics education and training to enhance research integrity and ethical research practices among lay and novice research staff. Camille's work is presently funded by NSF to develop and integrate ethics education within the Professional Science Master's degree programs.

Prem Pais, MD, is Dean and Professor of Medicine at St. John's Medical College, Bangalore, India. He also heads the Clinical Trials division of the St. John's Research Institute. His academic and research interests are cardiovascular epidemiology and clinical trials and research ethics. He is on the editorial boards of a number of cardiovascular journals and Davidson's *Textbook of Medicine*. He is on the peer-review committee of the Indian Council for Medical Research for cardiovascular disease.

Yasaswi Paruchuri is an undergraduate student at the School of Literature, Arts & Sciences, University of Michigan. She is the author of "Bioethics in a Neoliberal Society" (*Ivy Journal of Ethics*, 2009). Her studies focus on medical and cultural definitions of health and illness and inequality within global health systems. In addition to her work as a research assistant to Professor Raymond De Vries, she is researching the effects of mercury contamination on a mining community in northern Ghana.

Juleigh Petty, PhD, is Senior Lecturer in the Center for Medicine, Health, and Society in the College of Arts and Sciences at Vanderbilt University. Her research interests include the regulation of medicine and science, the ethics of research and HIV/AIDS. She is co-investigator with Elizabeth Heitman on an NSF-sponsored study of international science graduate students' experience of U.S. standards of practice in ethical research.

Leslie M. Rott is a PhD student in the Department of Sociology at the University of Michigan. She studies height as a social inequality, medical sociology, disability, and the body.

Marta A. Shaw is a PhD student in Comparative and International Development Education at the Department of Organizational Policy, Leadership, and Development at the University of Minnesota. She received her MA in English Philology from the Jagiellonian University, and taught at Tischner European University in Cracow, Poland. Her research interests focus primarily on innovation and higher-education development in transitional economies. She is currently serving as a research assistant on an NIH-funded study of international research collaborations.

Martha M. Sorenson, PhD, is Associate Professor in the Institute for Medical Biochemistry at the Federal University of Rio de Janeiro. Since emigrating to Brazil in 1983, she has supervised more than 30 MS and PhD theses, primarily in biophysics and biochemistry of muscle contraction and motility. In the last 10 years, she has developed an interest in questions related to evaluating productivity and research quality.

Andrew C. Stainthorpe, PhD, set up the UK Research Integrity Office in 2006. He reviewed the UK Research Councils' policies on research conduct, which led to their producing new guidance in 2009. He set up the European Network of Research Integrity Offices (ENRIO) in 2007 and was a member of the planning group for the First World Conference on Research Integrity (2007). He has worked in health research and research ethics within the United Kingdom and on European research projects. His main research interests include research integrity, ethics and health economics.

Herbert Stegemann, psychiatrist, graduated from the Universidad Central de Venezuela (1968) with postgraduate training at the Institute of Psychiatry, London. He was the co-founder of the Venezuelan Association of Medical Journal Editors (ASEREME, a pioneer group in Latin America) and served as its President for three terms. Dr. Stegemann is a former Director of the World Association of Medical Editors (WAME) and the former President of the Publications Committee, CONICIT. His main areas of interest include: ethics in scientific publications, aeronautical medicine and rural high-mountain psychiatry. Currently, he is a Médico Adjunto at the Hospital Vargas de Caracas.

Nicholas H. Steneck, PhD, is Director of the Research Ethics and Integrity Program of the Michigan Institute for Clinical and Health Research and Professor Emeritus of History at the University of Michigan. He has published articles on the history of research misconduct policy, responsible conduct of research instruction, the use of animals in research, classified research and academic freedom, the role of values in university research, and research on research integrity. Most recently, he authored the *ORI Introduction to the Responsible Conduct of Research* (2004, 2007; translated into Japanese, Chinese, Korean and Spanish). He initiated and co-chaired the First World Conference on Research Integrity (Lisbon, 2007) and is co-chairing the Second World Conference, which will be held in Singapore in July 2010.

Ingo Stolz is a doctoral candidate in the Department of Organizational Leadership, Policy, and Development at the University of Minnesota. His dissertation research focuses on organizational change dynamics in multinational corporations that result from the adoption of policies of corporate social responsibility. His most recent contribution in this area has been published in the journal, *Human Resource Development Review* (June 2009). As a partner of the international organization development consultancy, SGOCI, Ingo Stolz translates his research into organizational practice.

Ping Sun, PhD, is Researcher in the Institute of Scientific and Technical Information of China (ISTIC). He worked at the Chinese Ministry of

Education from 1984 to 2002, engaged mainly in international cooperation affairs. He joined the ISTIC in 2007, and his research interests are research integrity and research management issues.

Stacey R. Bolton Tsantir, MA, is the International Health, Safety and Compliance Coordinator at the University of Minnesota. She is responsible for international health, safety, security and liability issues for education-abroad students, faculty, staff and international students. She coordinates policy development and review, emergency preparedness, crisis management, international agreements and training across the five-campus University of Minnesota system. She works in close partnership with the university's General Council, Risk Management Office and Office of Institutional Compliance to support international activities, including research.

Sonia M. R. Vasconcelos, PhD, is Postdoctoral Fellow in the Science Education Program of the Institute for Medical Biochemistry at the Federal University of Rio de Janeiro (UFRJ). Her doctoral thesis focused on linguistic factors associated with research productivity in English-language international journals and looked at perceptions of plagiarism among Brazilian scientists. Her postdoctoral research, supported by the C. Chagas Filho Foundation for Research Support in the State of Rio de Janeiro, focuses on developing research-integrity policies in graduate programs in Brazil.

Denis Xavier, MD, is Professor and Head of the Department of Pharmacology at St. John's Medical College and the Coordinator of the Division of Clinical Trials at St. John's Research Institute. His special interest is in clinical cardiovascular pharmacology. With Dr. Prem Pais, he set up the Division of Clinical Trials and, for over a decade, has conducted several observation studies and clinical trials in over 150 centers in the country. He recently published the largest study on acute coronary syndromes of any developing country (*Lancet*, 2008). His focus in recent years has been on programs to prevent cardiovascular disease at both the primary- and secondary-care levels. He is the Principal Investigator of the Center of Excellence at St. John's on the National Heart, Lung and Blood Institute (NIH) program to combat chronic disease in developing countries.

Index

Printed in the USA/Agawam, MA
August 1, 2014
594376.060